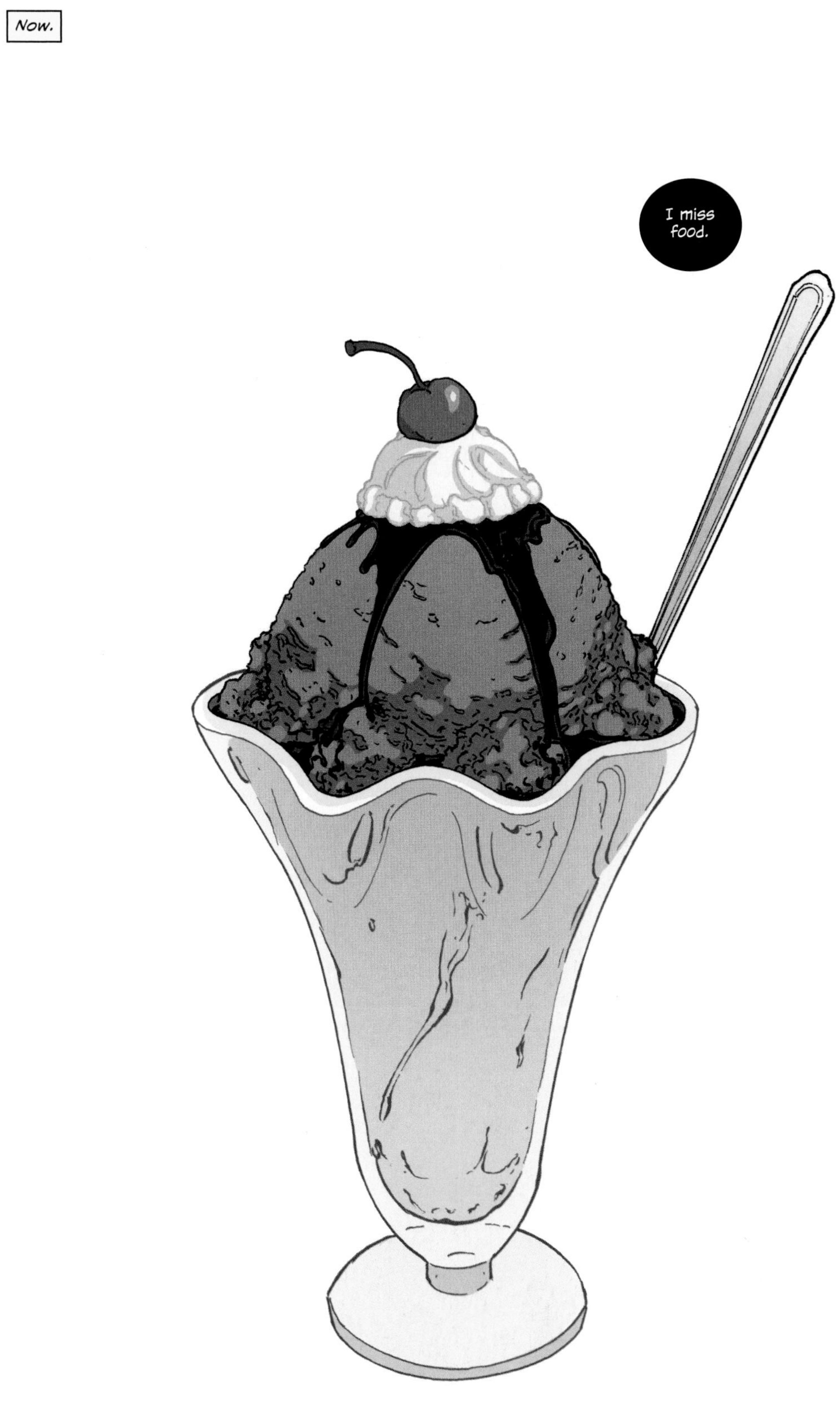
Now.
I miss food.

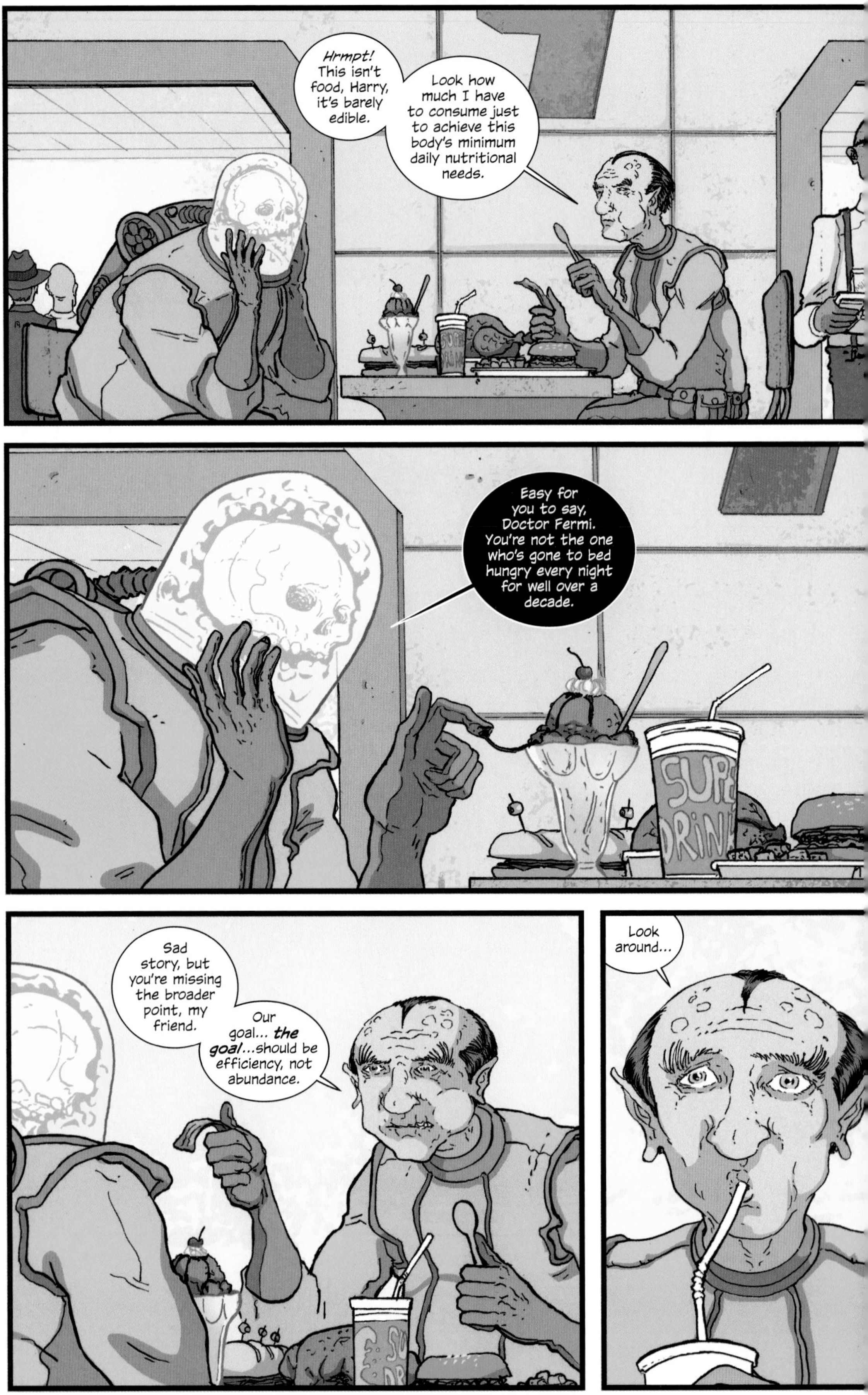
*Hrmpt!* This isn't food, Harry, it's barely edible.
Look how much I have to consume just to achieve this body's minimum daily nutritional needs.
Easy for you to say, Doctor Fermi. You're not the one who's gone to bed hungry every night for well over a decade.
Sad story, but you're missing the broader point, my friend.
Our goal... ***the goal***...should be efficiency, not abundance.
Look around...

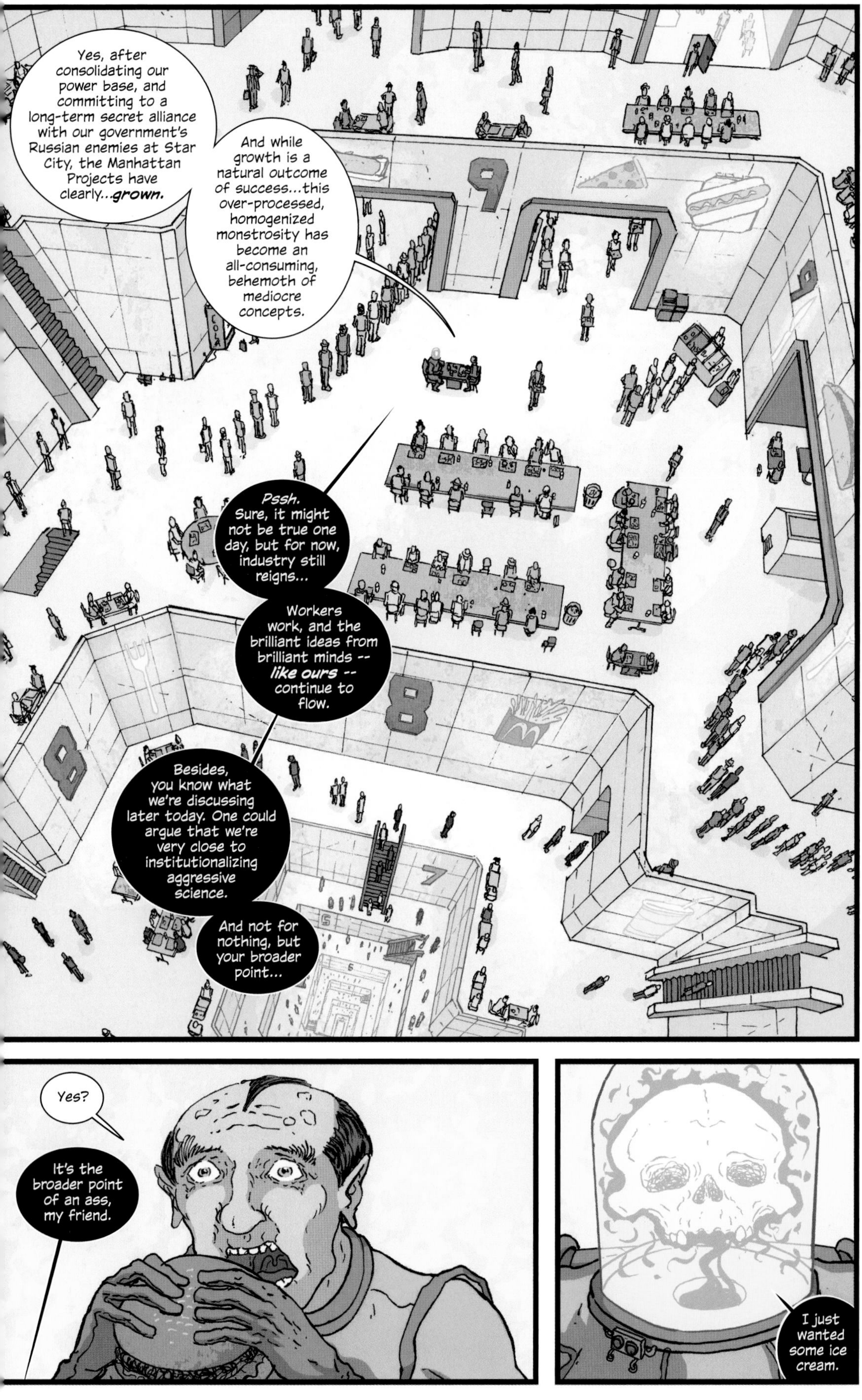
Yes, after consolidating our power base, and committing to a long-term secret alliance with our government's Russian enemies at Star City, the Manhattan Projects have clearly...*grown.*
And while growth is a natural outcome of success...this over-processed, homogenized monstrosity has become an all-consuming, behemoth of mediocre concepts.
*Pssh.* Sure, it might not be true one day, but for now, industry still reigns...
Workers work, and the brilliant ideas from brilliant minds -- *like ours* -- continue to flow.
Besides, you know what we're discussing later today. One could argue that we're very close to institutionalizing aggressive science.
And not for nothing, but your broader point...
Yes?
It's the broader point of an ass, my friend.
I just wanted some ice cream.

# 11

BUILDING

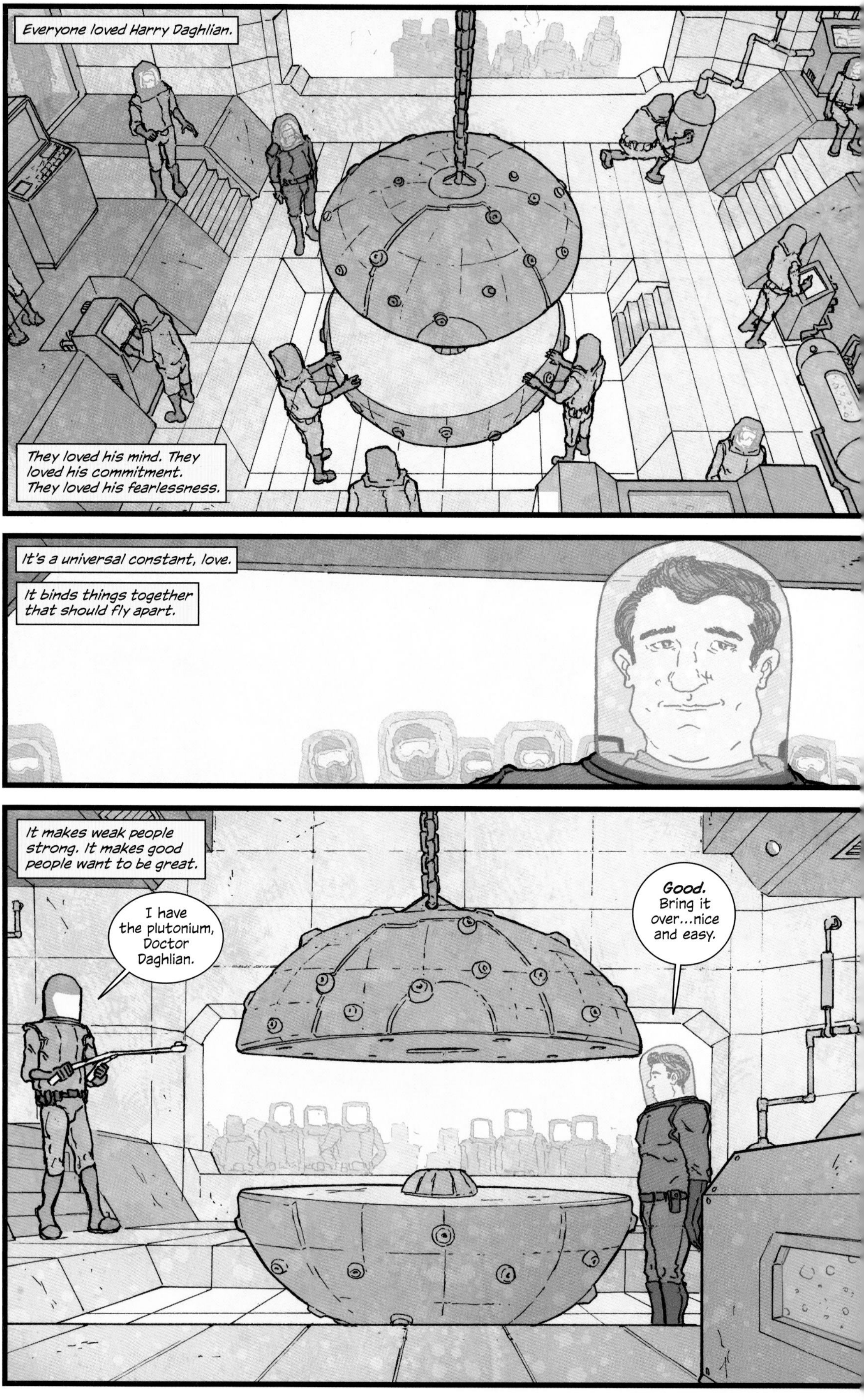
Everyone loved Harry Daghlian.
They loved his mind. They loved his commitment. They loved his fearlessness.
It's a universal constant, love.
It binds things together that should fly apart.
It makes weak people strong. It makes good people want to be great.
I have the plutonium, Doctor Daghlian.
Good. Bring it over...nice and easy.

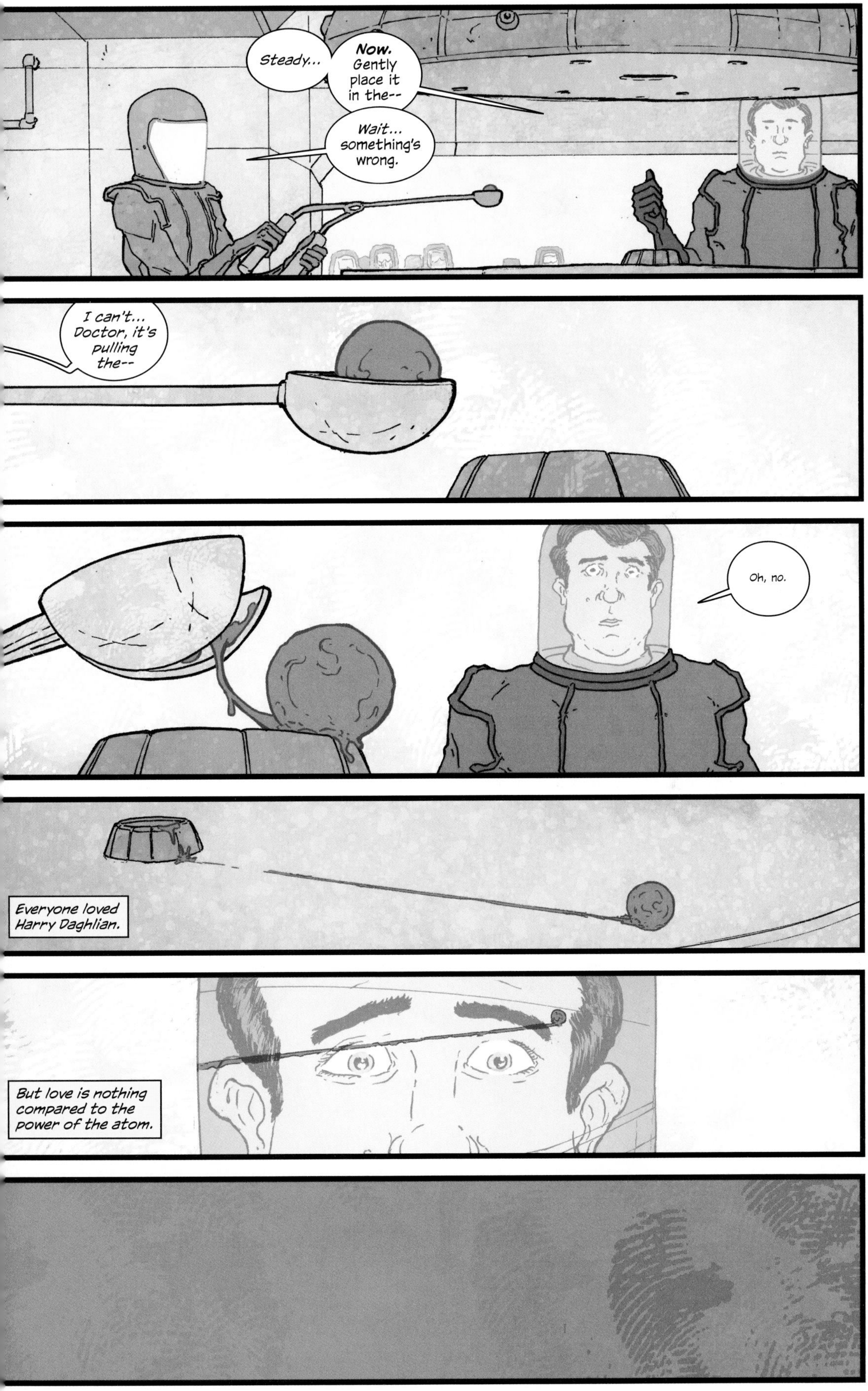
Steady...
Now. Gently place it in the--
Wait... something's wrong.
I can't... Doctor, it's pulling the--
Oh, no.
Everyone loved Harry Daghlian.
But love is nothing compared to the power of the atom.

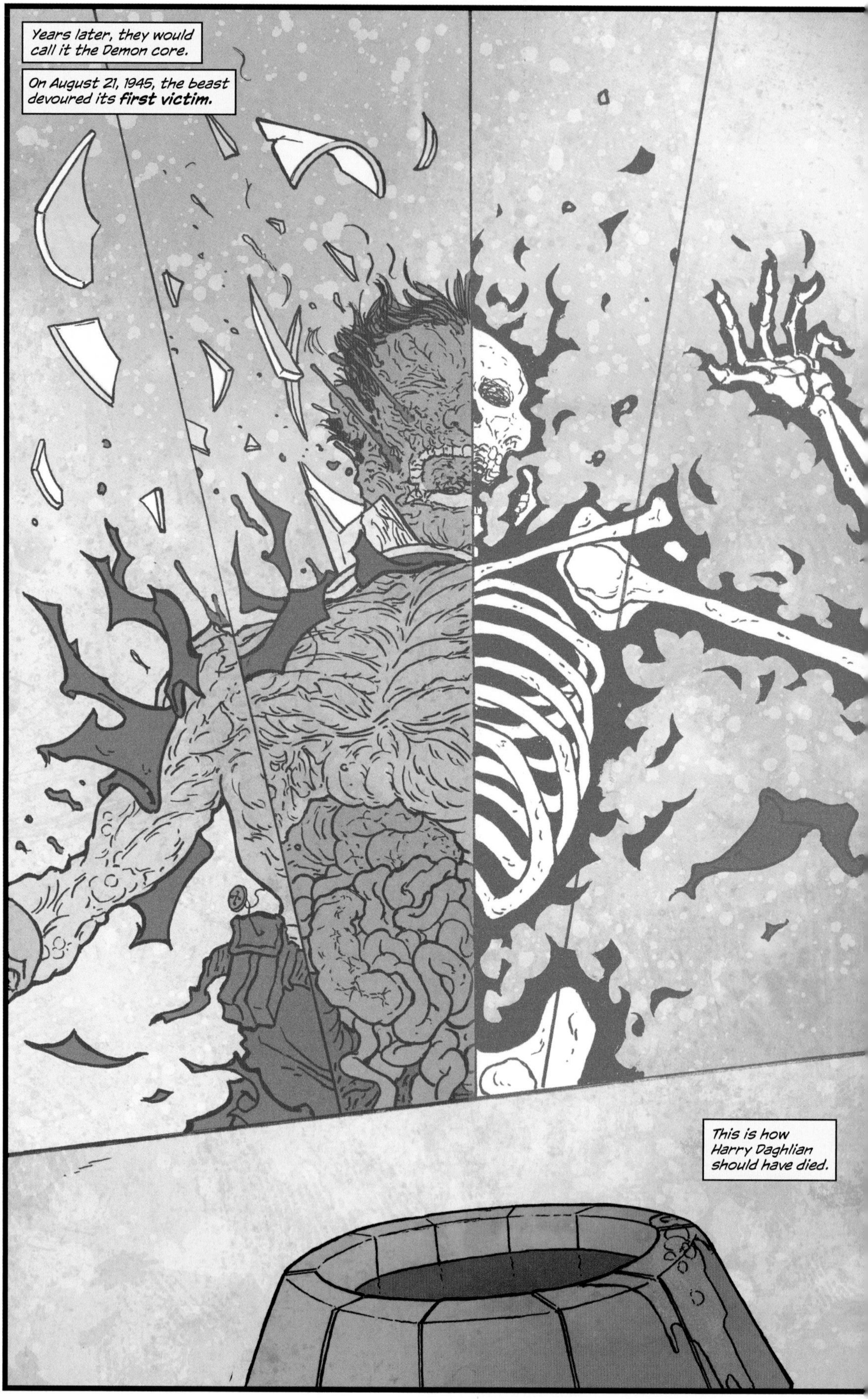
Years later, they would call it the Demon core.
On August 21, 1945, the beast devoured its **first victim.**
This is how Harry Daghlian should have died.

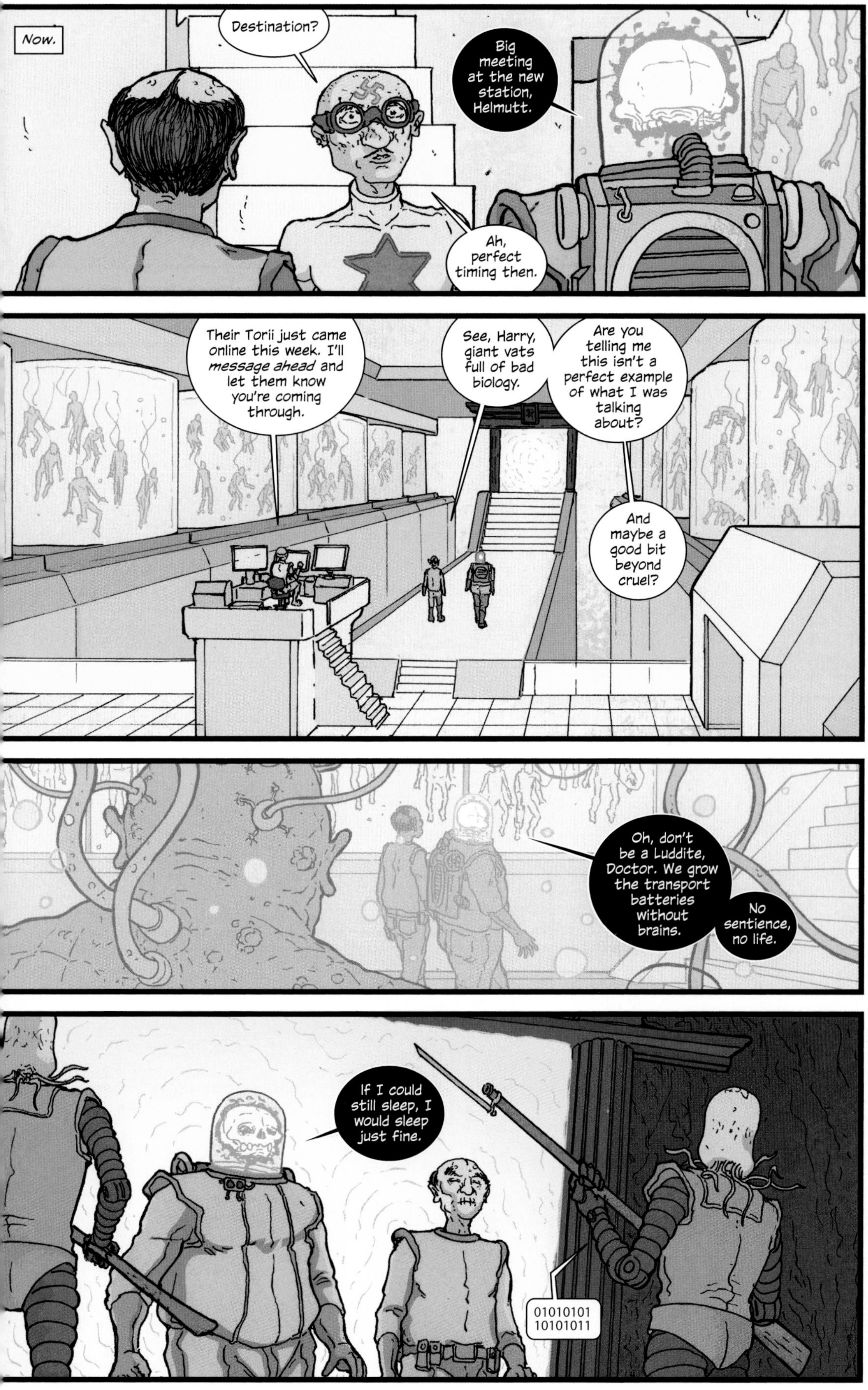
Now.
Destination?
Big meeting at the new station, Helmutt.
Ah, perfect timing then.
Their Torii just came online this week. I'll *message ahead* and let them know you're coming through.
See, Harry, giant vats full of bad biology.
Are you telling me this isn't a perfect example of what I was talking about?
And maybe a good bit beyond cruel?
Oh, don't be a Luddite, Doctor. We grow the transport batteries without brains.
No sentience, no life.
If I could still sleep, I would sleep just fine.
01010101
10101011

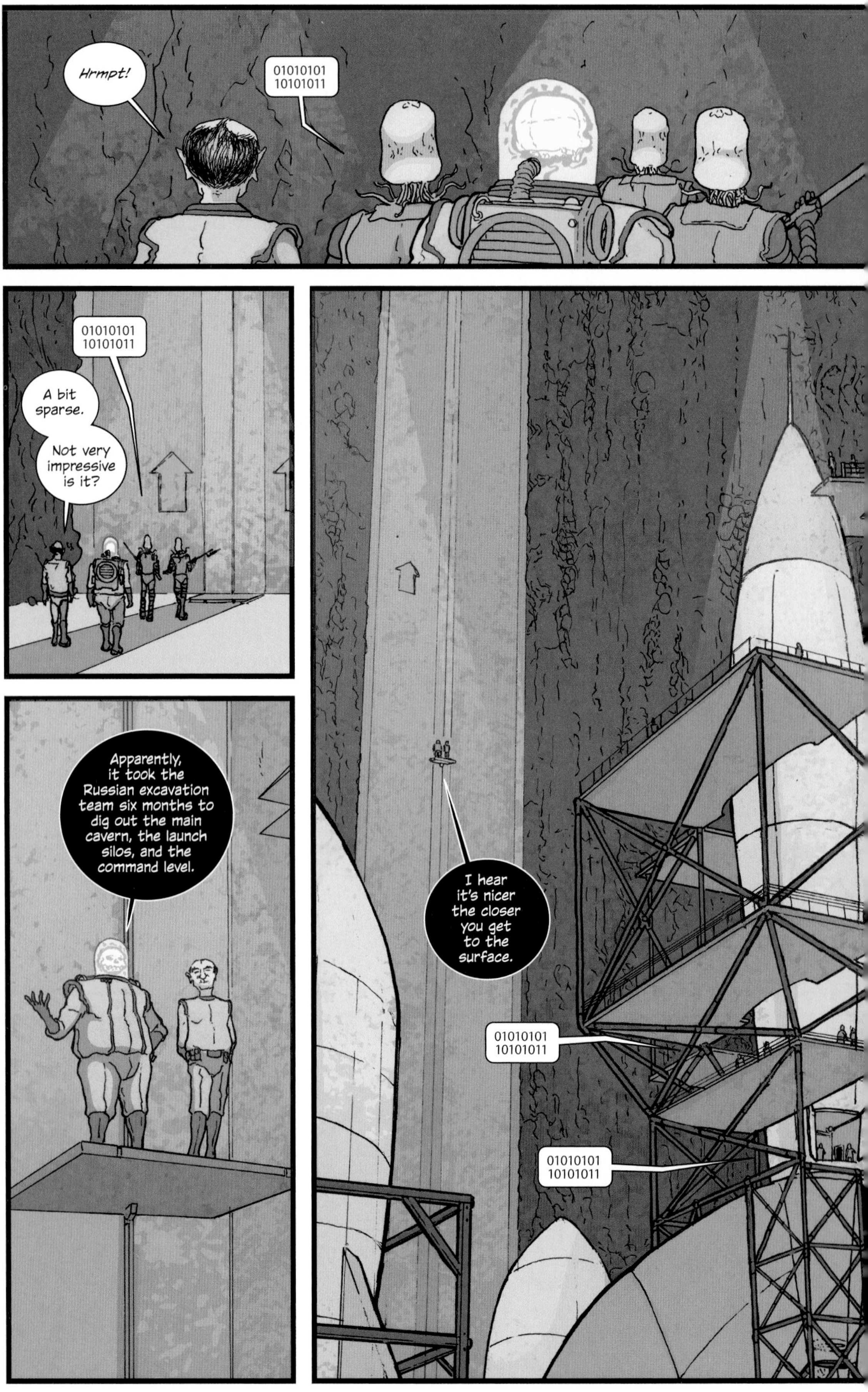
Hrmpt!
01010101 10101011
01010101 10101011
A bit sparse.
Not very impressive is it?
Apparently, it took the Russian excavation team six months to dig out the main cavern, the launch silos, and the command level.
I hear it's nicer the closer you get to the surface.
01010101 10101011
01010101 10101011

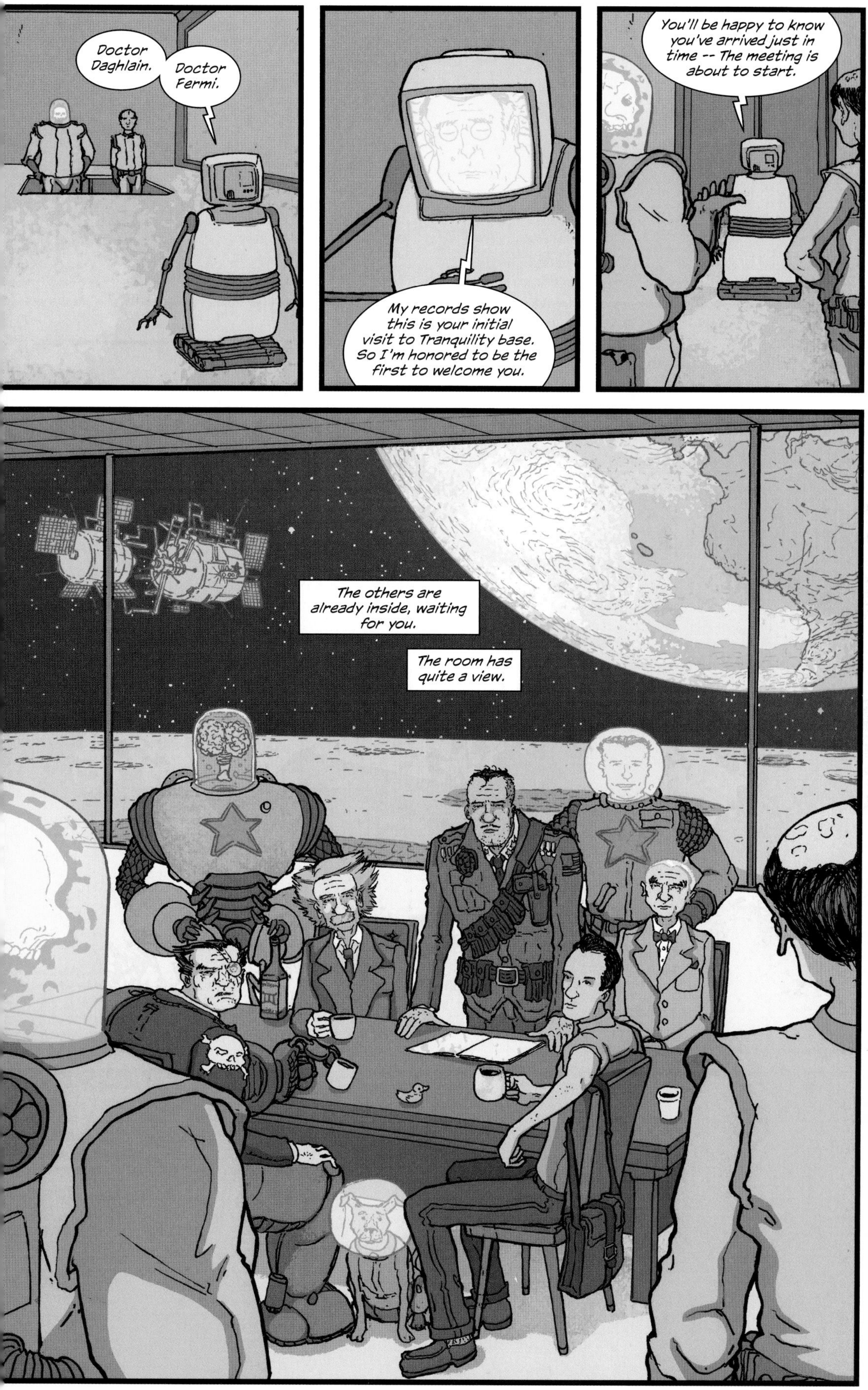
Doctor Daghlain.
Doctor Fermi.
My records show this is your initial visit to Tranquility base. So I'm honored to be the first to welcome you.
You'll be happy to know you've arrived just in time -- The meeting is about to start.
The others are already inside, waiting for you.
The room has quite a view.

Everyone feared Harry Daghlian.

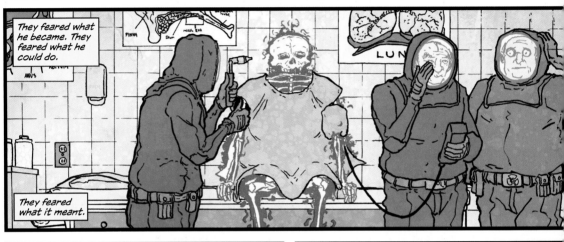

They feared what he became. They feared what he could do.

They feared what it meant.

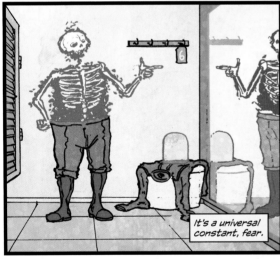

It's a universal constant, fear.

It destroys the mind and eats at hope, which rests in all men's hearts.

It makes the strong weak. It steals life and leaves you for dead.

Harry Daghlian should have died.

And he should have died alone.

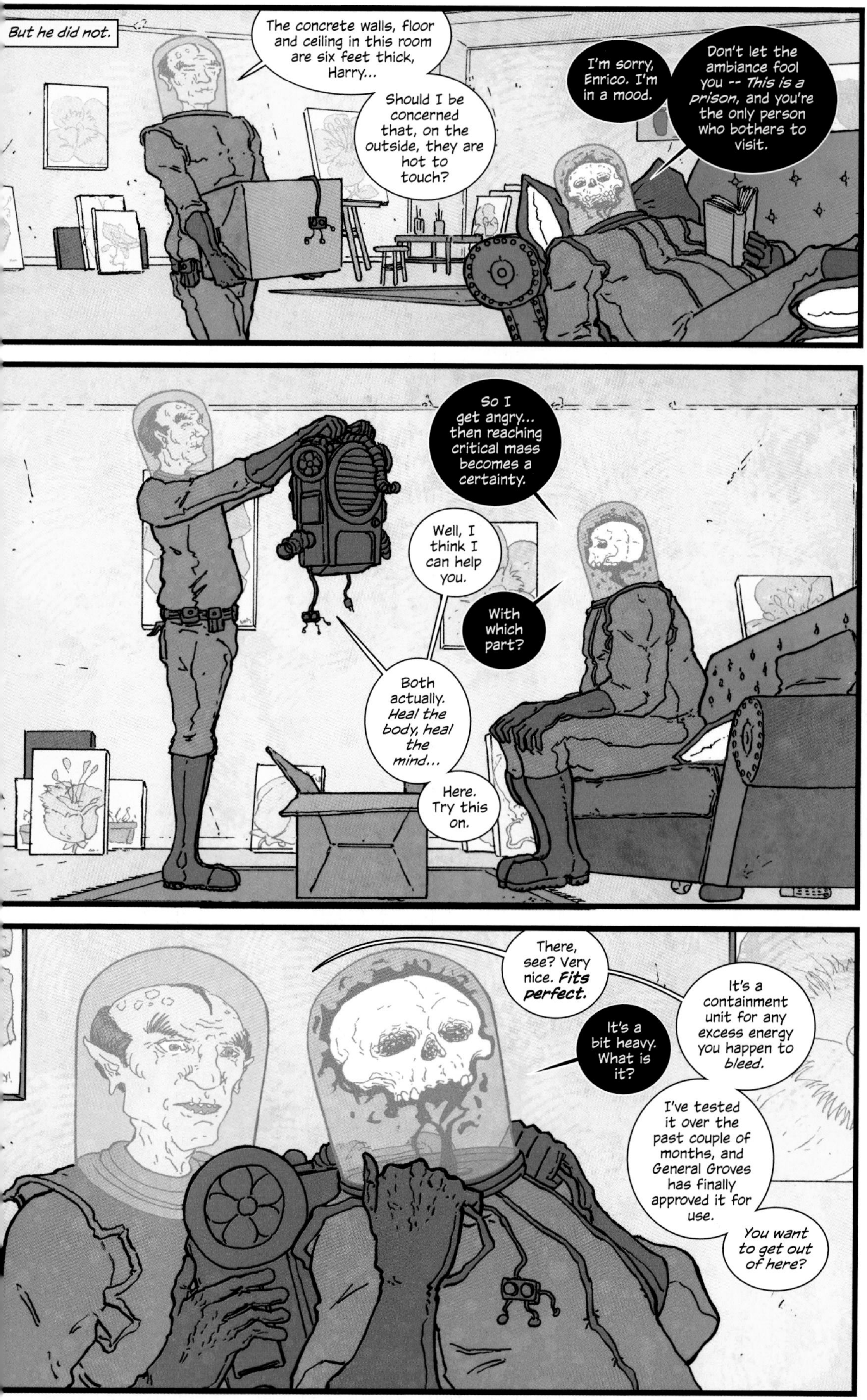

But he did not.
The concrete walls, floor and ceiling in this room are six feet thick, Harry...
Should I be concerned that, on the outside, they are hot to touch?
I'm sorry, Enrico. I'm in a mood.
Don't let the ambiance fool you -- *This is a prison*, and you're the only person who bothers to visit.
So I get angry... then reaching critical mass becomes a certainty.
Well, I think I can help you.
With which part?
Both actually. *Heal the body, heal the mind...*
Here. Try this on.
There, see? Very nice. ***Fits perfect.***
It's a bit heavy. What is it?
It's a containment unit for any excess energy you happen to *bleed.*
I've tested it over the past couple of months, and General Groves has finally approved it for use.
*You want to get out of here?*

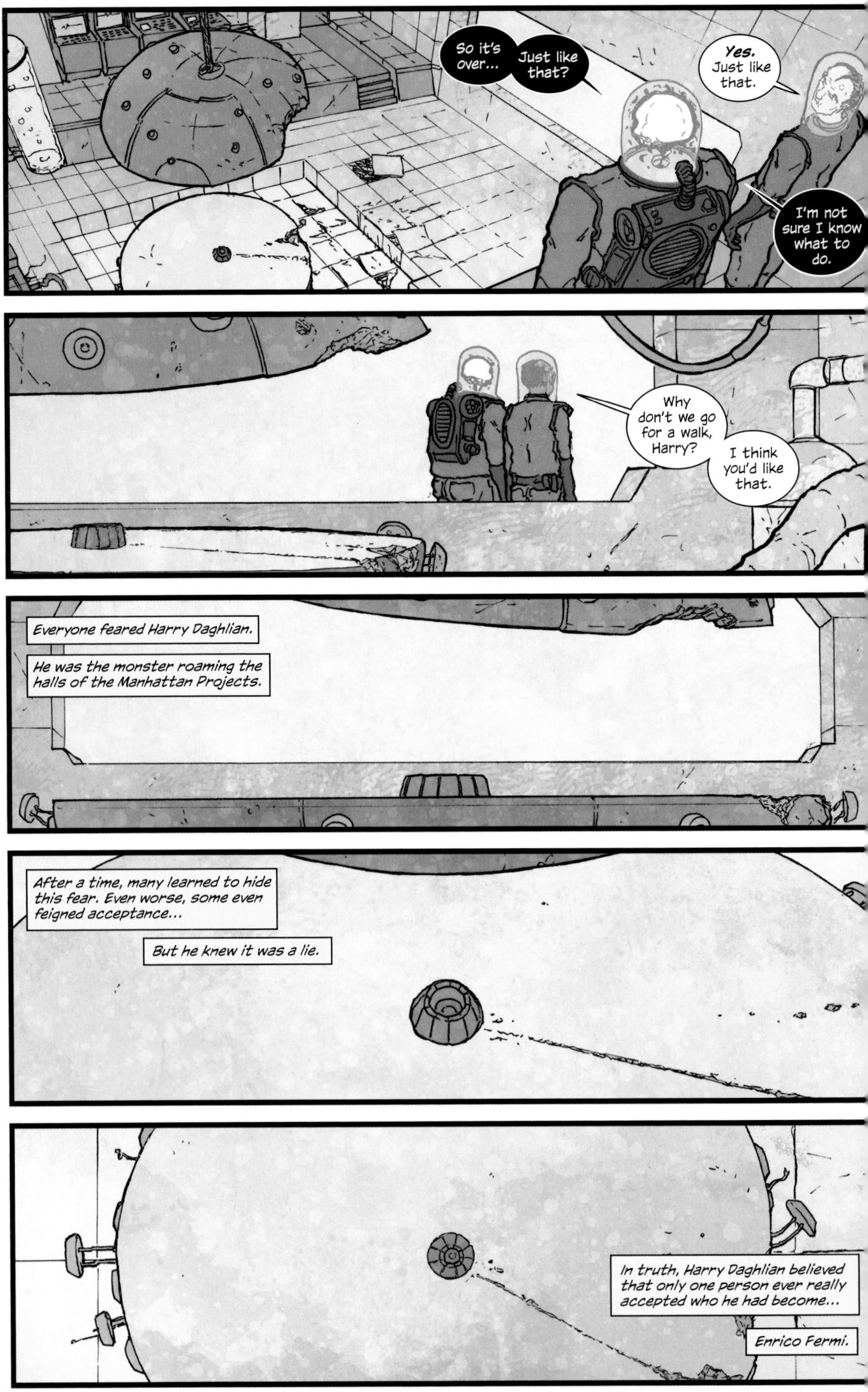
So it's over...
Just like that?
Yes. Just like that.
I'm not sure I know what to do.
Why don't we go for a walk, Harry?
I think you'd like that.
Everyone feared Harry Daghlian.
He was the monster roaming the halls of the Manhattan Projects.
After a time, many learned to hide this fear. Even worse, some even feigned acceptance...
But he knew it was a lie.
In truth, Harry Daghlian believed that only one person ever really accepted who he had become...
Enrico Fermi.

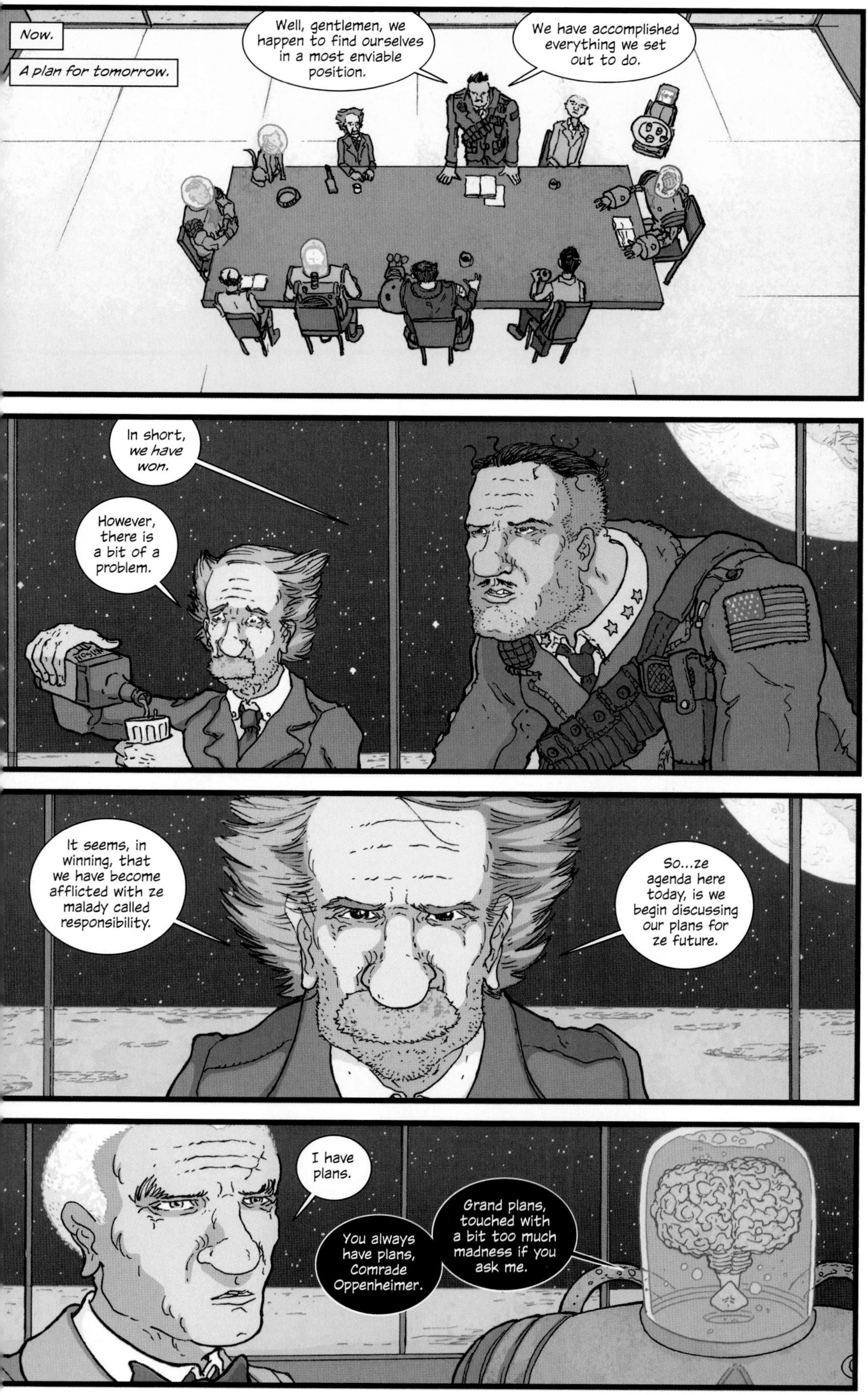
Now.
A plan for tomorrow.
Well, gentlemen, we happen to find ourselves in a most enviable position.
We have accomplished everything we set out to do.
In short, *we have* won.
However, there is a bit of a problem.
It seems, in winning, that we have become afflicted with ze malady called responsibility.
So...ze agenda here today, is we begin discussing our plans for ze future.
I have plans.
You always have plans, Comrade Oppenheimer.
Grand plans, touched with a bit too much madness if you ask me.

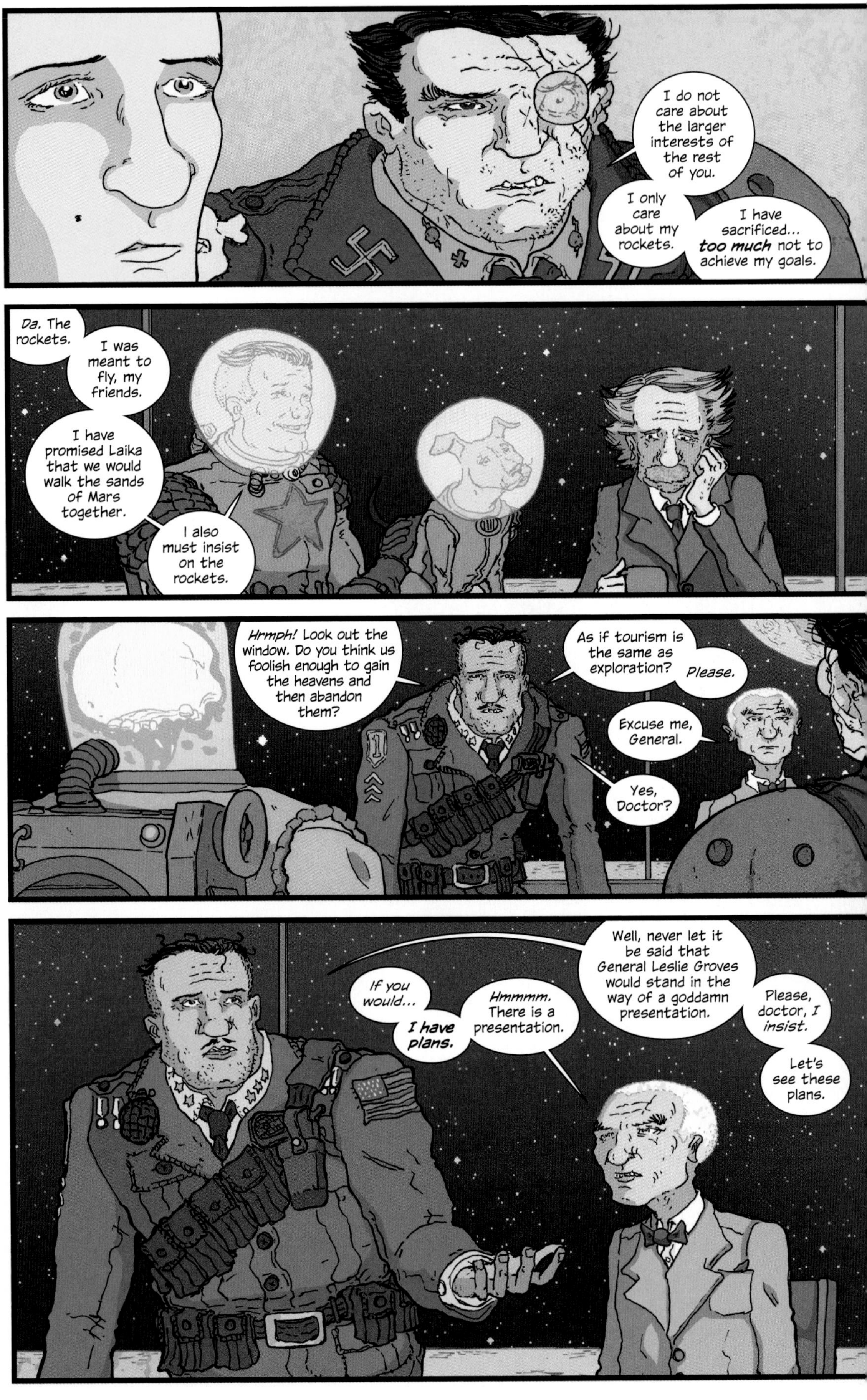
I do not care about the larger interests of the rest of you.
I only care about my rockets.
I have sacrificed... **too much** not to achieve my goals.
*Da.* The rockets.
I was meant to fly, my friends.
I have promised Laika that we would walk the sands of Mars together.
I also must insist on the rockets.
*Hrmph!* Look out the window. Do you think us foolish enough to gain the heavens and then abandon them?
As if tourism is the same as exploration?
*Please.*
Excuse me, General.
Yes, Doctor?
*If you would...*
***I have plans.***
*Hmmmm.* There is a presentation.
Well, never let it be said that General Leslie Groves would stand in the way of a goddamn presentation.
Please, doctor, *I insist.*
Let's see these plans.

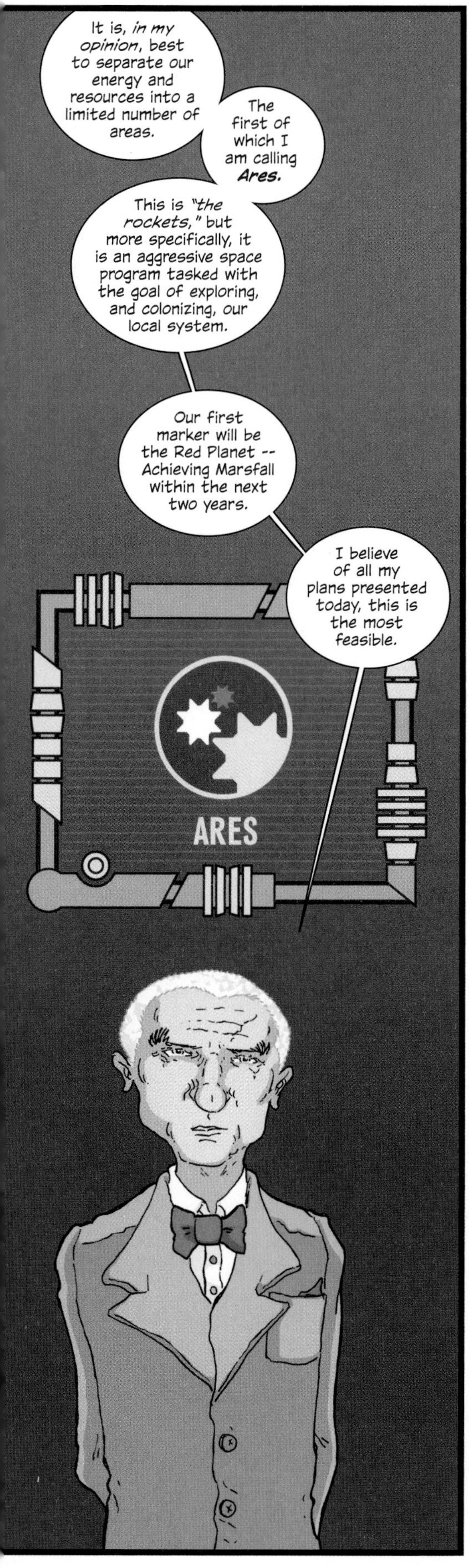
It is, *in my opinion*, best to separate our energy and resources into a limited number of areas.
The first of which I am calling ***Ares.***
This is *"the rockets,"* but more specifically, it is an aggressive space program tasked with the goal of exploring, and colonizing, our local system.
Our first marker will be the Red Planet -- Achieving Marsfall within the next two years.
I believe of all my plans presented today, this is the most feasible.
ARES

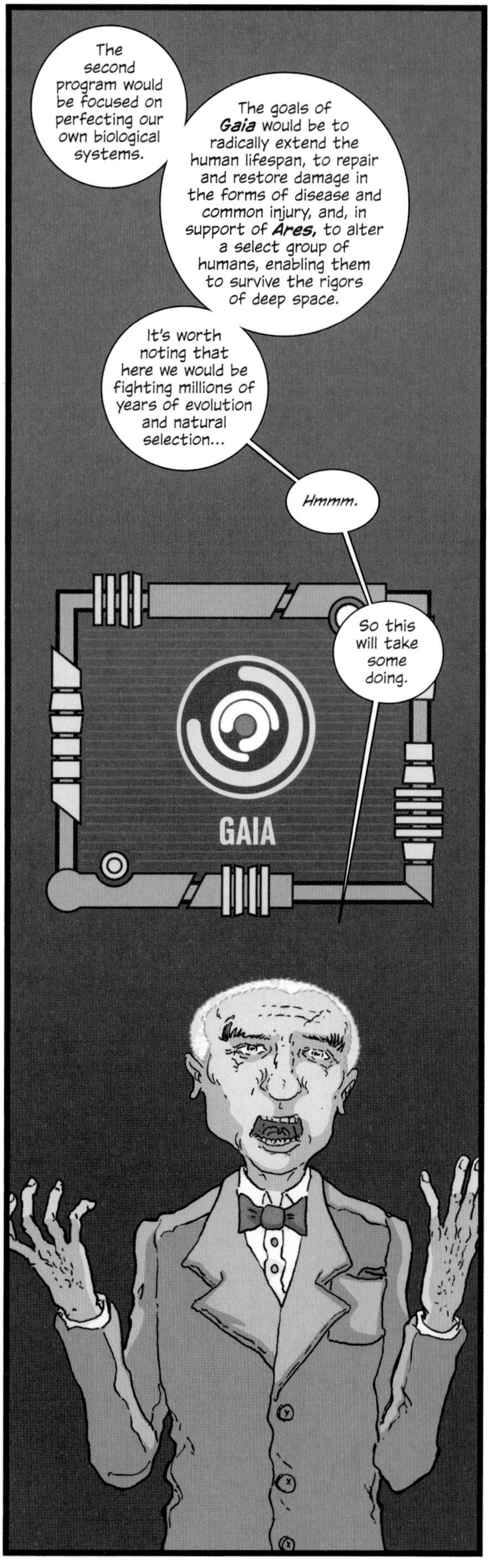
The second program would be focused on perfecting our own biological systems.
The goals of ***Gaia*** would be to radically extend the human lifespan, to repair and restore damage in the forms of disease and common injury, and, in support of ***Ares,*** to alter a select group of humans, enabling them to survive the rigors of deep space.
It's worth noting that here we would be fighting millions of years of evolution and natural selection...
*Hmmm.*
So this will take some doing.
GAIA

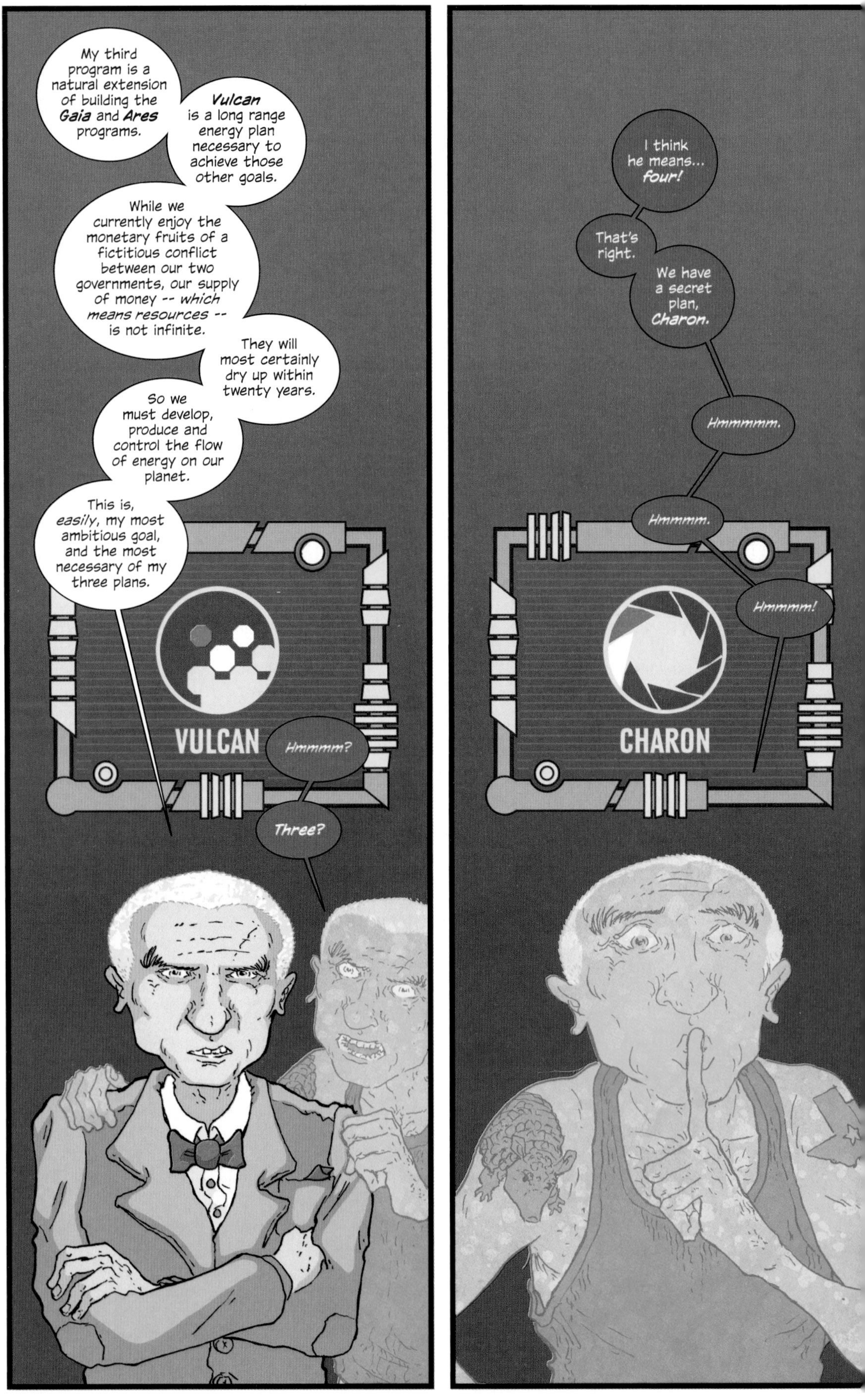
My third program is a natural extension of building the *Gaia* and *Ares* programs.
*Vulcan* is a long range energy plan necessary to achieve those other goals.
While we currently enjoy the monetary fruits of a fictitious conflict between our two governments, our supply of money -- *which means resources* -- is not infinite.
They will most certainly dry up within twenty years.
So we must develop, produce and control the flow of energy on our planet.
This is, *easily*, my most ambitious goal, and the most necessary of my three plans.
VULCAN
*Hmmmm?*
*Three?*
I think he means... *four!*
That's right.
We have a secret plan, *Charon.*
*Hmmmmm.*
*Hmmmm.*
*Hmmmm!*
CHARON

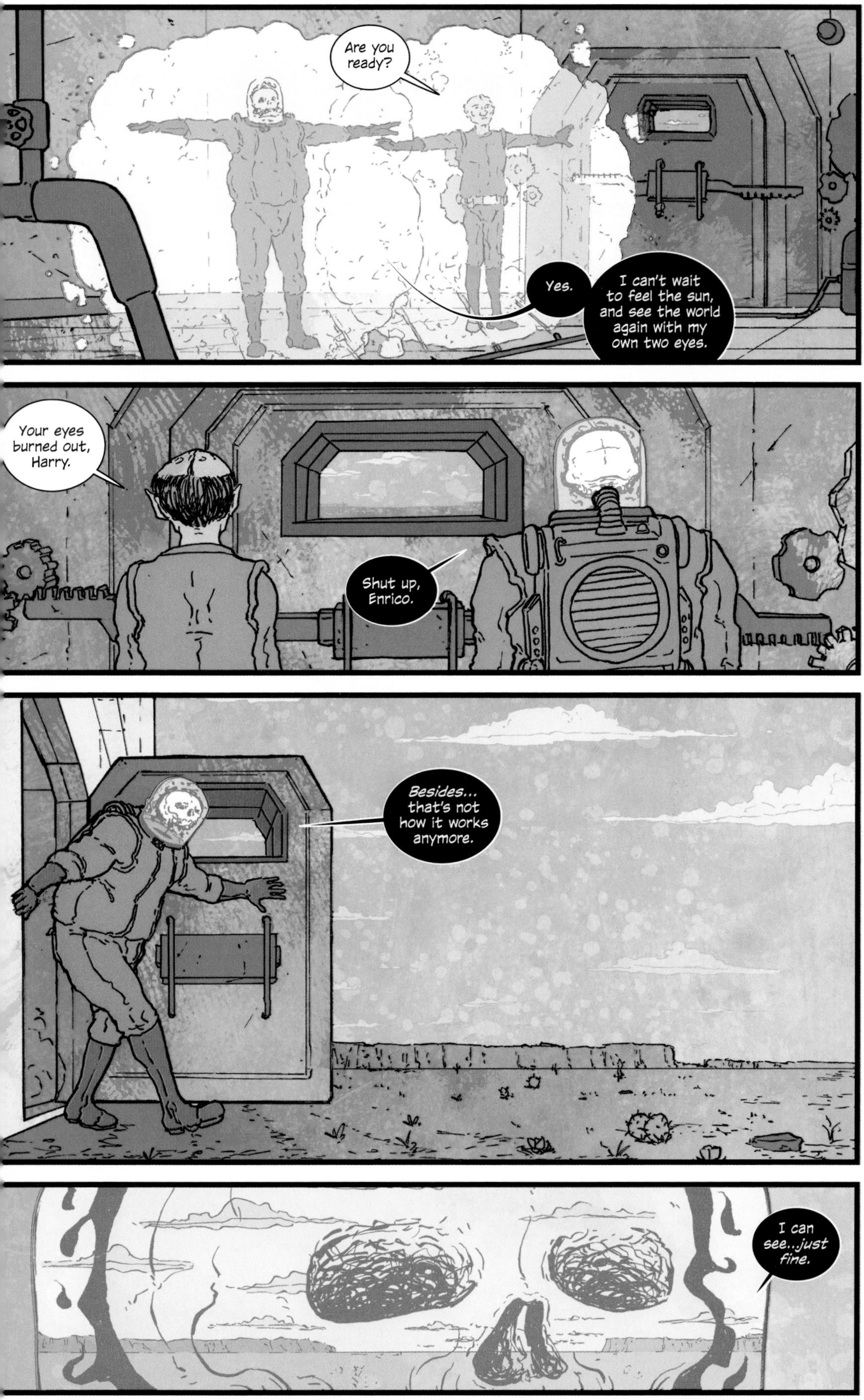
Are you ready?
Yes.
I can't wait to feel the sun, and see the world again with my own two eyes.
Your eyes burned out, Harry.
Shut up, Enrico.
*Besides...* that's not how it works anymore.
I can see...*just fine.*

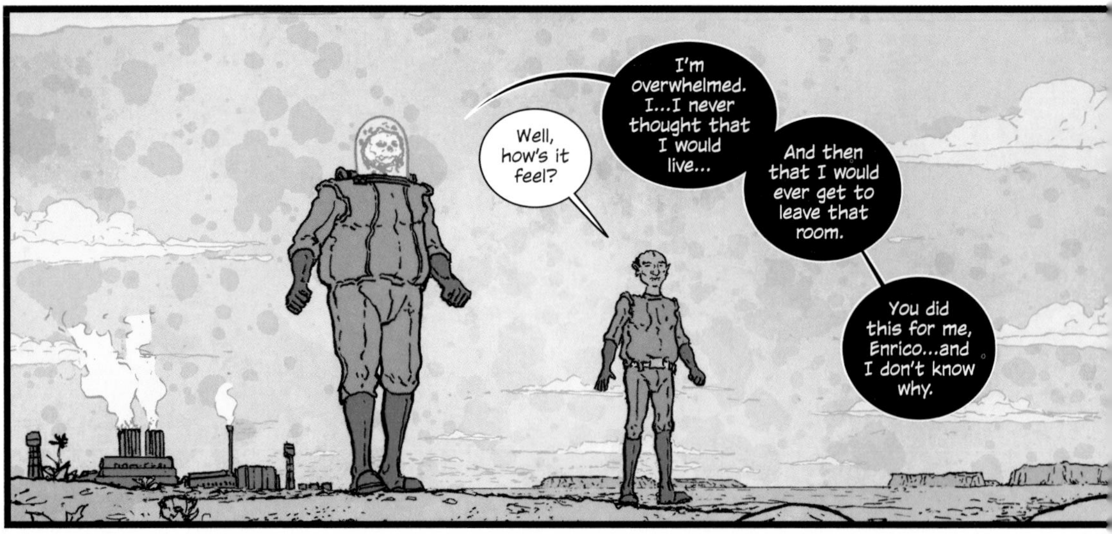
Well, how's it feel?
I'm overwhelmed. I...I never thought that I would live...
And then that I would ever get to leave that room.
You did this for me, Enrico...and I don't know why.

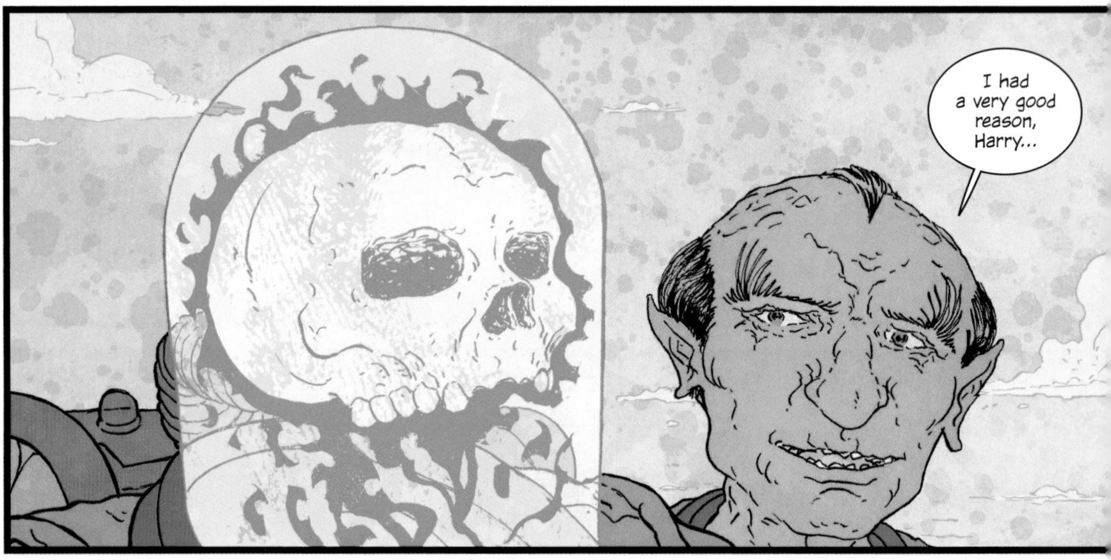
I had a very good reason, Harry...

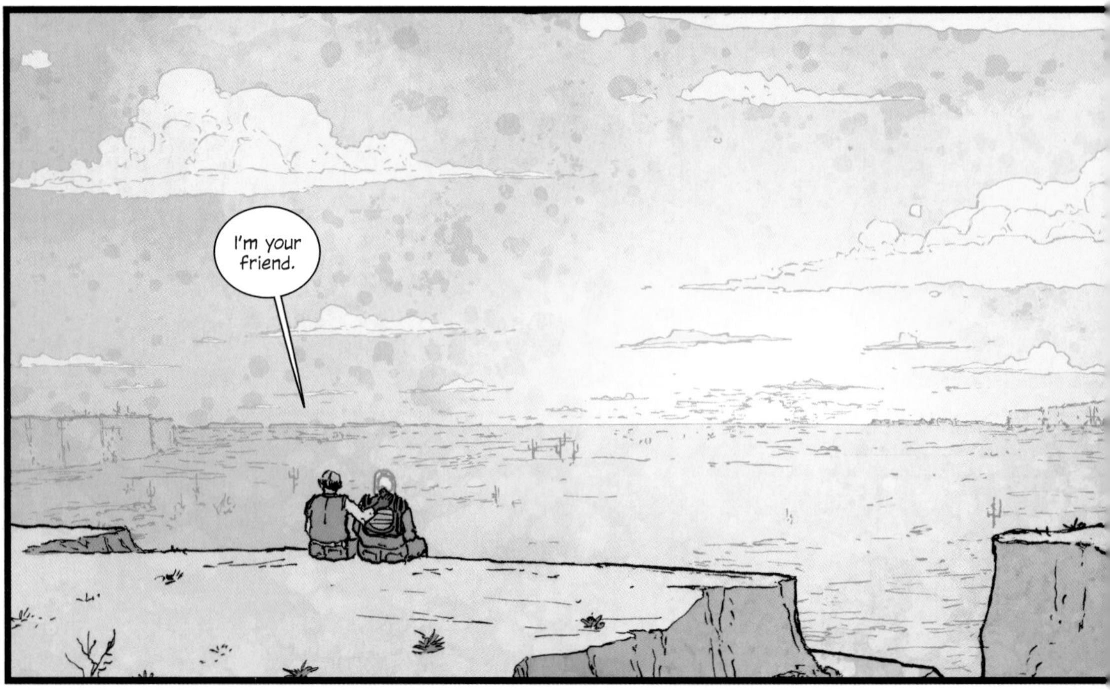
I'm your friend.

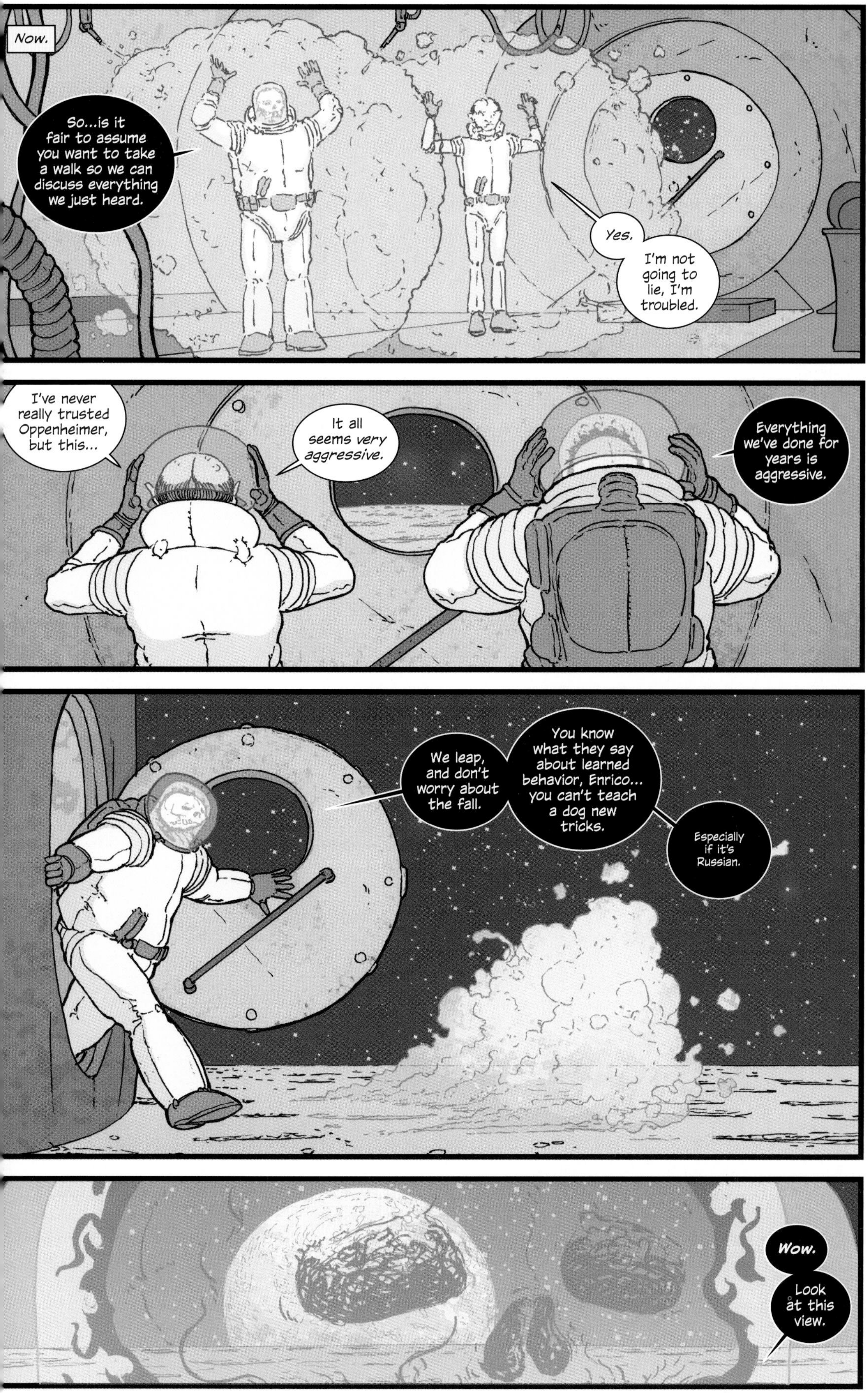
Now.
So...is it fair to assume you want to take a walk so we can discuss everything we just heard.
Yes.
I'm not going to lie, I'm troubled.
I've never really trusted Oppenheimer, but this...
It all seems very aggressive.
Everything we've done for years is aggressive.
We leap, and don't worry about the fall.
You know what they say about learned behavior, Enrico... you can't teach a dog new tricks.
Especially if it's Russian.
Wow.
Look at this view.

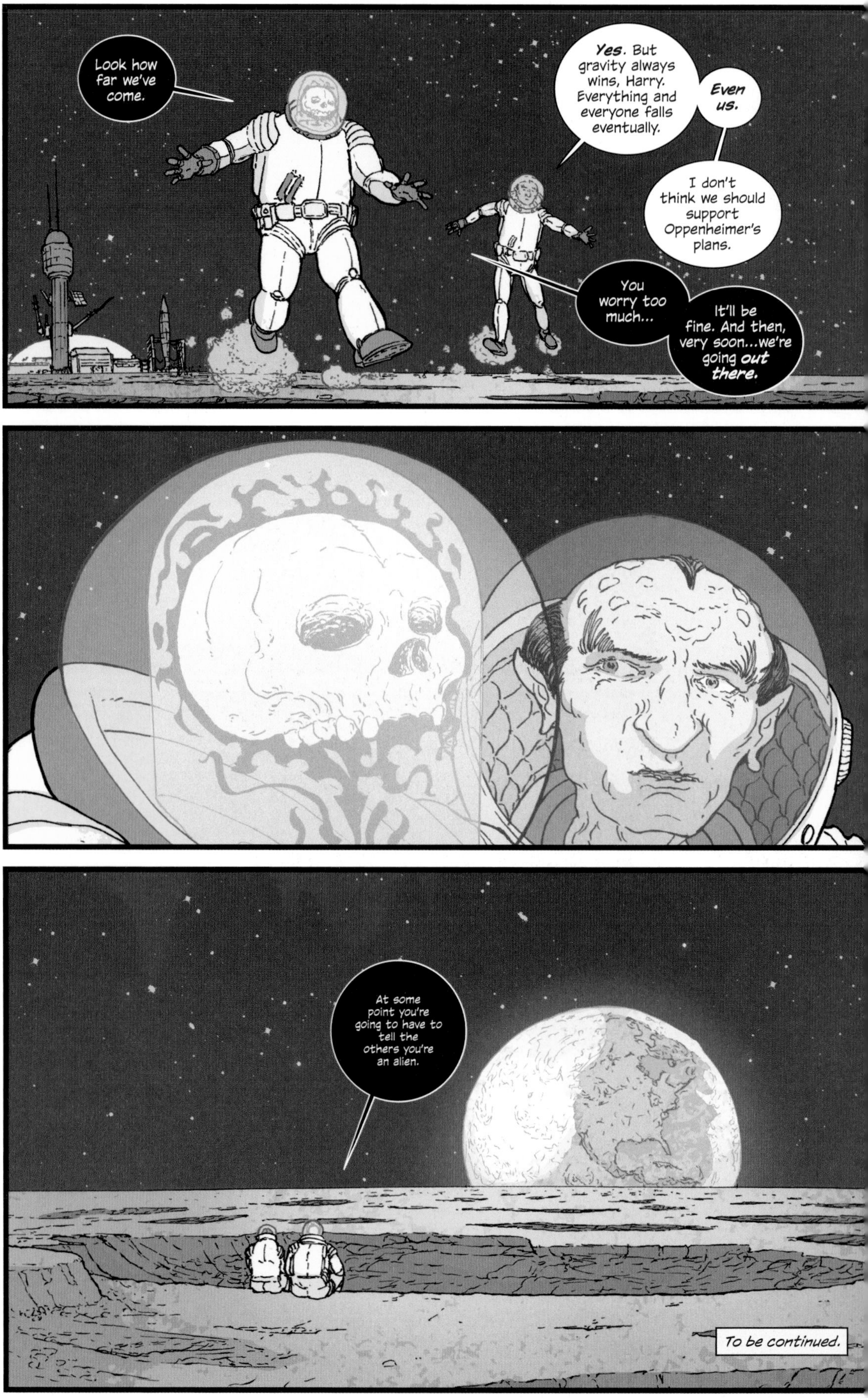

Look how far we've come.
Yes. But gravity always wins, Harry. Everything and everyone falls eventually.
Even us.
I don't think we should support Oppenheimer's plans.
You worry too much...
It'll be fine. And then, very soon...we're going out there.
At some point you're going to have to tell the others you're an alien.
To be continued.

"ALL HAIL THE DEMON CORE."

- FERMI

*CLAVIS AUREA*
THE RECORDED FEYNMAN | **VOL. 3**

# DRONE STATUS:
## ONLINE

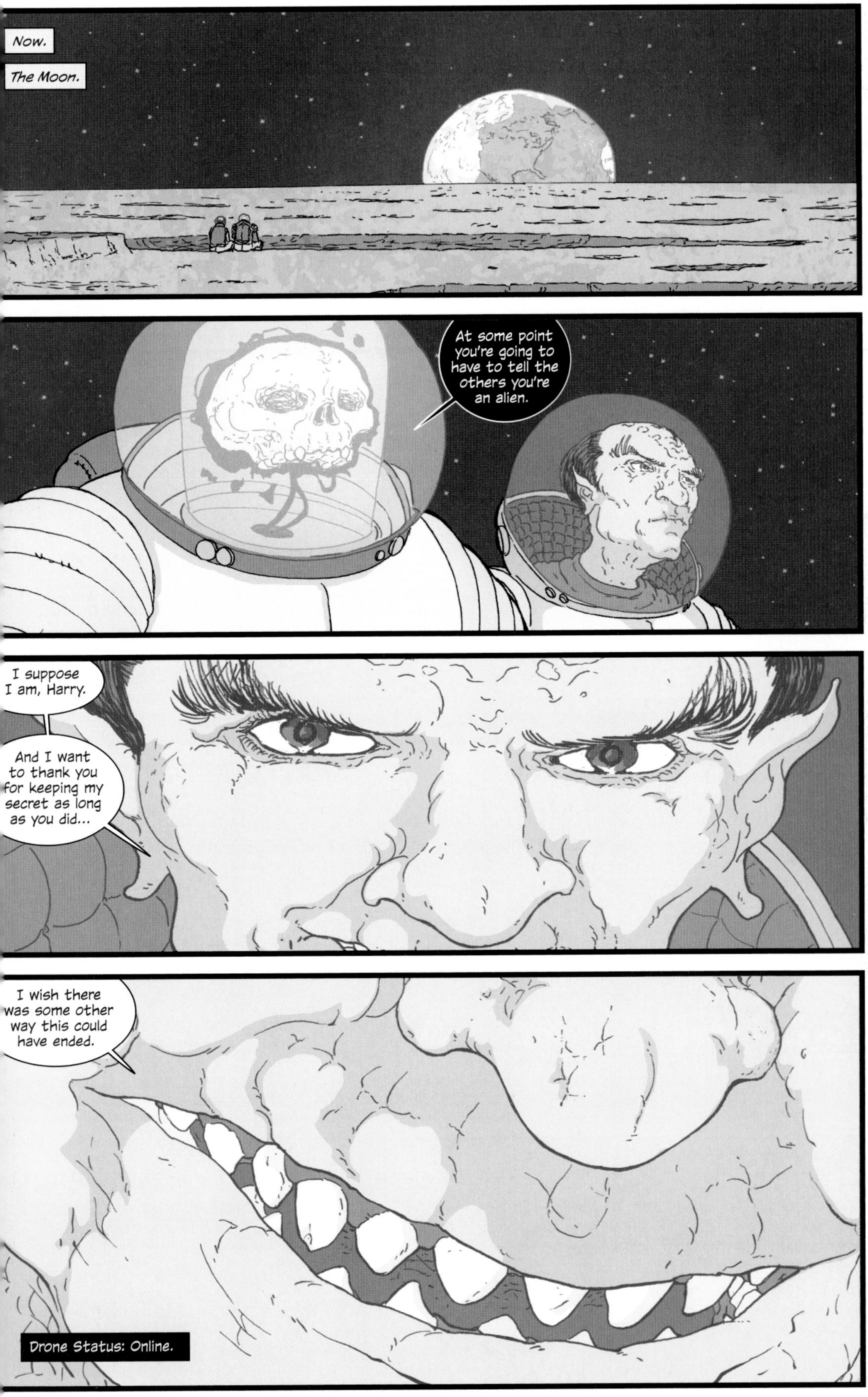
Now.
The Moon.
At some point you're going to have to tell the others you're an alien.
I suppose I am, Harry.
And I want to thank you for keeping my secret as long as you did...
I wish there was some other way this could have ended.
Drone Status: Online.

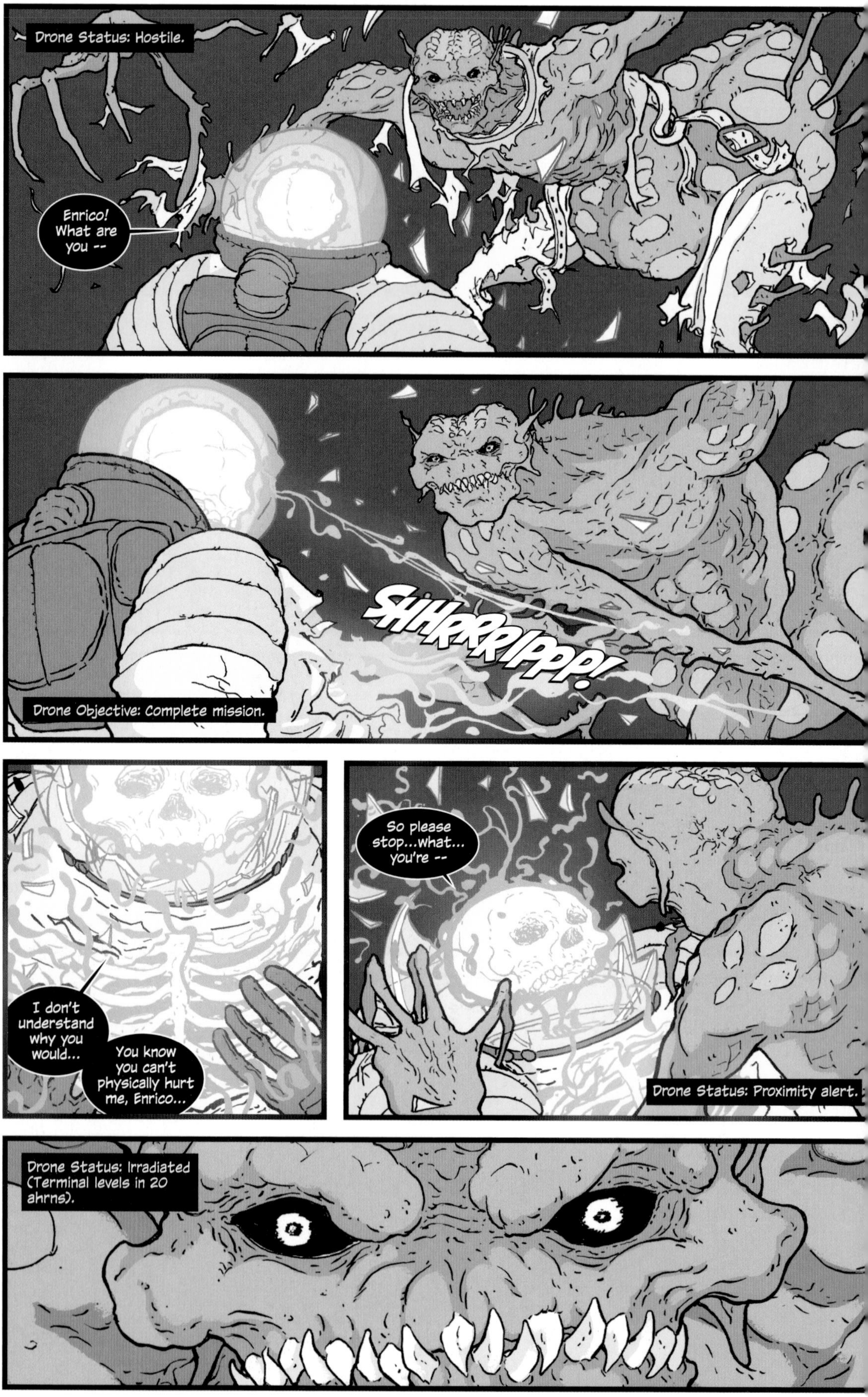
Drone Status: Hostile.
Enrico! What are you --
SHHRRRIPPP!
Drone Objective: Complete mission.
I don't understand why you would...
You know you can't physically hurt me, Enrico...
So please stop...what... you're --
Drone Status: Proximity alert.
Drone Status: Irradiated (Terminal levels in 20 ahrns).

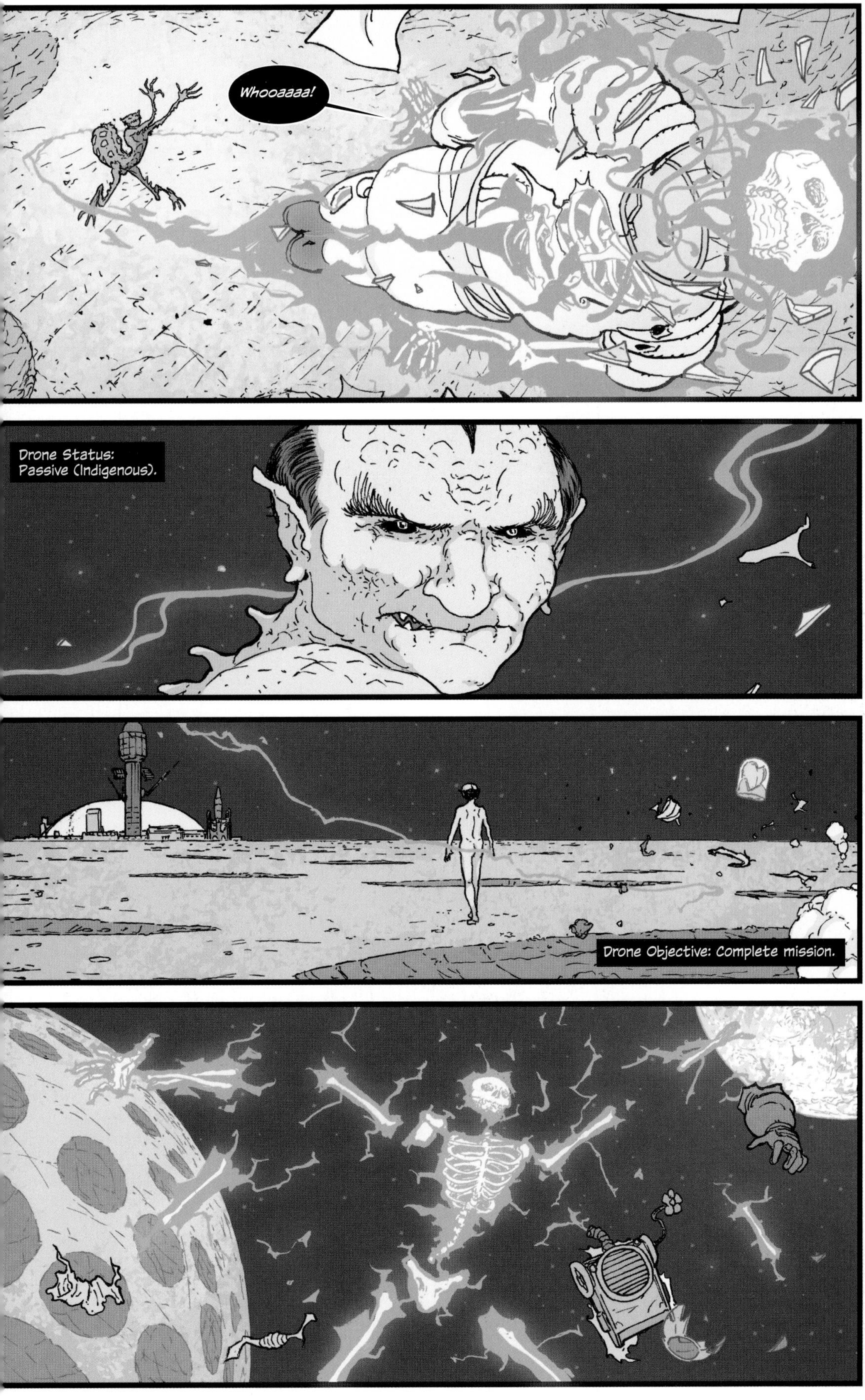
Whooaaaa!
Drone Status:
Passive (Indigenous).
Drone Objective: Complete mission.

# 12

## THE FERMI PARADOX

"COSMETIC SURGERY HAS COME A LONG
WAY. "

*CLAVIS AUREA*
THE RECORDED FEYNMAN | **VOL. 3**

Then.

Probe: Habitable zone, industrialized planet detected.

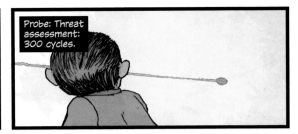

Probe: Threat assessment: 300 cycles.

Probe Action: Observe.

Probe Action: Send Drone.

Drone Status: Online.

<Hey, look. You done fell from up in the sky. You weird-looking, and I ain't too smart, but I betcha you're some kinda birdsnake.>

<My daddy don't like no snakes, so let's keeps things quiet. Okay? My name's, Enrico, I like eating worms too.>

Drone Status: Assimilate.

<Okay.>

<Fuh-whu!>

Drone Objective: Complete mission.

Mission Objective: Observe.

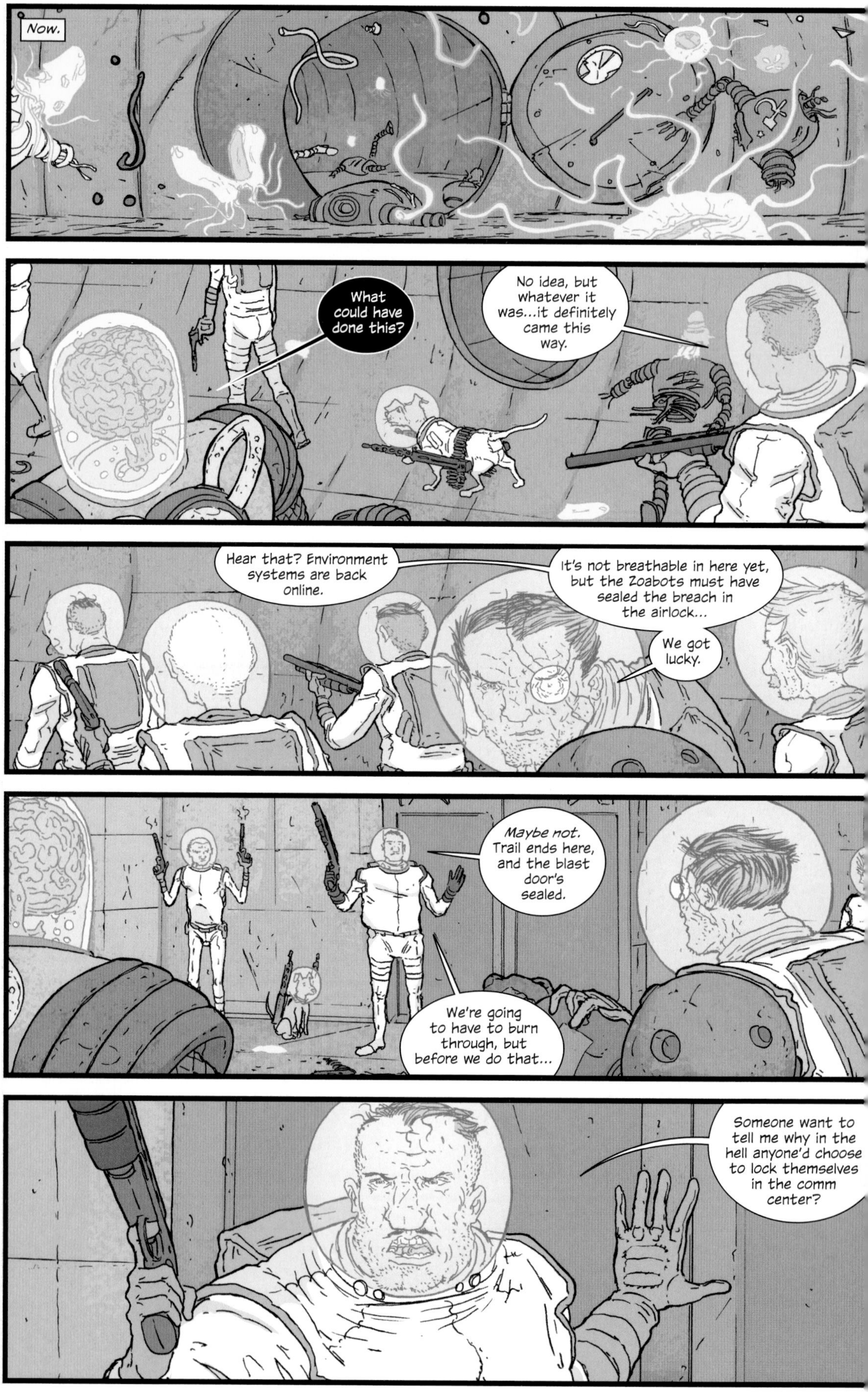
Now.
What could have done this?
No idea, but whatever it was...it definitely came this way.
Hear that? Environment systems are back online.
It's not breathable in here yet, but the Zoabots must have sealed the breach in the airlock...
We got lucky.
*Maybe not.* Trail ends here, and the blast door's sealed.
We're going to have to burn through, but before we do that...
Someone want to tell me why in the hell anyone'd choose to lock themselves in the comm center?

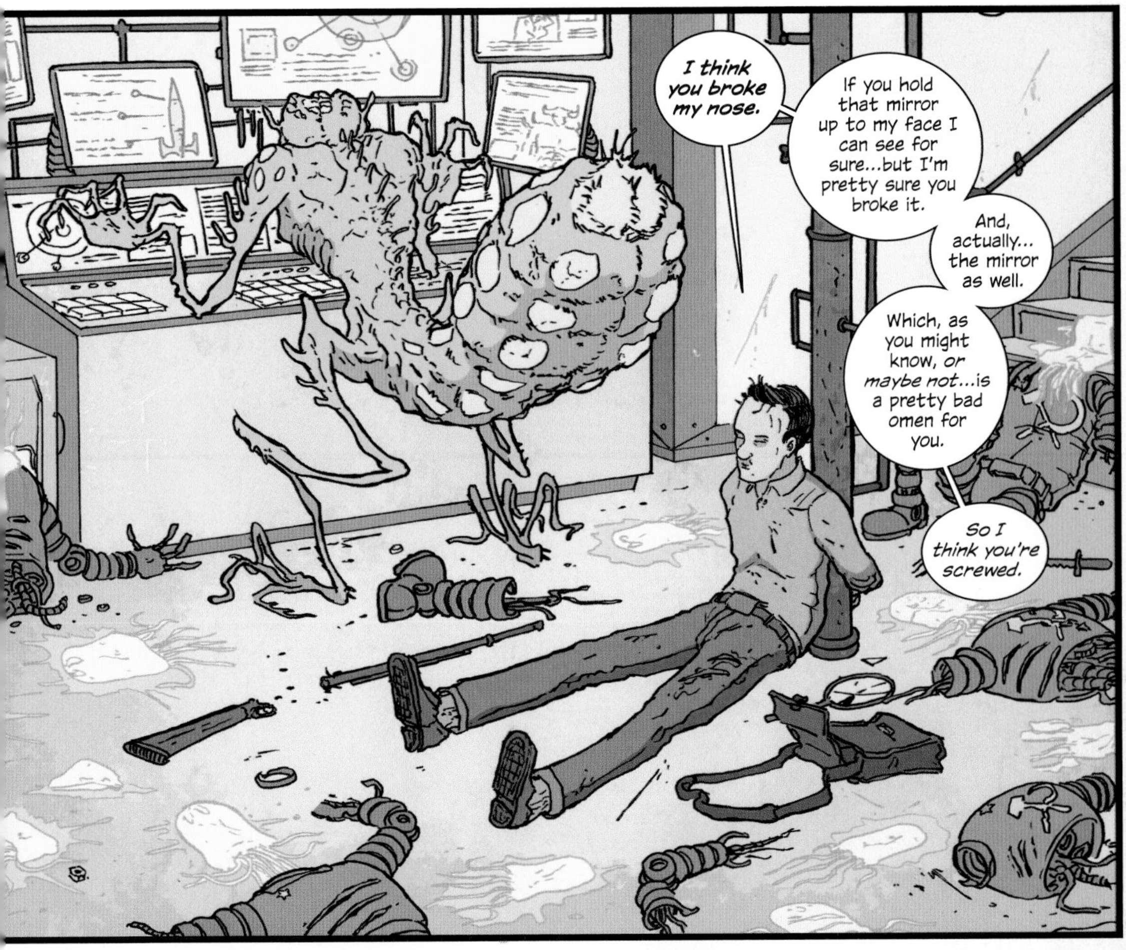
I think you broke my nose.
If you hold that mirror up to my face I can see for sure...but I'm pretty sure you broke it.
And, actually... the mirror as well.
Which, as you might know, or maybe not...is a pretty bad omen for you.
So I think you're screwed.

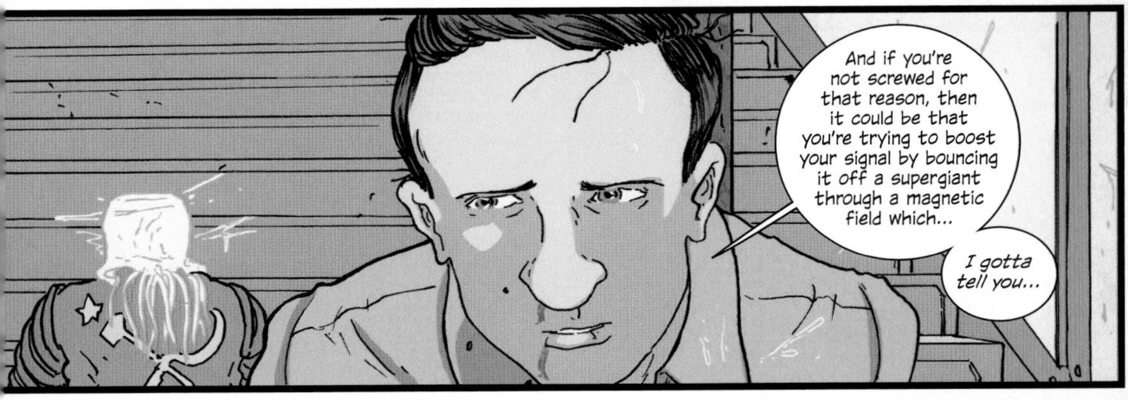
And if you're not screwed for that reason, then it could be that you're trying to boost your signal by bouncing it off a supergiant through a magnetic field which...
I gotta tell you...

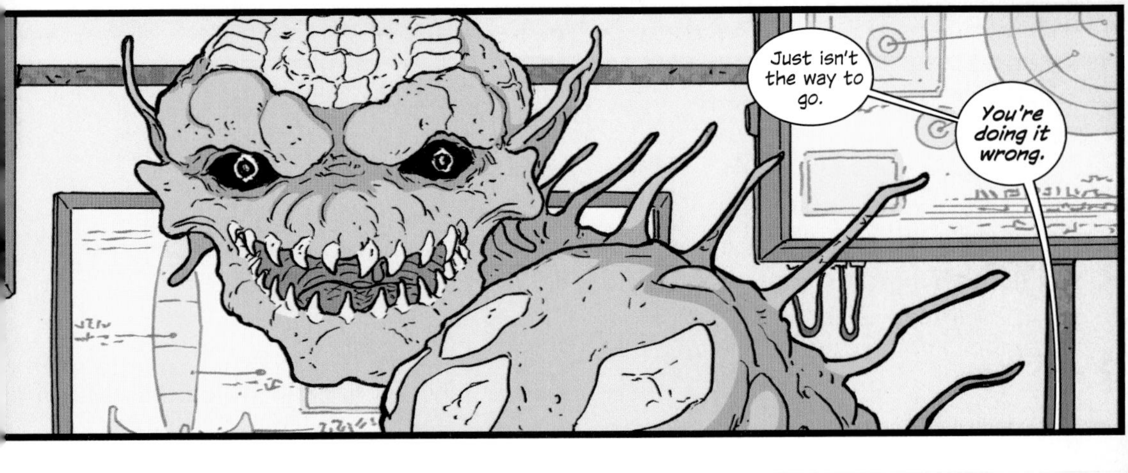
Just isn't the way to go.
You're doing it wrong.

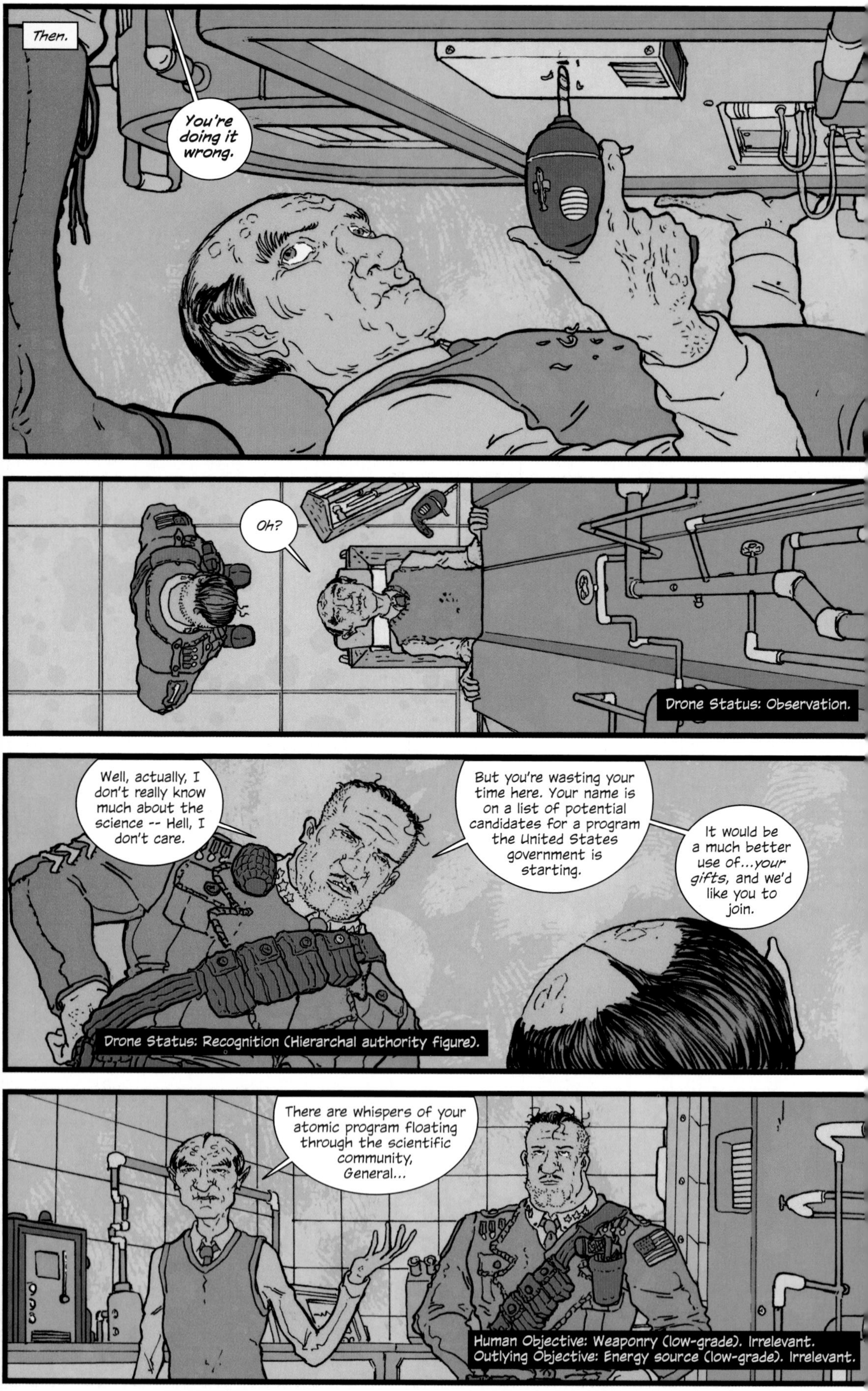
Then.
You're doing it wrong.
Oh?
Drone Status: Observation.
Well, actually, I don't really know much about the science -- Hell, I don't care.
But you're wasting your time here. Your name is on a list of potential candidates for a program the United States government is starting.
It would be a much better use of...your gifts, and we'd like you to join.
Drone Status: Recognition (Hierarchal authority figure).
There are whispers of your atomic program floating through the scientific community, General...
Human Objective: Weaponry (low-grade). Irrelevant.
Outlying Objective: Energy source (low-grade). Irrelevant.

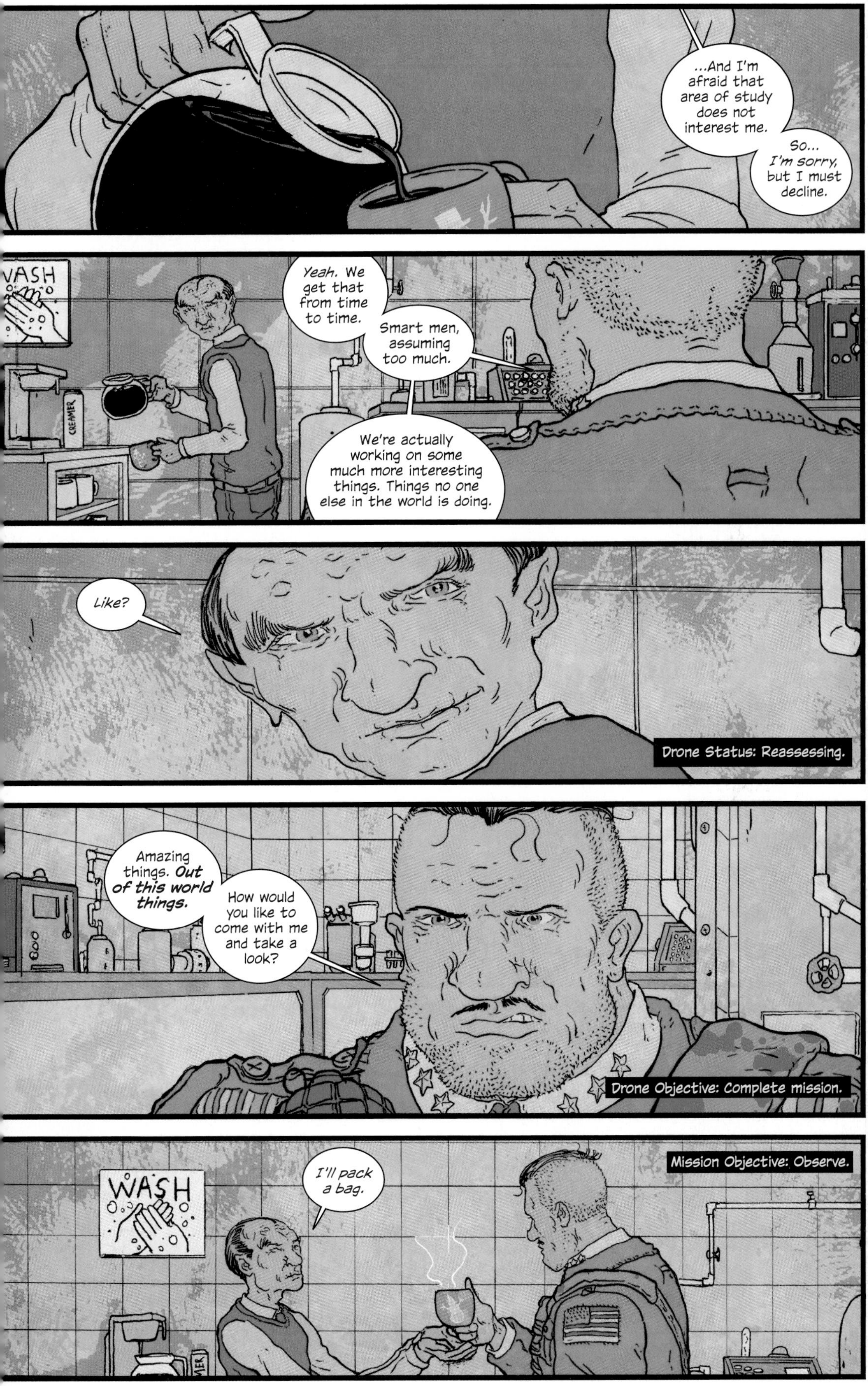

...And I'm afraid that area of study does not interest me.
So... *I'm sorry,* but I must decline.
*Yeah.* We get that from time to time.
Smart men, assuming too much.
We're actually working on some much more interesting things. Things no one else in the world is doing.
VASH
CREAMER
*Like?*
Drone Status: Reassessing.
Amazing things. ***Out of this world things.***
How would you like to come with me and take a look?
Drone Objective: Complete mission.
Mission Objective: Observe.
*I'll pack a bag.*
WASH

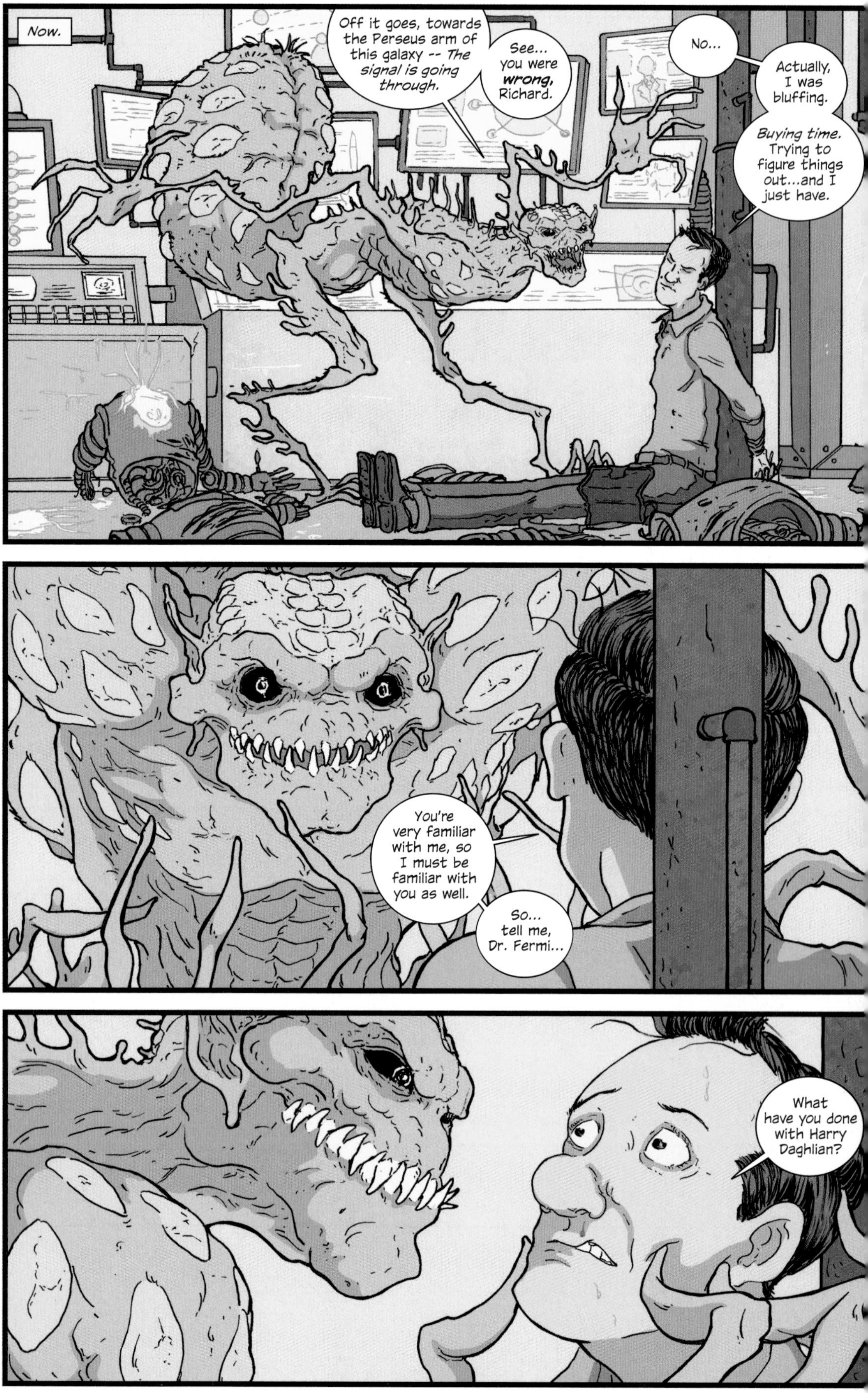
Now.
Off it goes, towards the Perseus arm of this galaxy -- *The signal is going through.*
See... you were ***wrong,*** Richard.
No...
Actually, I was bluffing.
*Buying time.* Trying to figure things out...and I just have.
You're very familiar with me, so I must be familiar with you as well.
So... tell me, Dr. Fermi...
What have you done with Harry Daghlian?

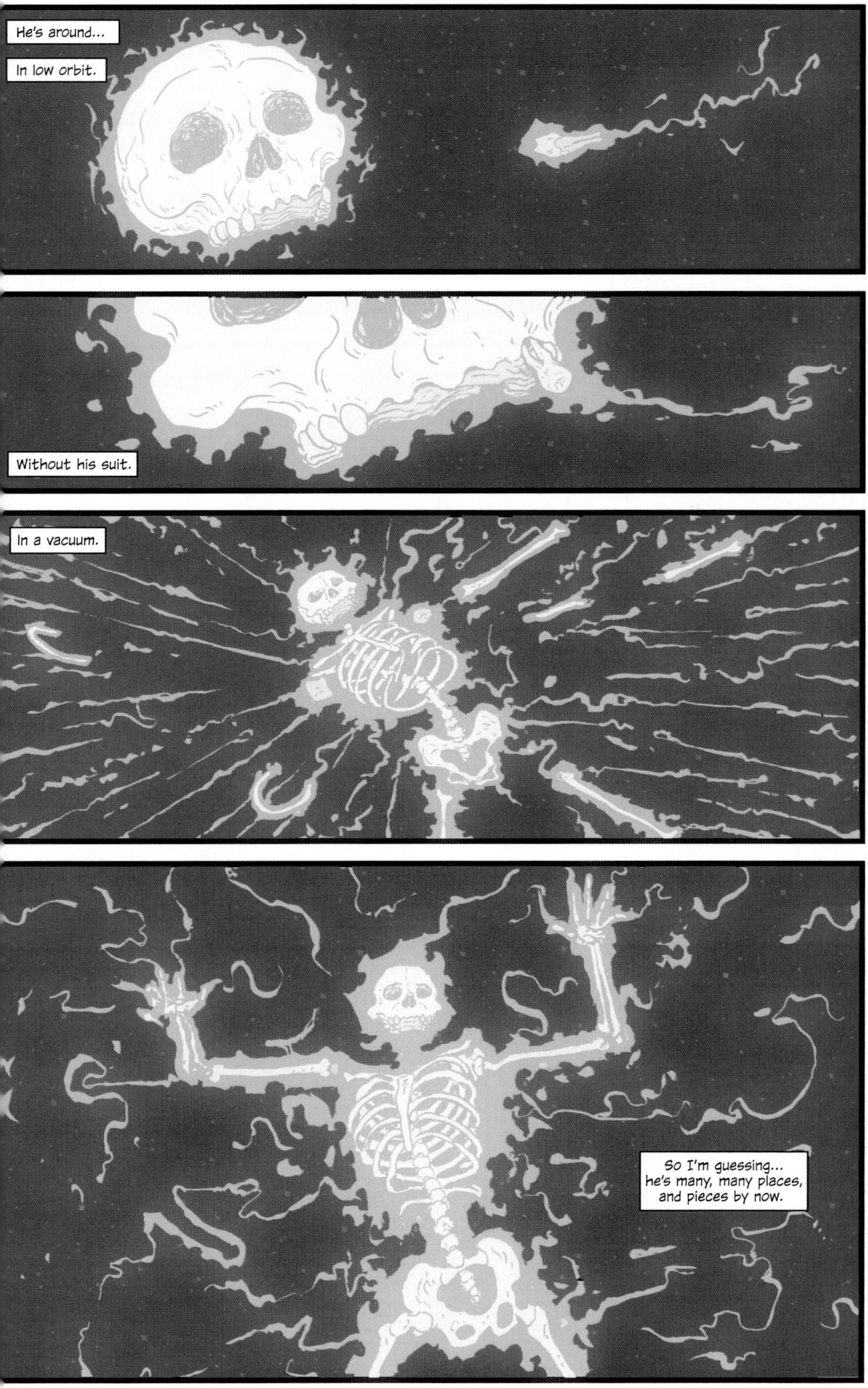
He's around...
In low orbit.
Without his suit.
In a vacuum.
So I'm guessing... he's many, many places, and pieces by now.

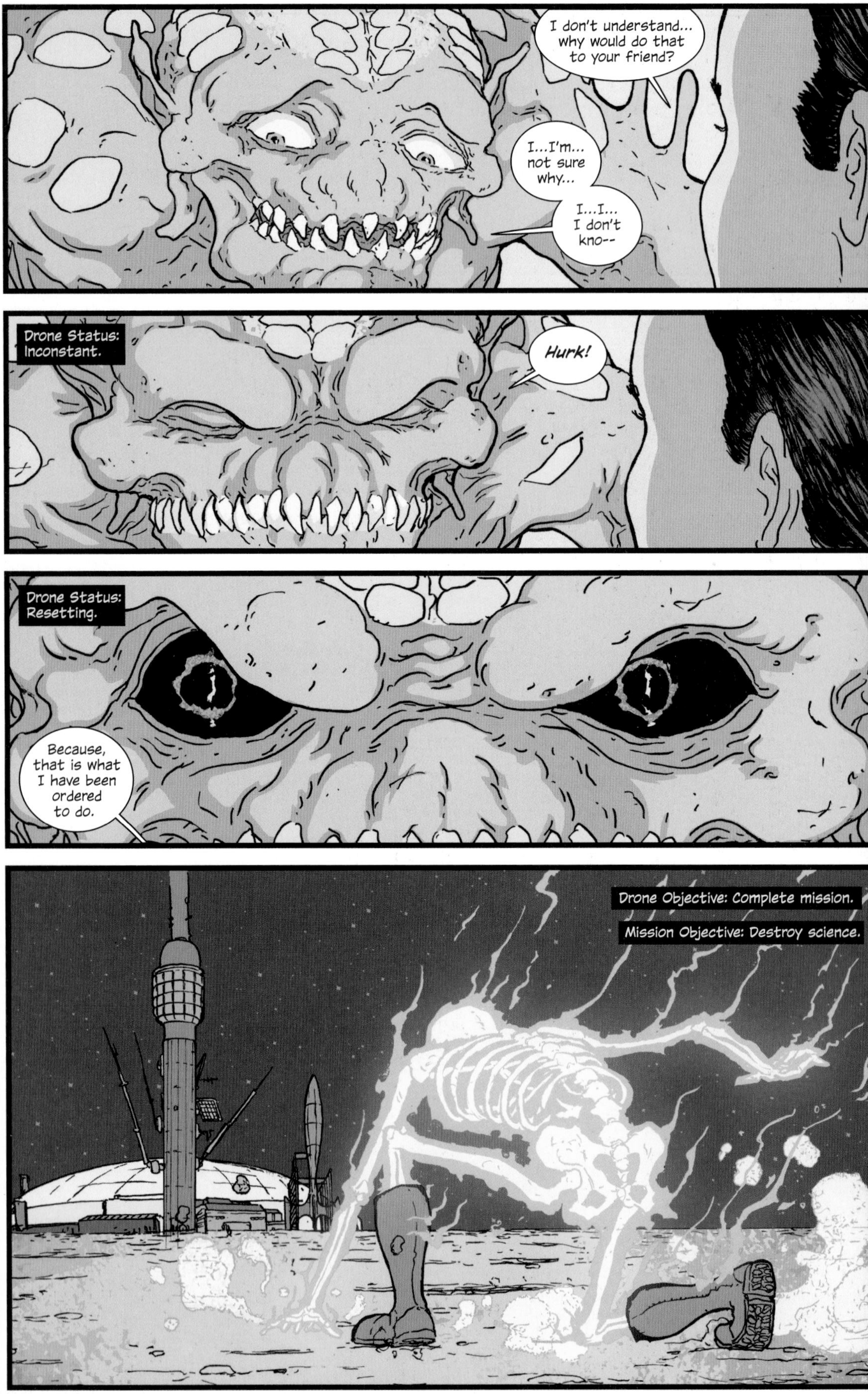
I don't understand... why would do that to your friend?
I...I'm... not sure why...
I...I... I don't kno--
Drone Status: Inconstant.
Hurk!
Drone Status: Resetting.
Because, that is what I have been ordered to do.
Drone Objective: Complete mission.
Mission Objective: Destroy science.

Then.

Mission Objective: Observation (sub-designation: Top level science programs).

Drone Status: Ineffectual (assigned to atomics).

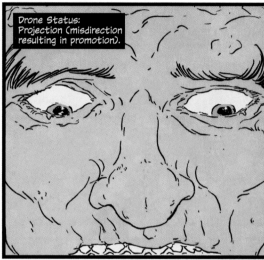

Drone Status: Projection (misdirection resulting in promotion).

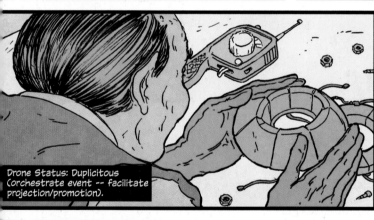

Drone Status: Duplicitous (orchestrate event -- facilitate projection/promotion).

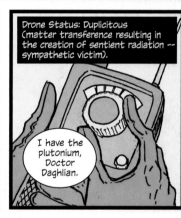

Drone Status: Duplicitous (matter transference resulting in the creation of sentient radiation -- sympathetic victim).

I have the plutonium, Doctor Daghlian.

Good. Bring it over...nice and easy.

Steady...

Mission Objective: Observation.

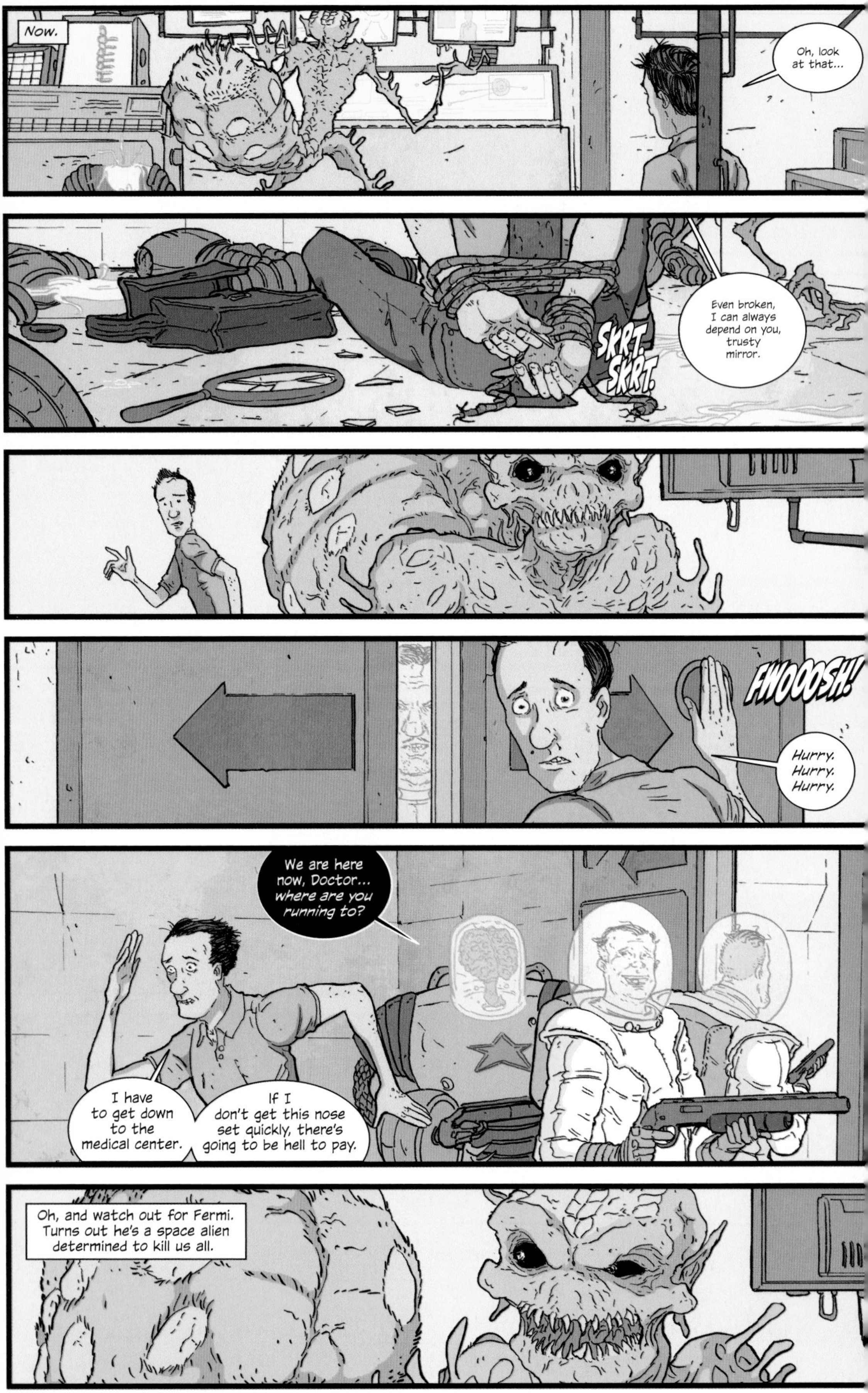
Now.
Oh, look at that...
Even broken, I can always depend on you, trusty mirror.
SKRT. SKRT.
FWOOOSH!
Hurry. Hurry. Hurry.
We are here now, Doctor... where are you running to?
I have to get down to the medical center.
If I don't get this nose set quickly, there's going to be hell to pay.
Oh, and watch out for Fermi. Turns out he's a space alien determined to kill us all.

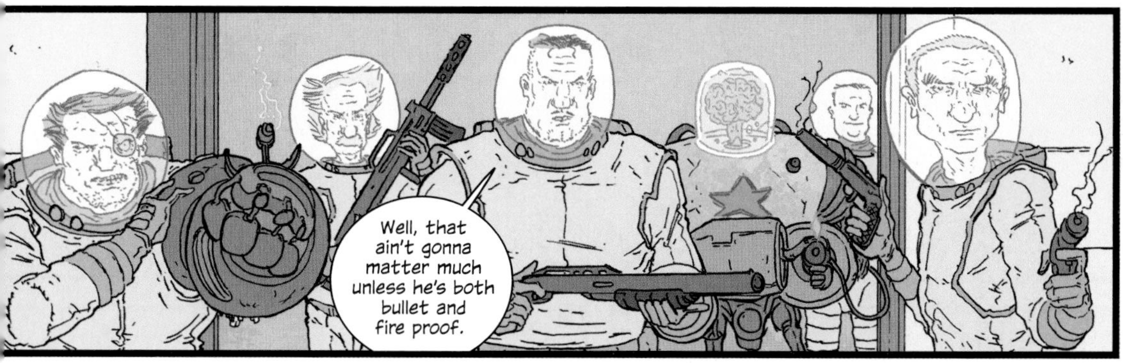
Well, that ain't gonna matter much unless he's both bullet and fire proof.

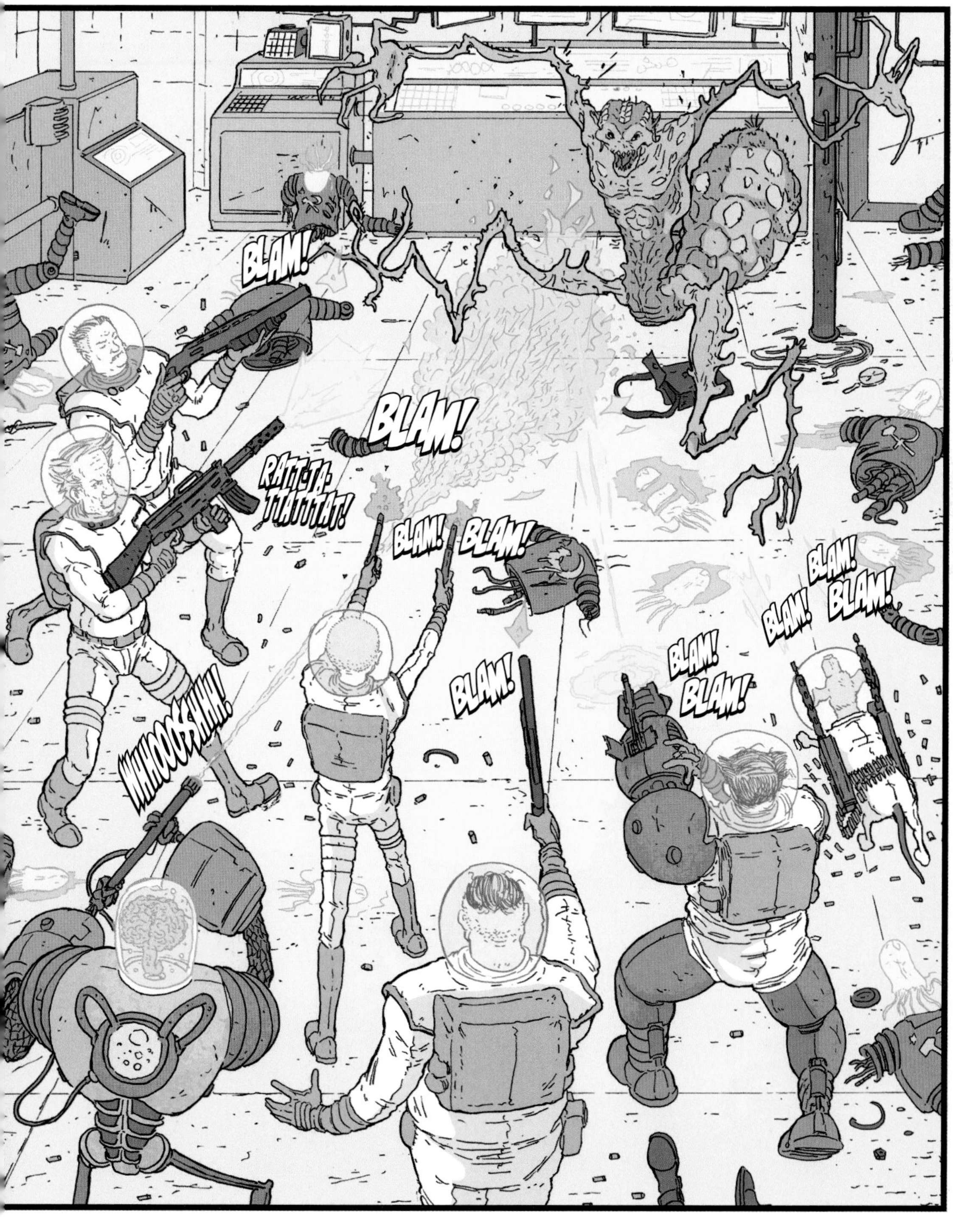
BLAM!
BLAM!
RATT-TA-TTATTTAT!
BLAM!
BLAM!
BLAM!
BLAM!
BLAM!
BLAM!
BLAM!
BLAM!
BLAM!
WHHOOOSHHH!

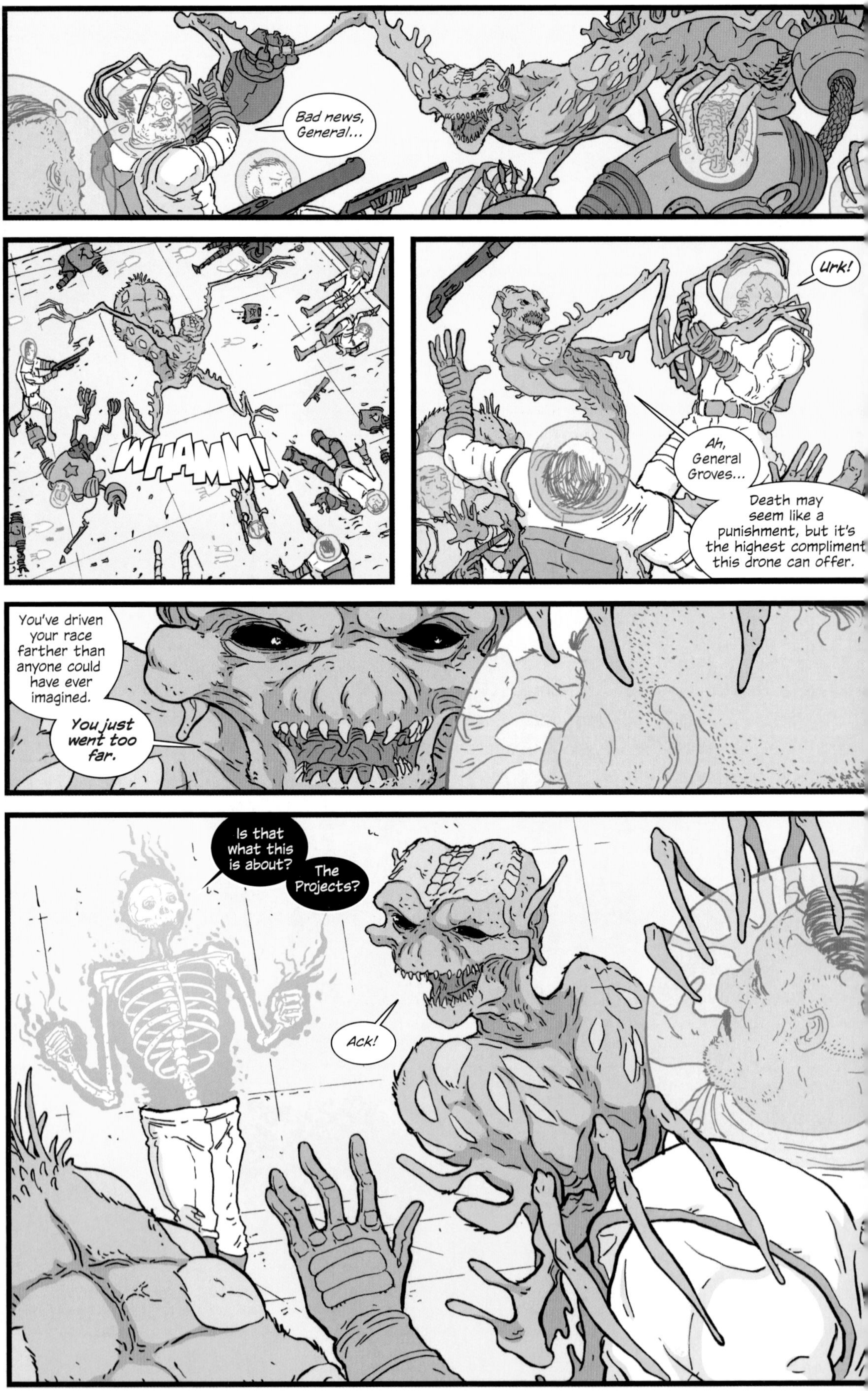
Bad news, General...
WHAMM!
Urk!
Ah, General Groves...
Death may seem like a punishment, but it's the highest compliment this drone can offer.
You've driven your race farther than anyone could have ever imagined.
You just went too far.
Is that what this is about?
The Projects?
Ack!

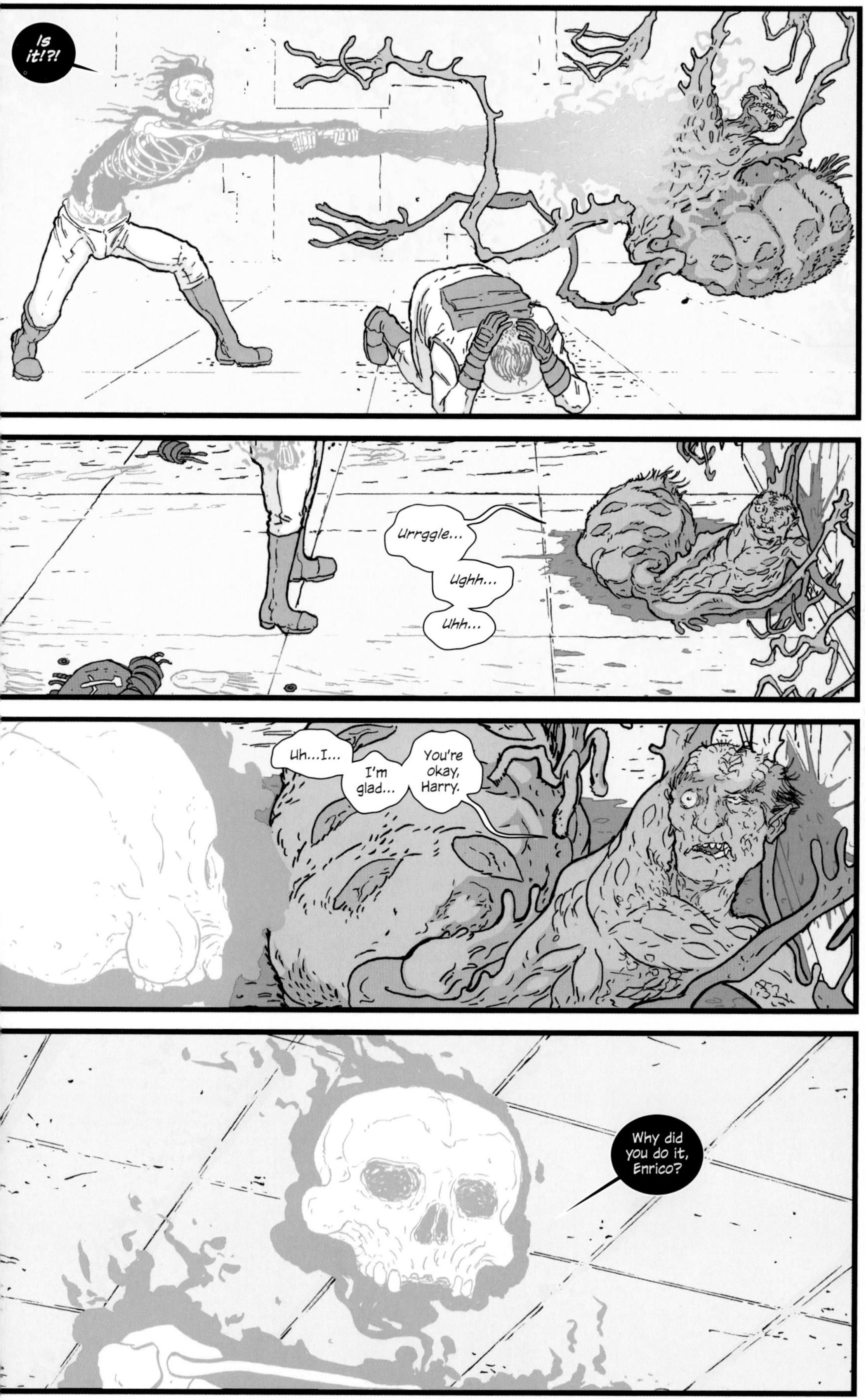
Is it!?!
Urrggle...
Ughh...
Uhh...
Uh...I...
I'm glad...
You're okay, Harry.
Why did you do it, Enrico?

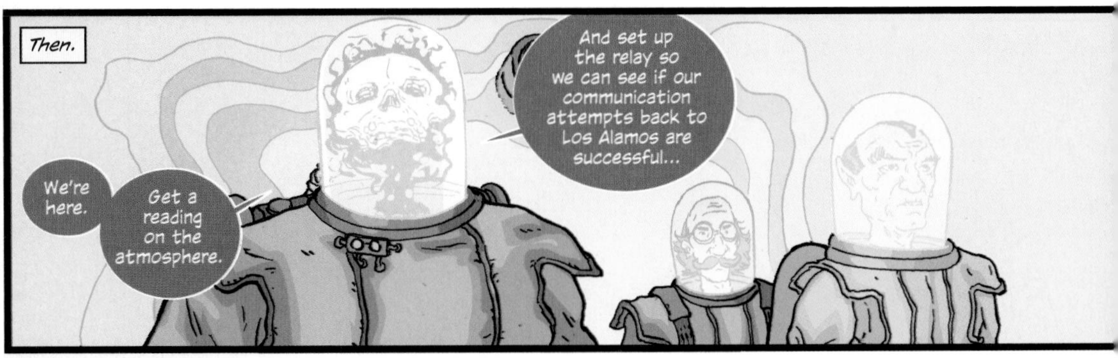
Then.
We're here.
Get a reading on the atmosphere.
And set up the relay so we can see if our communication attempts back to Los Alamos are successful...

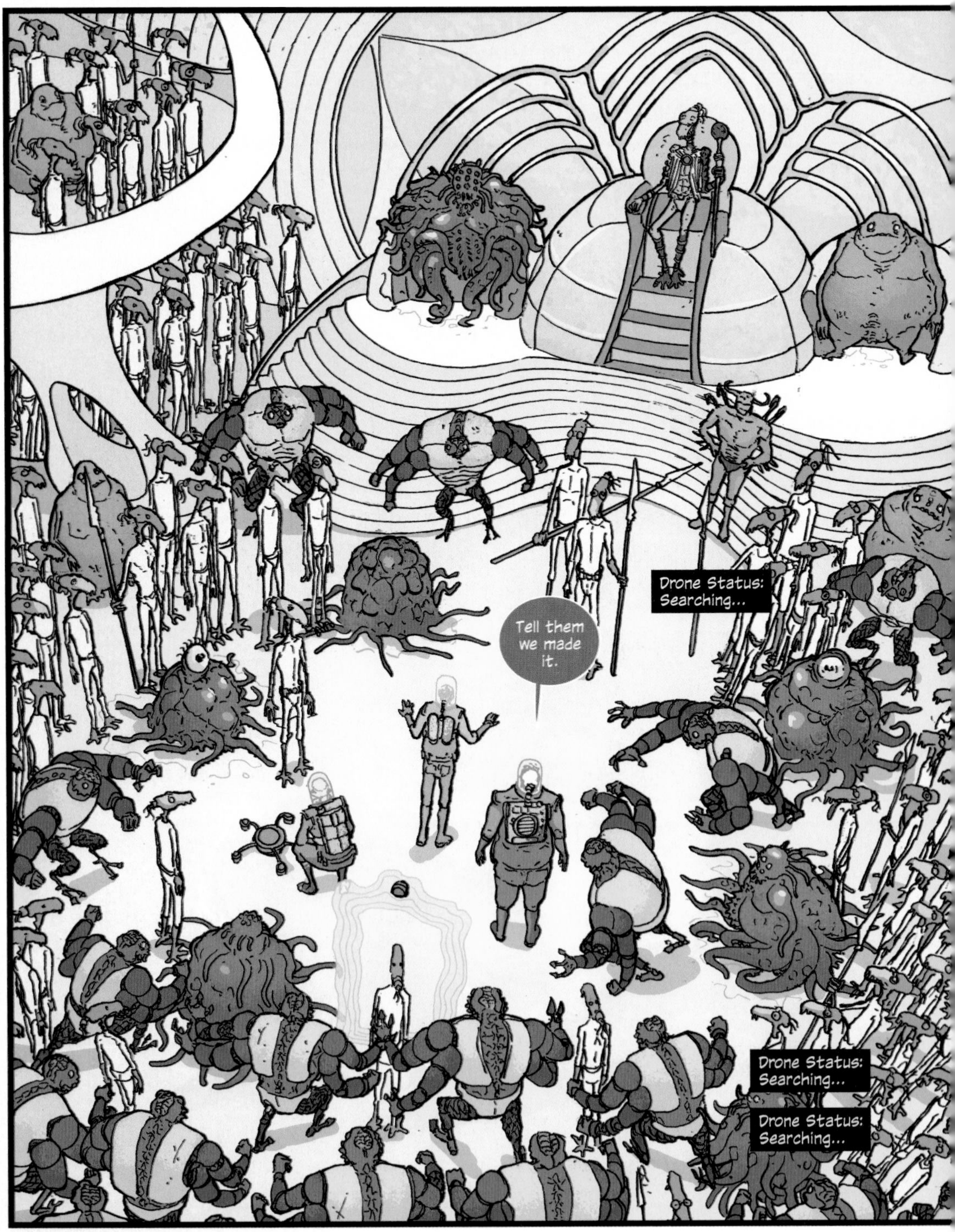
Drone Status: Searching...
Tell them we made it.
Drone Status: Searching...
Drone Status: Searching...

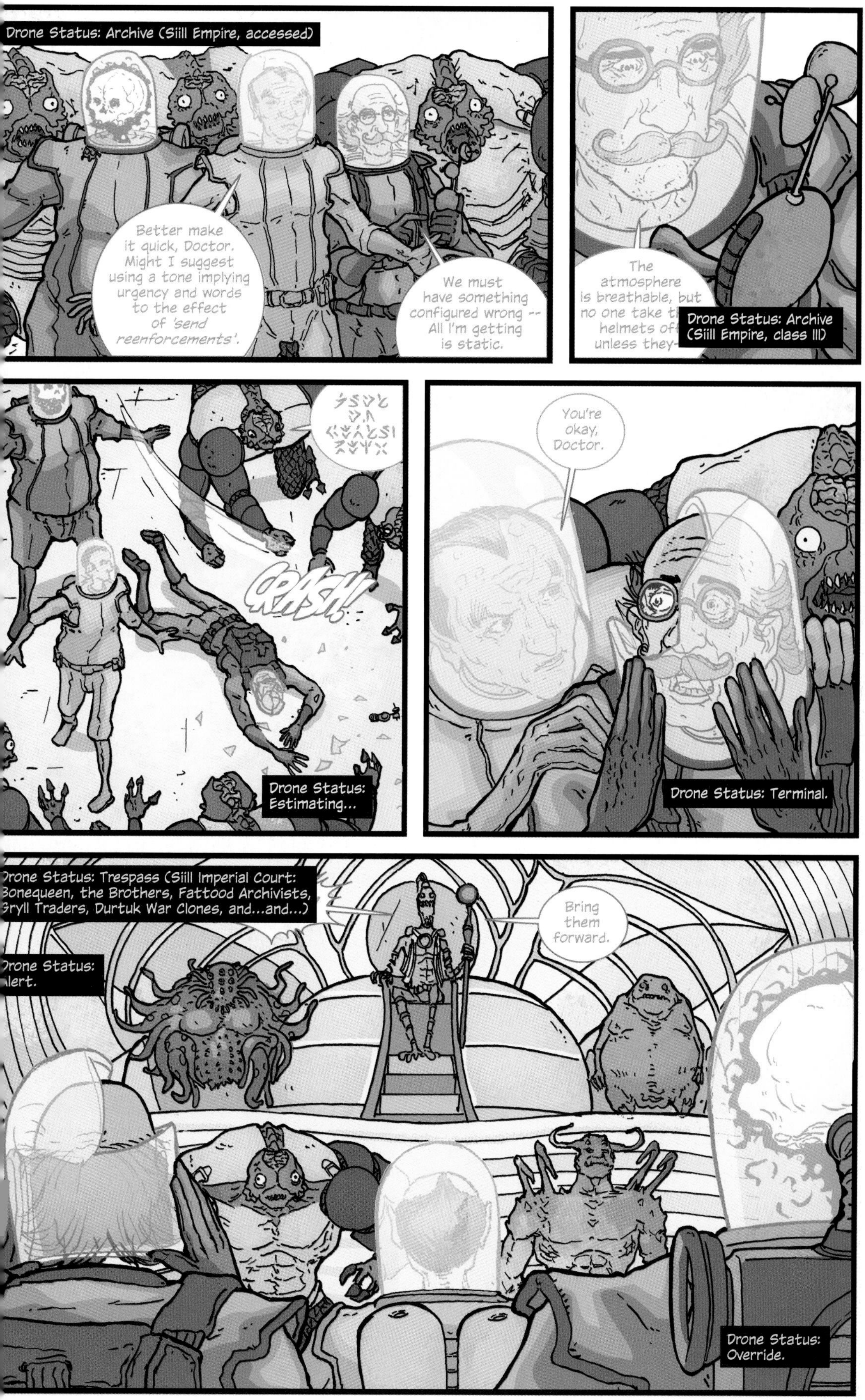

Drone Status: Archive (Siill Empire, accessed)
Better make it quick, Doctor. Might I suggest using a tone implying urgency and words to the effect of 'send reenforcements'.
We must have something configured wrong -- All I'm getting is static.
The atmosphere is breathable, but no one take t helmets off unless they-
Drone Status: Archive (Siill Empire, class III)
CRASH!
Drone Status: Estimating...
You're okay, Doctor.
Drone Status: Terminal.
rone Status: Trespass (Siill Imperial Court: onequeen, the Brothers, Fattood Archivists, ryll Traders, Durtuk War Clones, and...and...)
Bring them forward.
rone Status: lert.
Drone Status: Override.

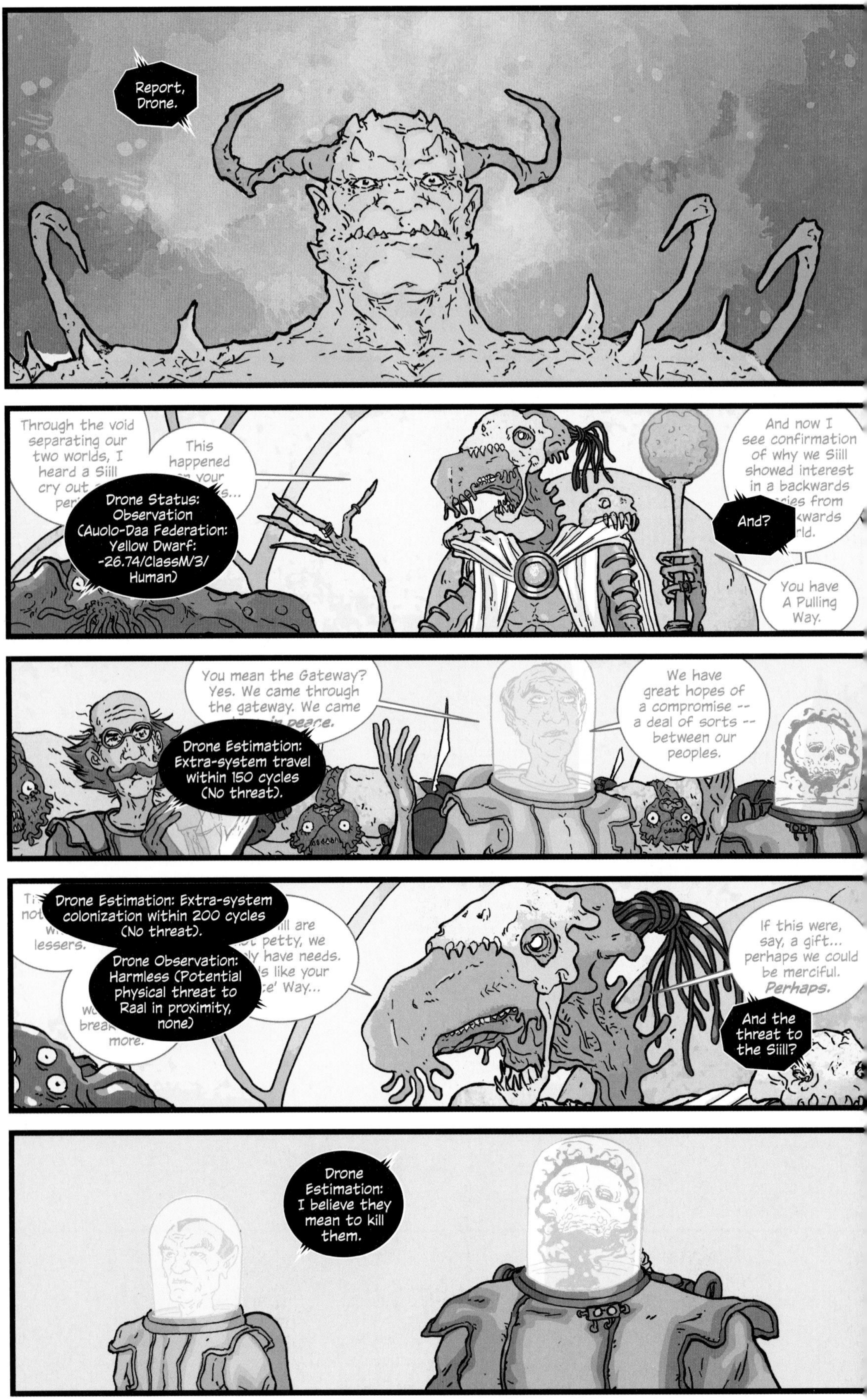

Report, Drone.
Through the void separating our two worlds, I heard a Siill cry out
This happened
Drone Status: Observation (Auolo-Daa Federation: Yellow Dwarf: -26.74/ClassM/3/Human)
And now I see confirmation of why we Siill showed interest in a backwards
And?
You have A Pulling Way.
You mean the Gateway? Yes. We came through the gateway. We came
Drone Estimation: Extra-system travel within 150 cycles (No threat).
We have great hopes of a compromise -- a deal of sorts -- between our peoples.
Drone Estimation: Extra-system colonization within 200 cycles (No threat).
lessers.
Drone Observation: Harmless (Potential physical threat to Raal in proximity, none)
have needs.
more.
If this were, say, a gift... perhaps we could be merciful. *Perhaps.*
And the threat to the Siill?
Drone Estimation: I believe they mean to kill them.

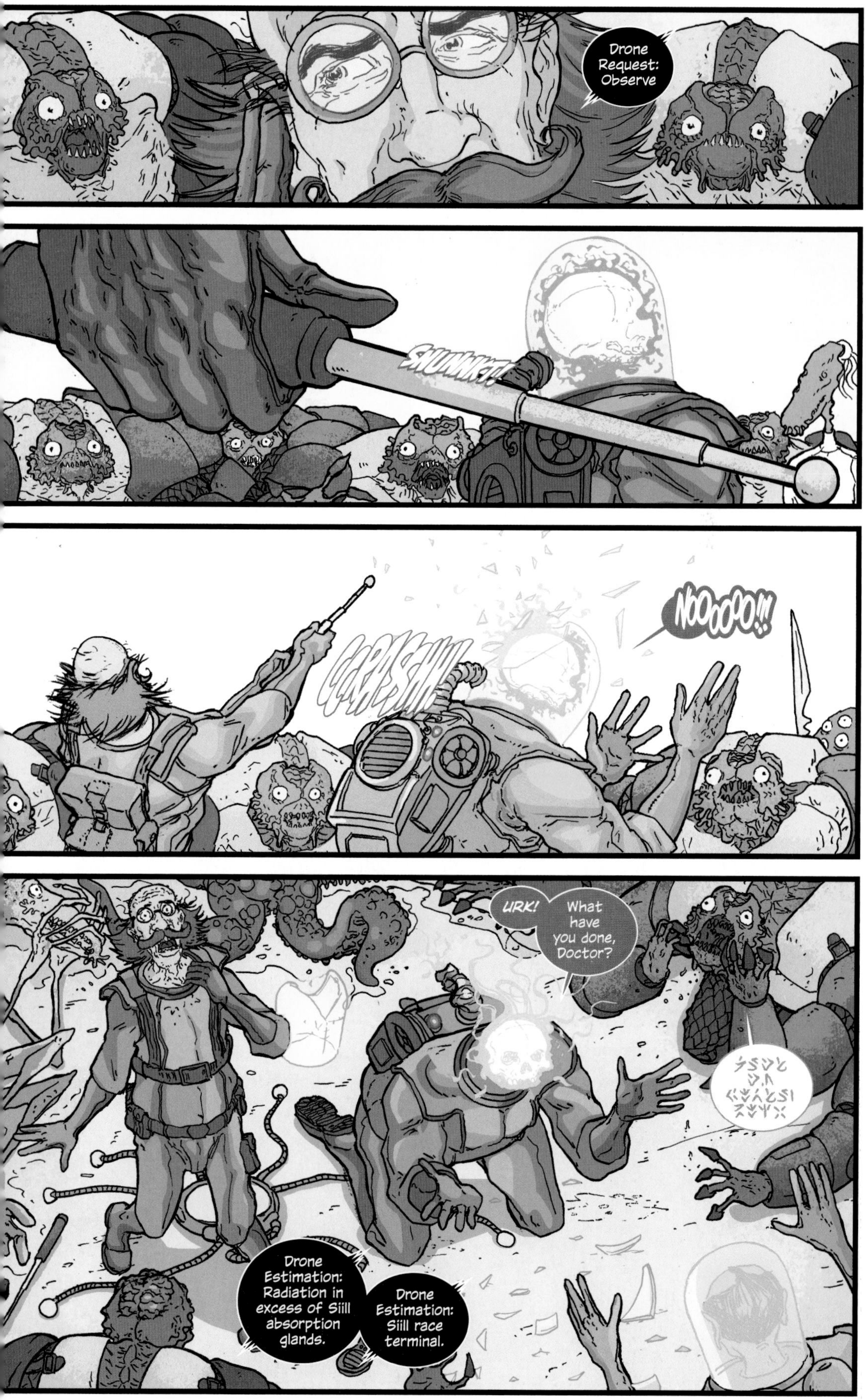
Drone Request: Observe
SNUNKT!
CCRASHH!
NOOOOOO!!!
URK!
What have you done, Doctor?
Drone Estimation: Radiation in excess of Siill absorption glands.
Drone Estimation: Siill race terminal.

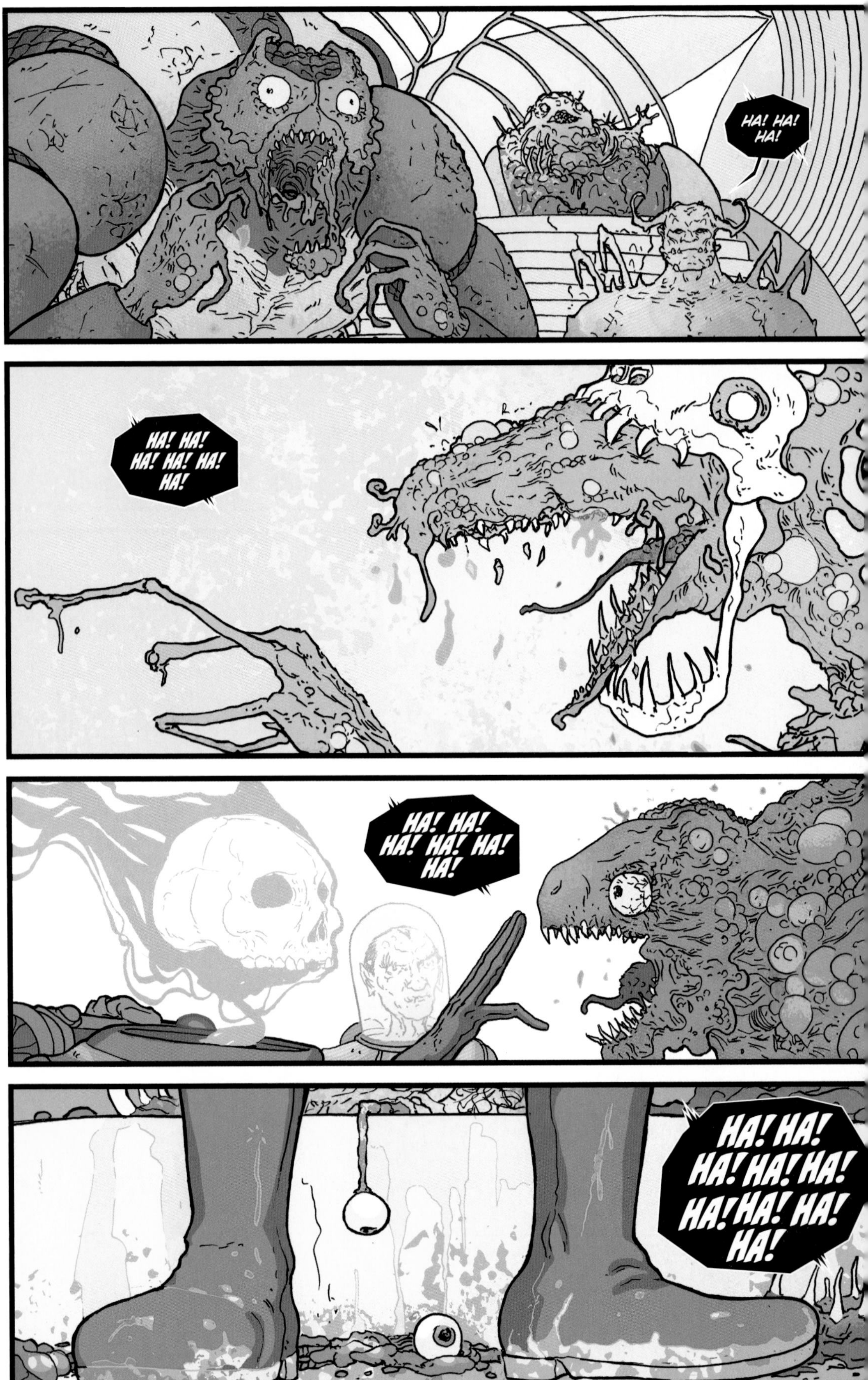
HA! HA! HA!
HA! HA! HA! HA! HA! HA!
HA! HA! HA! HA! HA! HA!
HA! HA! HA! HA! HA! HA! HA! HA! HA! HA!

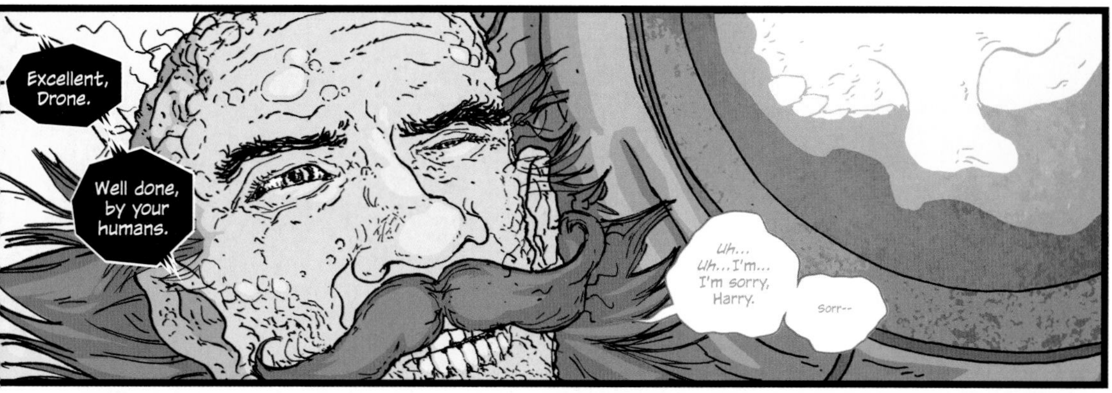
Excellent, Drone.
Well done, by your humans.
Uh... Uh... I'm... I'm sorry, Harry.
Sorr--

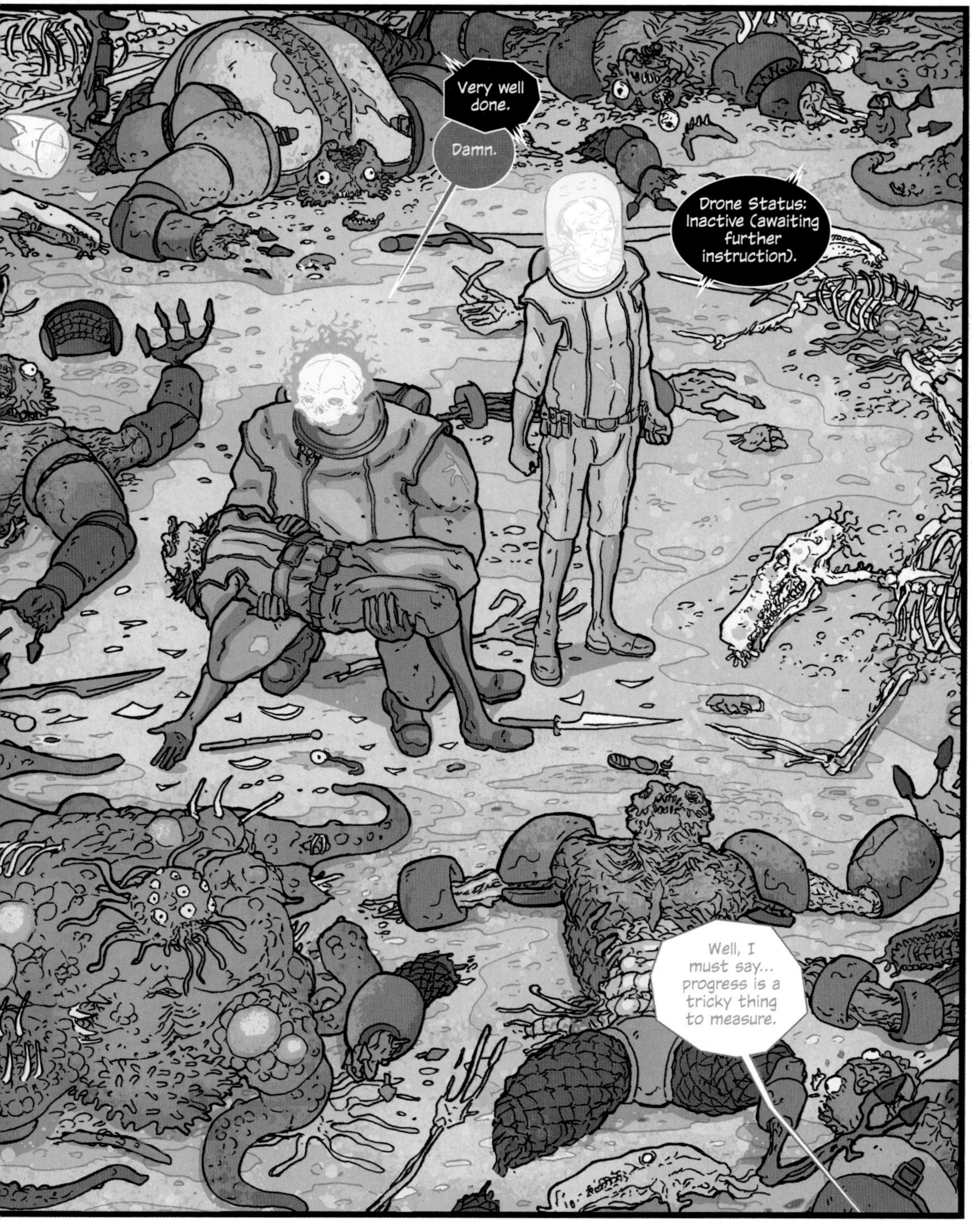
Very well done.
Damn.
Drone Status: Inactive (awaiting further instruction).
Well, I must say... progress is a tricky thing to measure.

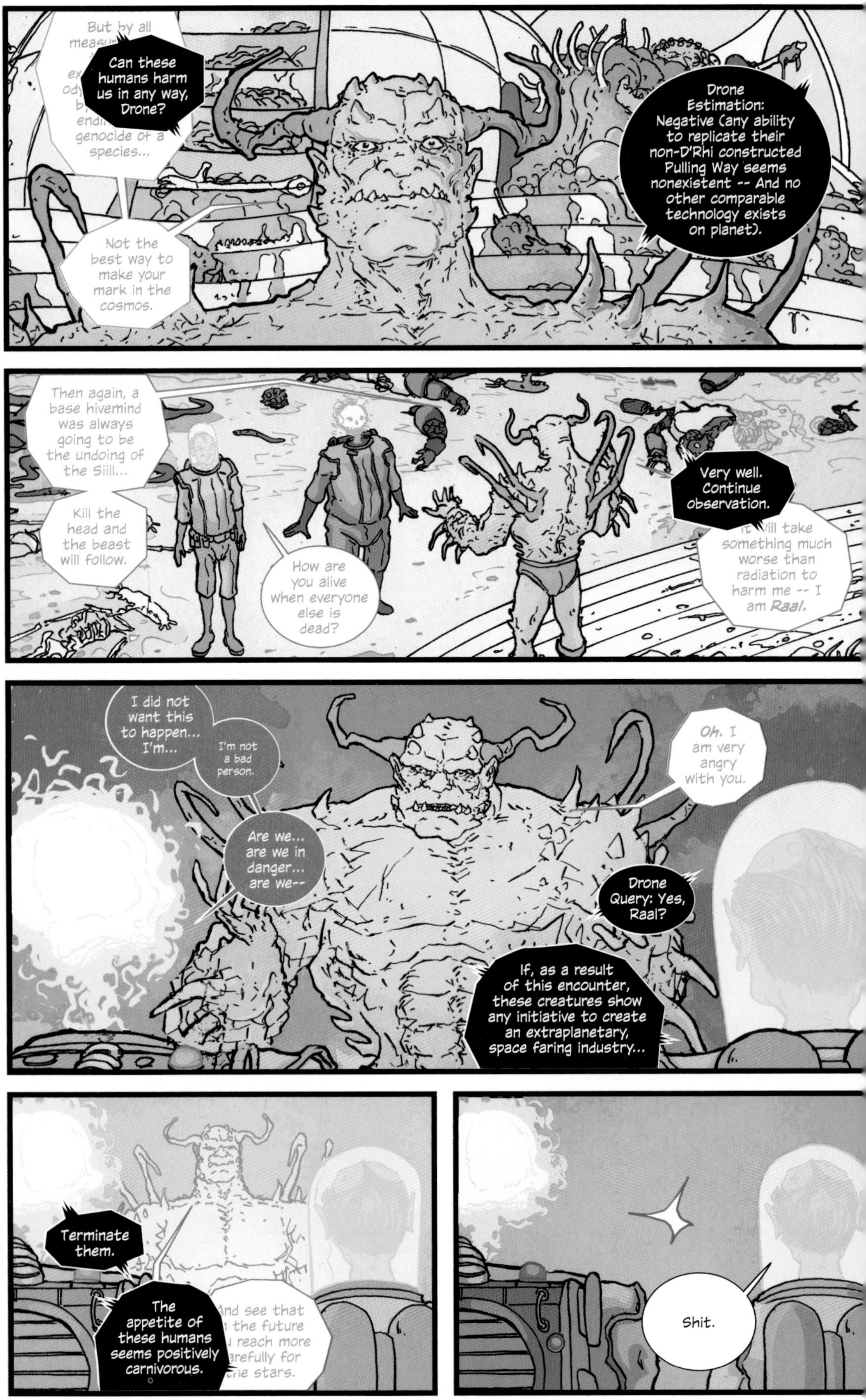

But by all
genocide of a species...
Can these humans harm us in any way, Drone?
Drone Estimation: Negative (any ability to replicate their non-D'Rhi constructed Pulling Way seems nonexistent -- And no other comparable technology exists on planet).
Not the best way to make your mark in the cosmos.
Then again, a base hivemind was always going to be the undoing of the Siill...
Kill the head and the beast will follow.
How are you alive when everyone else is dead?
Very well. Continue observation.
something much worse than radiation to harm me -- I am *Raal.*
I did not want this to happen... I'm...
I'm not a bad person.
Are we... are we in danger... are we--
*Oh.* I am very angry with you.
Drone Query: Yes, Raal?
If, as a result of this encounter, these creatures show any initiative to create an extraplanetary, space faring industry...
Terminate them.
The appetite of these humans seems positively carnivorous.
And see that
the stars.
Shit.

Now.

So...what are we gonna do with you?

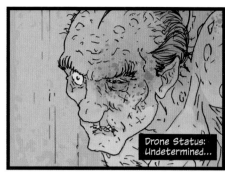

Drone Status: Undetermined...

Doctor Feynman?

Oh, the bastard broke my nose. I say at the very least we skin it.

Harry?

I...I'm just so sad about all this...

I don't know.

Well. I think I know ze answer to ze question.

Drone Status: Conflicted.

Harry!

Harry! I'm sorry!

I had to do it. It was what they made me for.

We considered feeding you to ze Oppenheimer... finding out ze knowledge hidden in your head.

But then we thought about it...

And who wants to keep around a traitor?

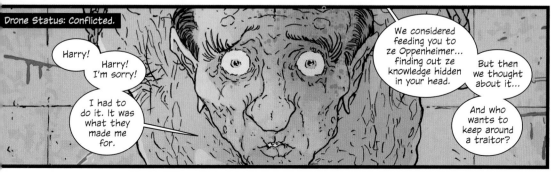

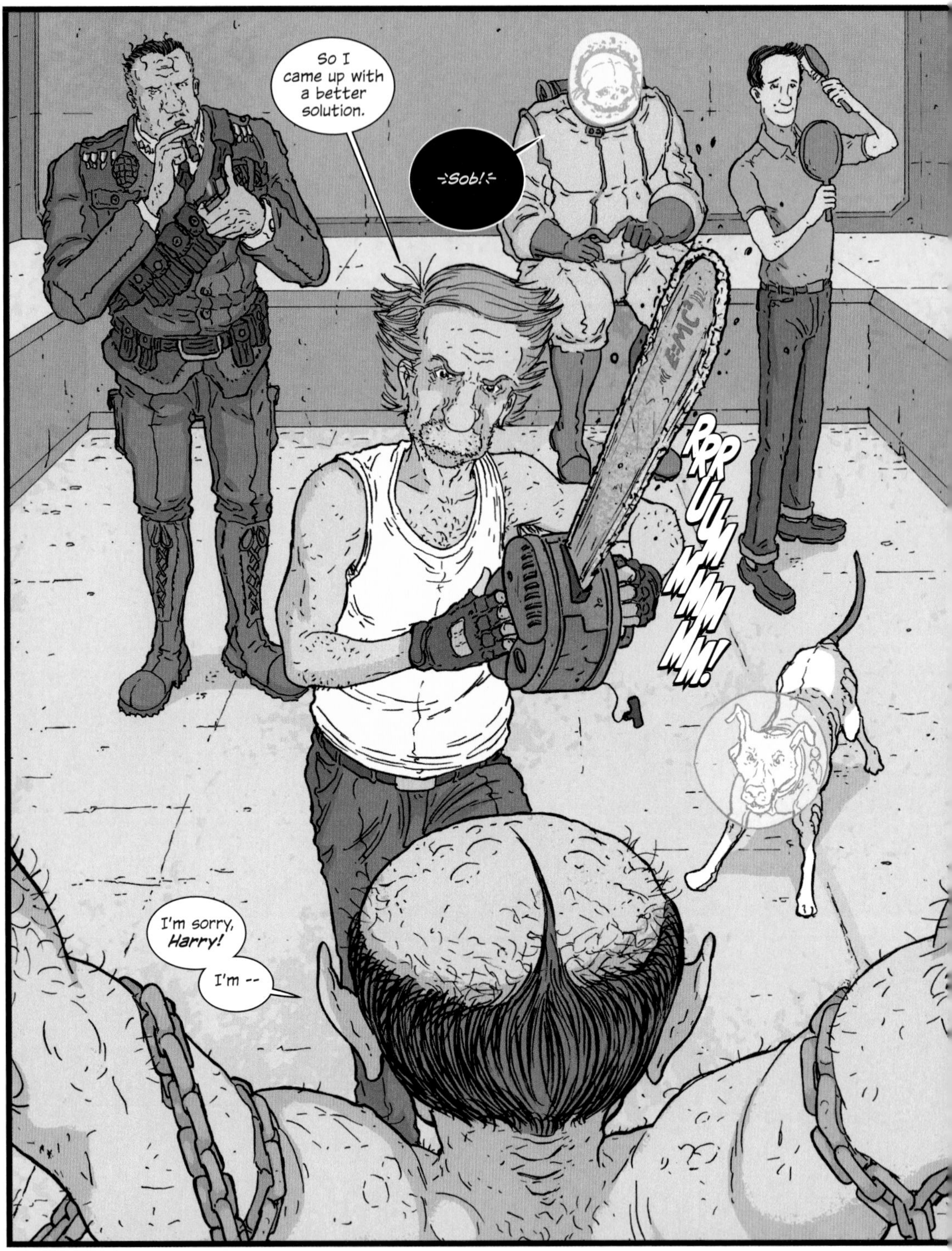
So I came up with a better solution.
Sob!
RRRUUUMMMMMM!
I'm sorry, Harry!
I'm --

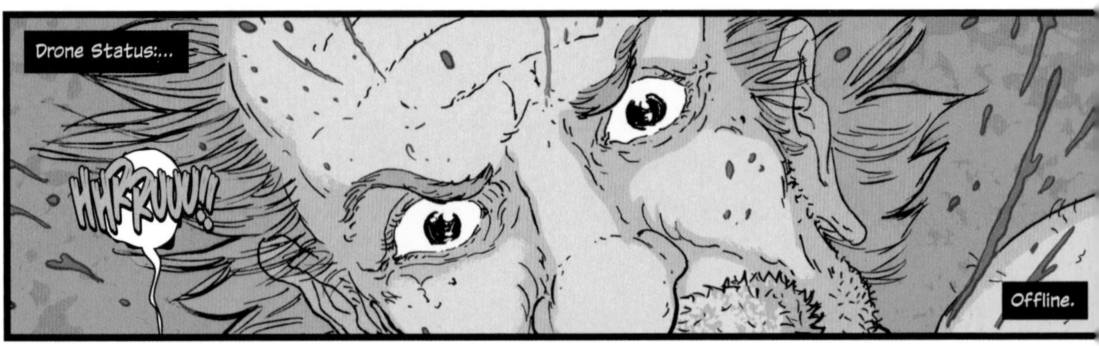
Drone Status:...
HHRUUU!!
Offline.

# YOU WERE AN
# INSPIRATION

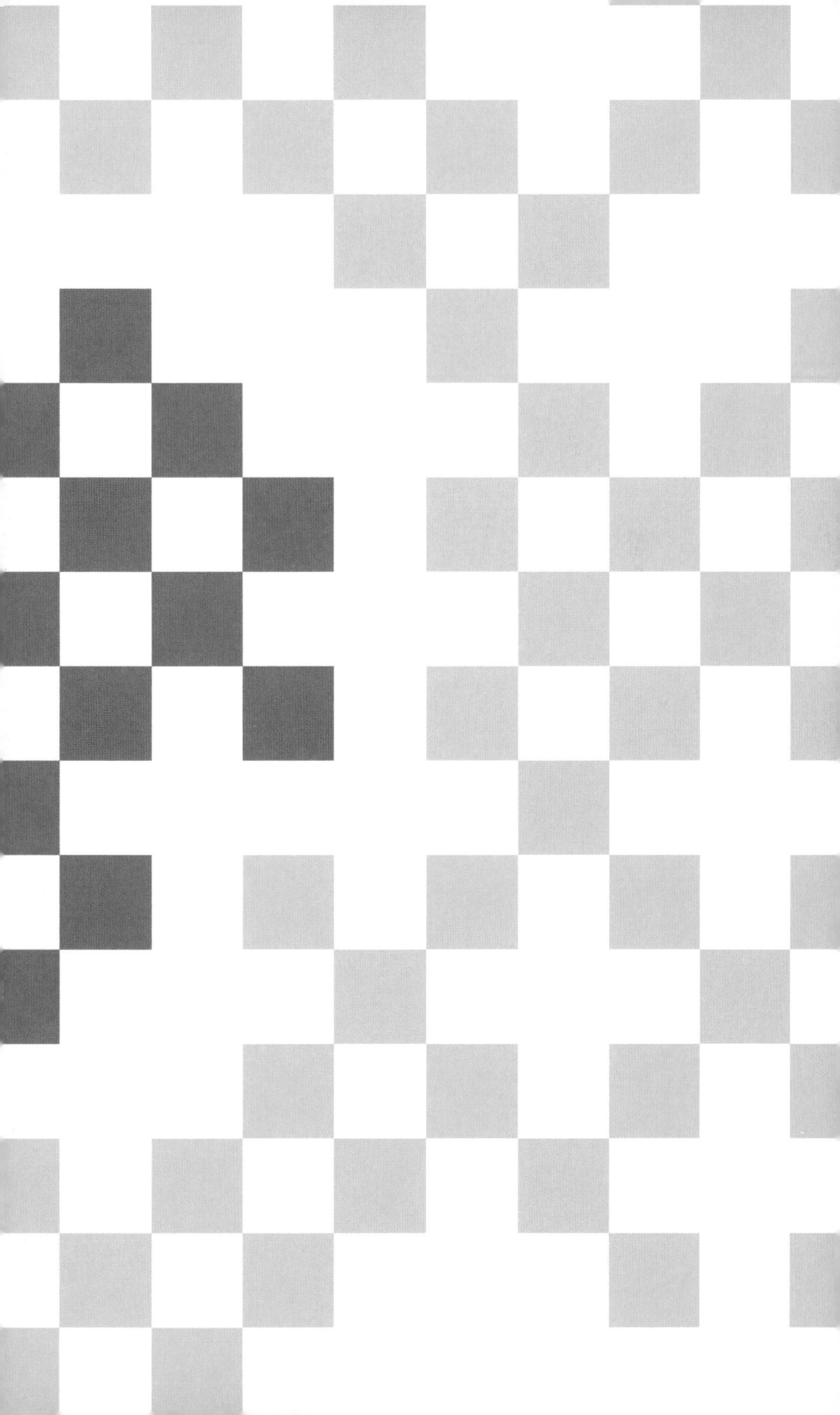

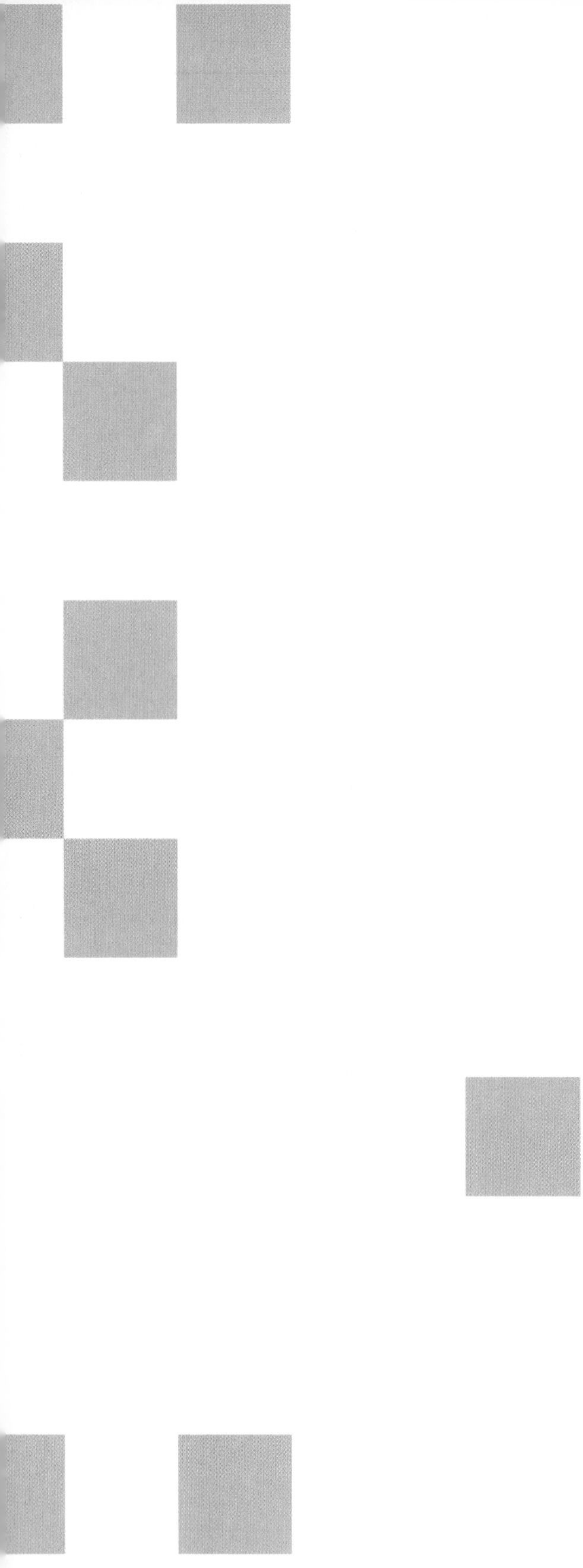

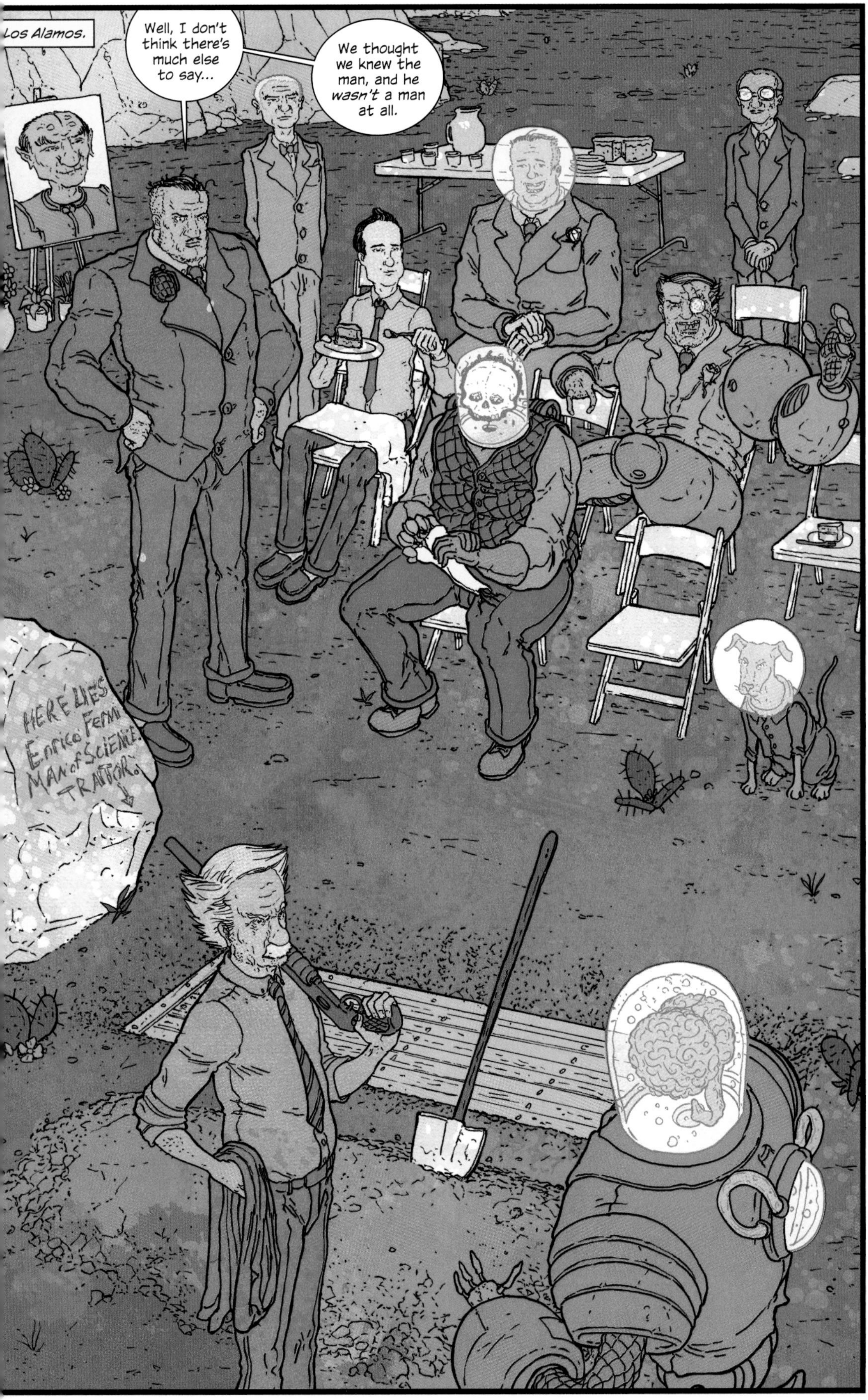

Los Alamos.
Well, I don't think there's much else to say...
We thought we knew the man, and he *wasn't* a man at all.
HERE LIES Enrico Fermi MAN of SCIENCE TRAITOR.

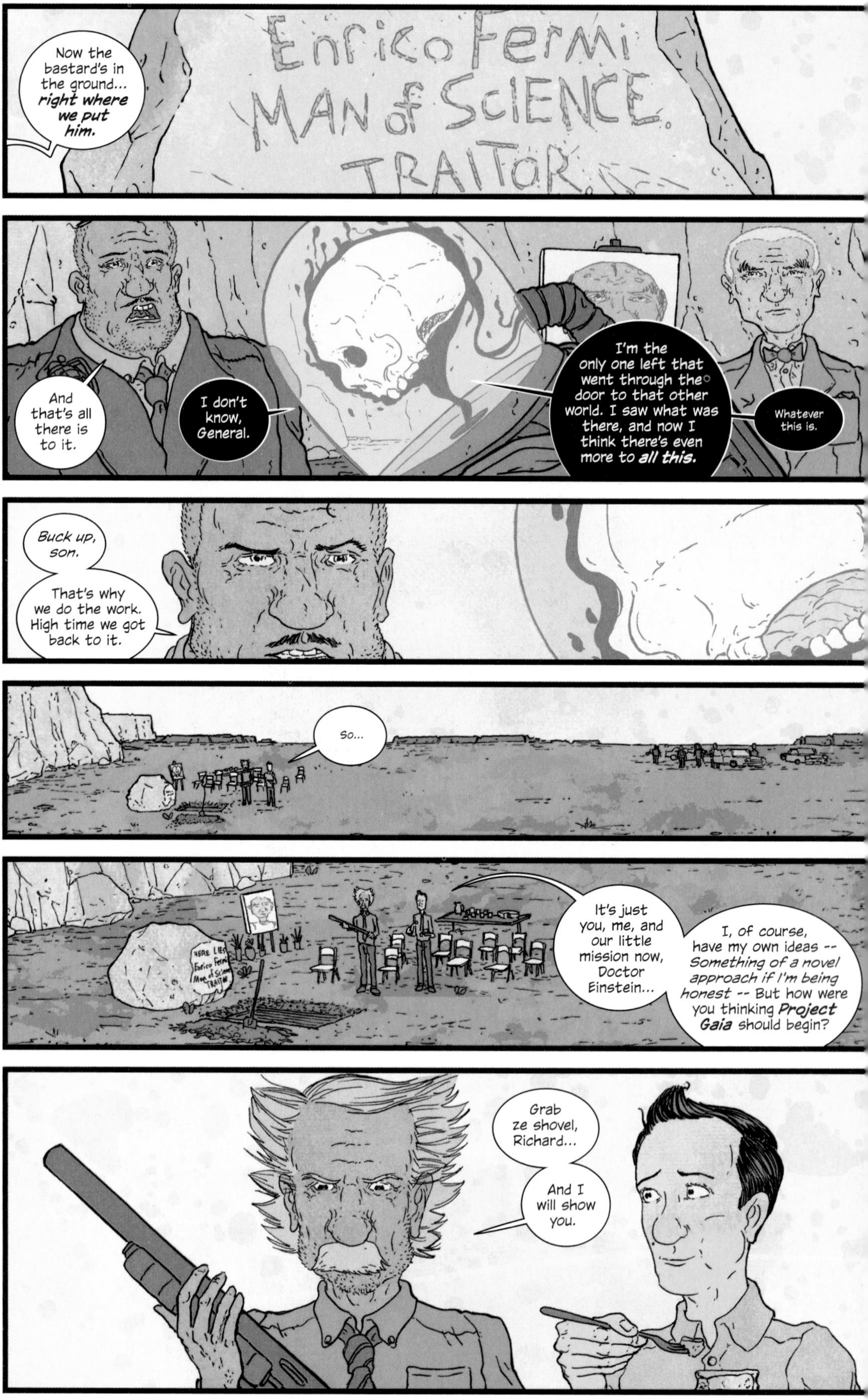
Enrico Fermi
MAN of SCIENCE.
TRAITOR.
Now the bastard's in the ground... ***right where we put him.***
And that's all there is to it.
I don't know, General.
I'm the only one left that went through the door to that other world. I saw what was there, and now I think there's even more to ***all this.***
Whatever this is.
*Buck up, son.*
That's why we do the work. High time we got back to it.
So...
HERE LIES Enrico Fermi Man of Science TRAITOR
It's just you, me, and our little mission now, Doctor Einstein...
I, of course, have my own ideas -- *Something of a novel approach if I'm being honest* -- But how were you thinking ***Project Gaia*** should begin?
Grab ze shovel, Richard...
And I will show you.

"EARTH, FIRE, WATER, AIR...ALL OF THESE, AT MY COMMAND."

- OPPENHEIMER

*CLAVIS AUREA*
THE RECORDED FEYNMAN

VOL. 4

# 13

## PIECE BY PIECE

"THE EARTH, THE STARS, THE SUN, FOREVER...ALL OF THESE, IN MY HAND."

- OPPENHEIMER

*CLAVIS AUREA*
THE RECORDED FEYNMAN | **VOL. 4**

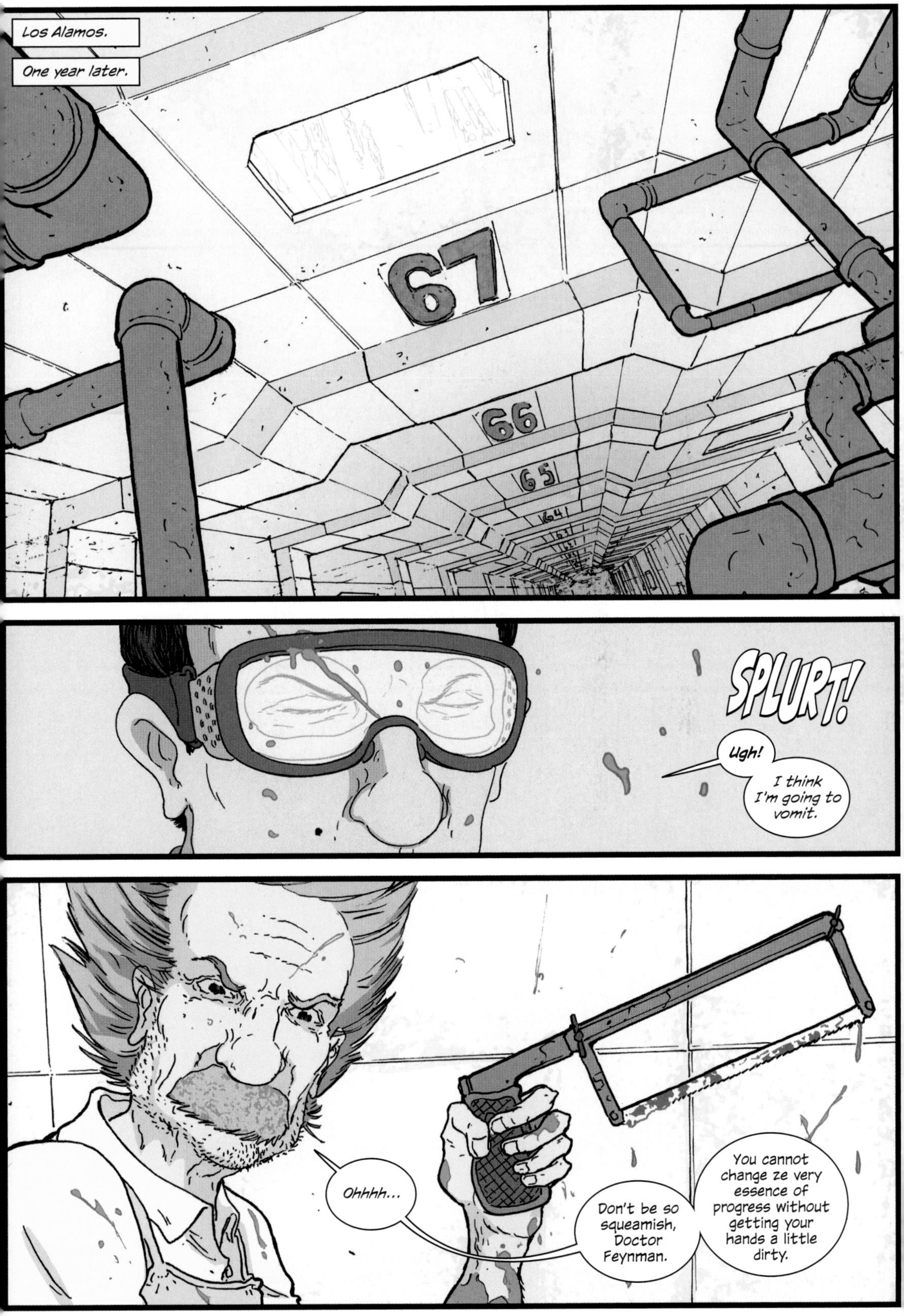
Los Alamos.
One year later.
67
66
65
64
SPLURT!
Ugh!
I think I'm going to vomit.
Ohhhh...
Don't be so squeamish, Doctor Feynman.
You cannot change ze very essence of progress without getting your hands a little dirty.

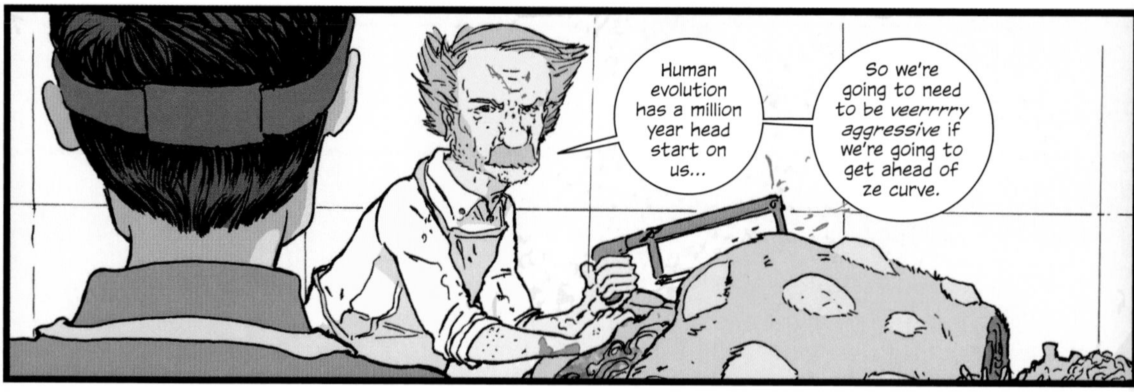
Human evolution has a million year head start on us...
So we're going to need to be *veerrrry aggressive* if we're going to get ahead of ze curve.

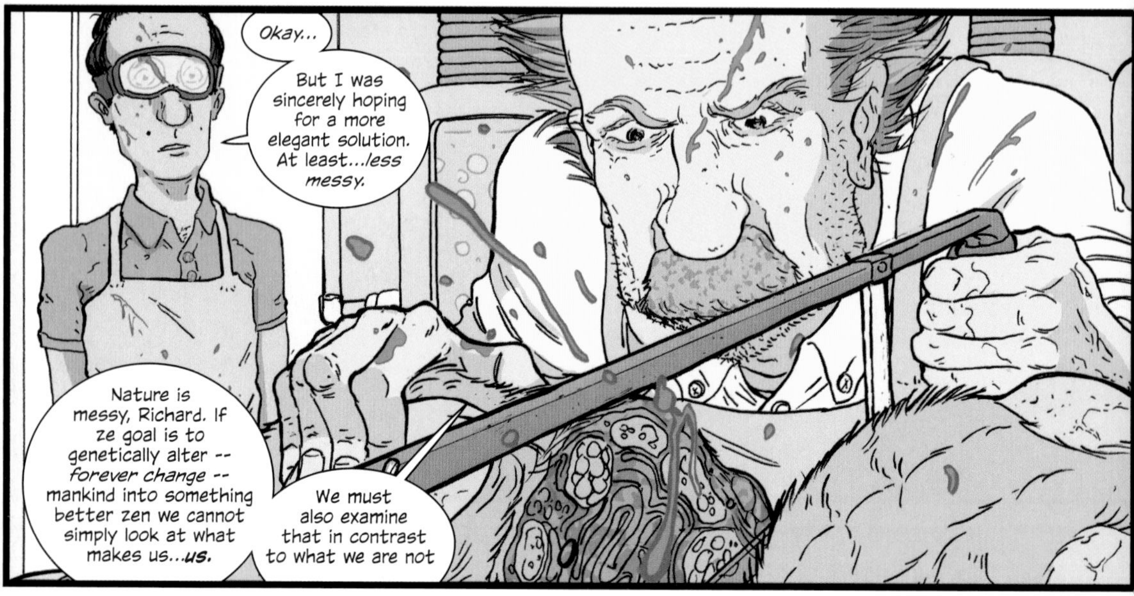
*Okay...*
But I was sincerely hoping for a more elegant solution. At least...*less messy.*
Nature is messy, Richard. If ze goal is to genetically alter -- *forever change* -- mankind into something better zen we cannot simply look at what makes us...***us.***
We must also examine that in contrast to what we are not

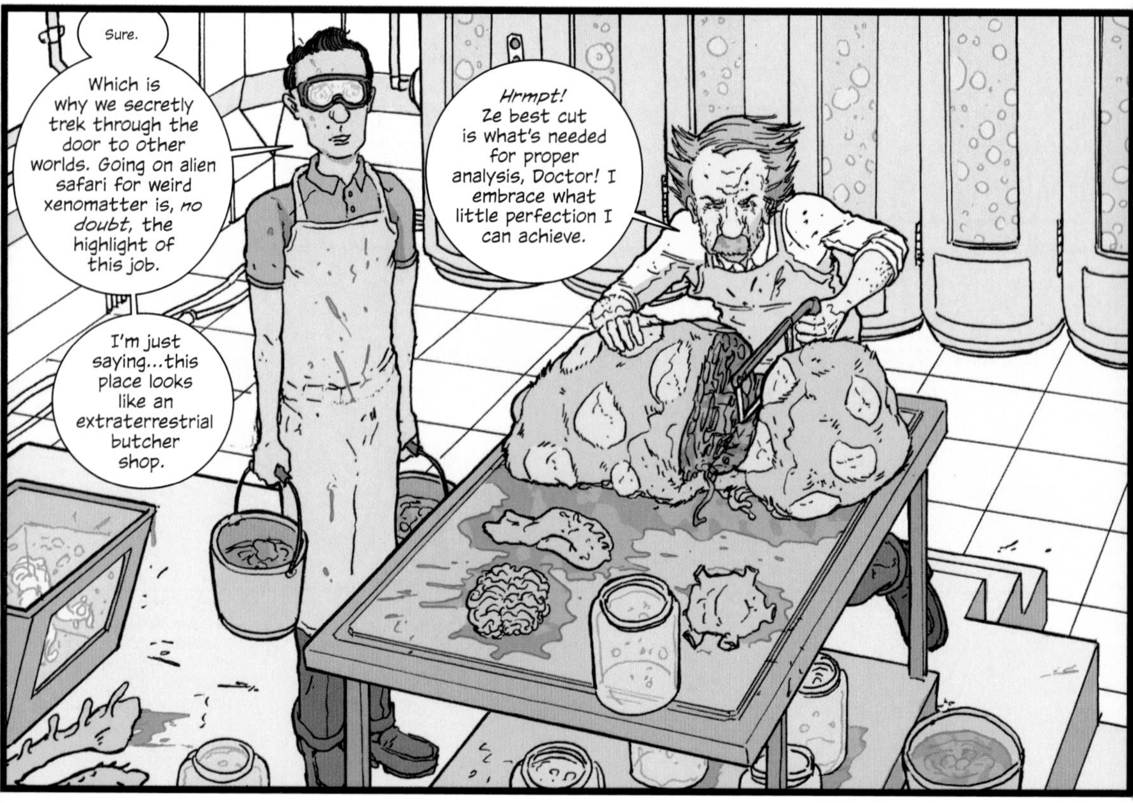
Sure.
Which is why we secretly trek through the door to other worlds. Going on alien safari for weird xenomatter is, *no doubt,* the highlight of this job.
I'm just saying...this place looks like an extraterrestrial butcher shop.
*Hrmpt!* Ze best cut is what's needed for proper analysis, Doctor! I embrace what little perfection I can achieve.

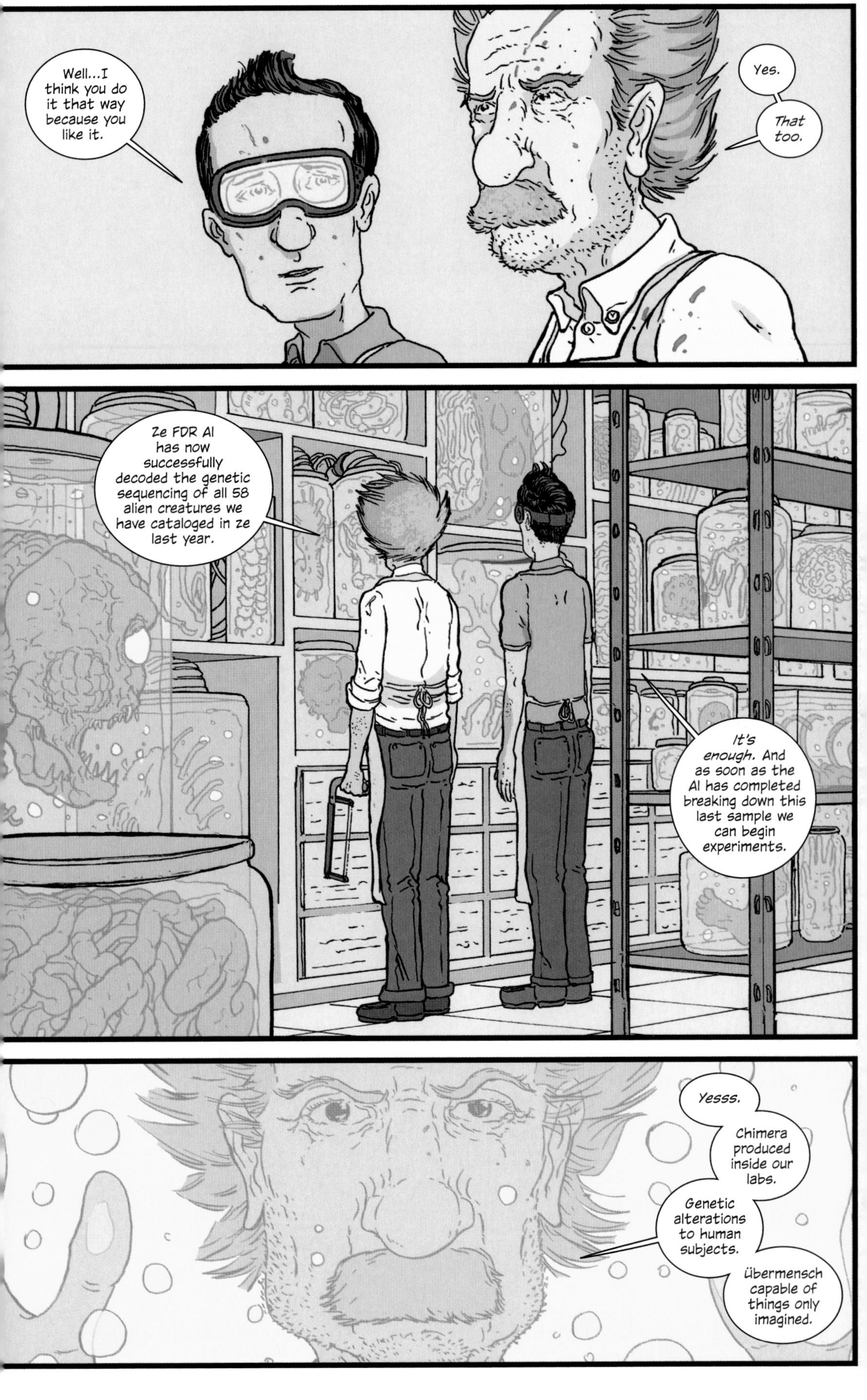
Well...I think you do it that way because you like it.
Yes.
*That too.*
Ze FDR AI has now successfully decoded the genetic sequencing of all 58 alien creatures we have cataloged in ze last year.
*It's enough.* And as soon as the AI has completed breaking down this last sample we can begin experiments.
*Yesss.*
Chimera produced inside our labs.
Genetic alterations to human subjects.
Übermensch capable of things only imagined.

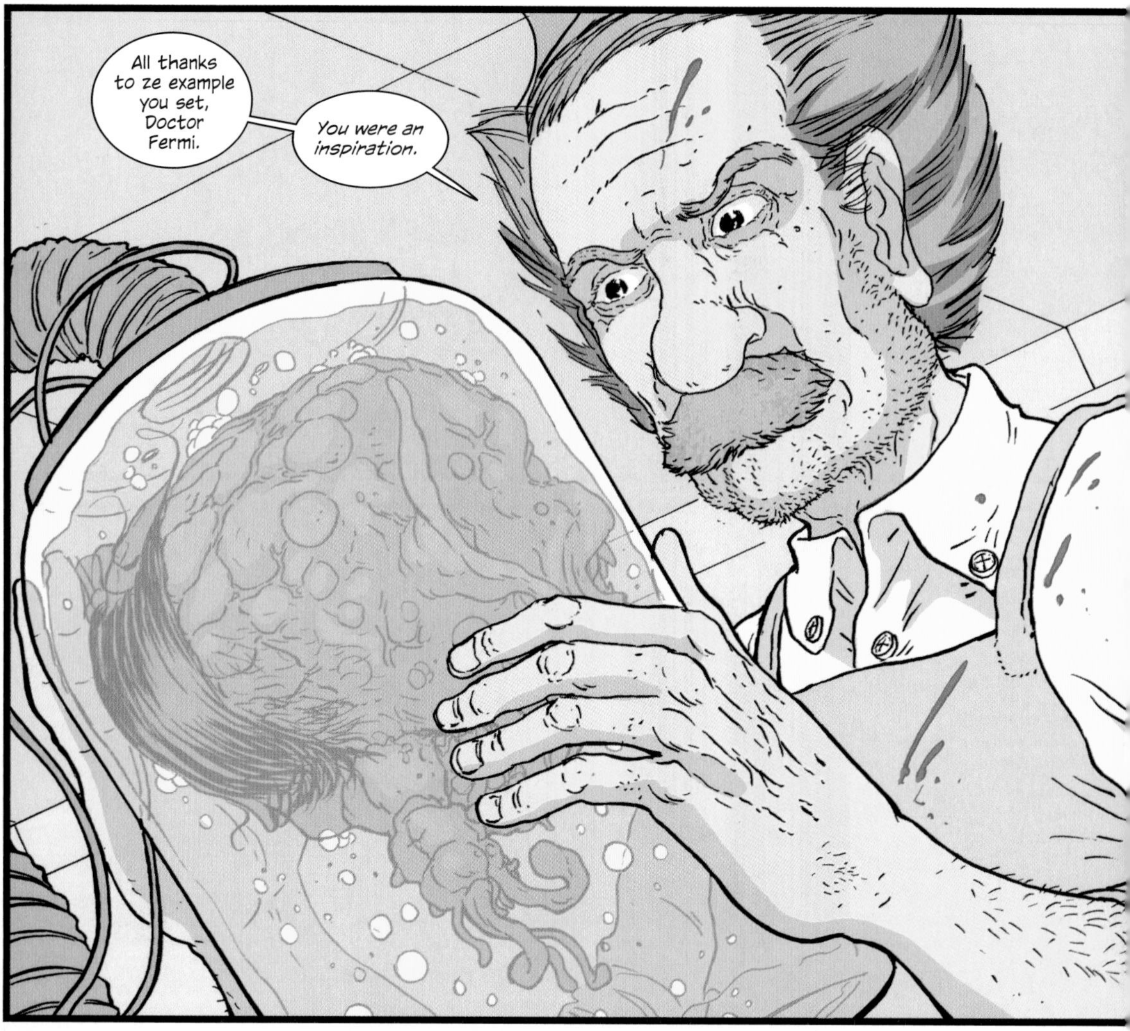
All thanks to ze example you set, Doctor Fermi.
You were an inspiration.

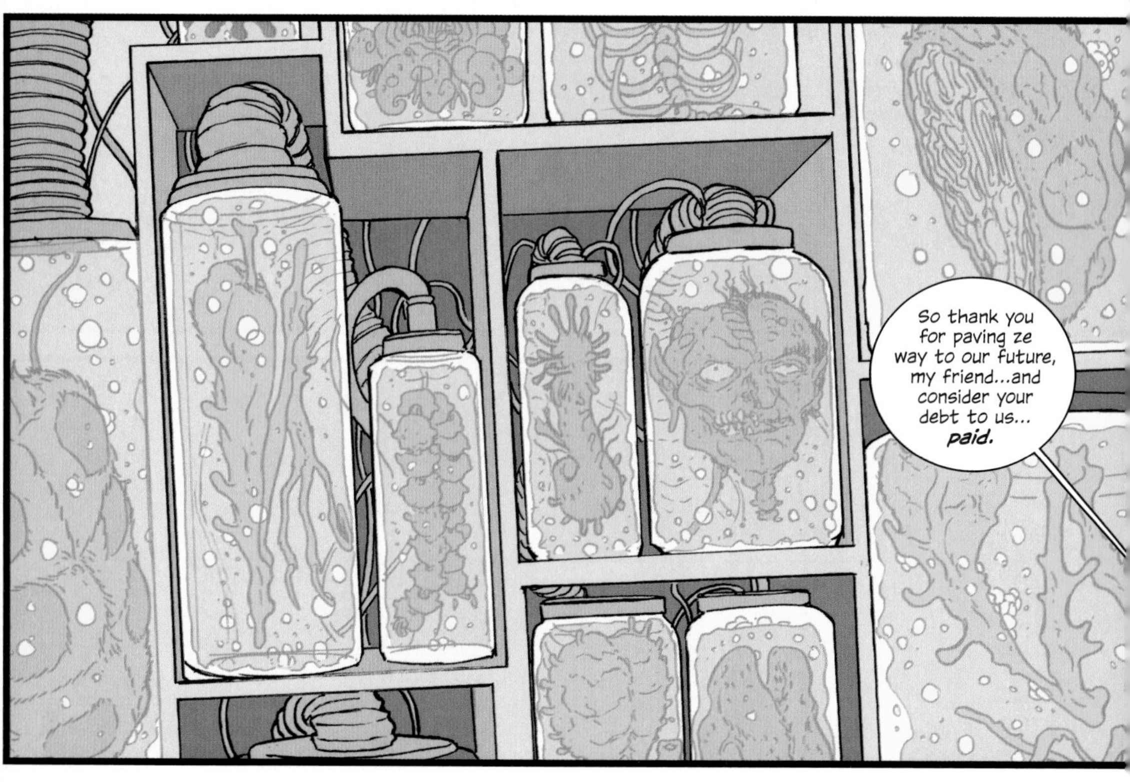
So thank you for paving ze way to our future, my friend...and consider your debt to us... **paid.**

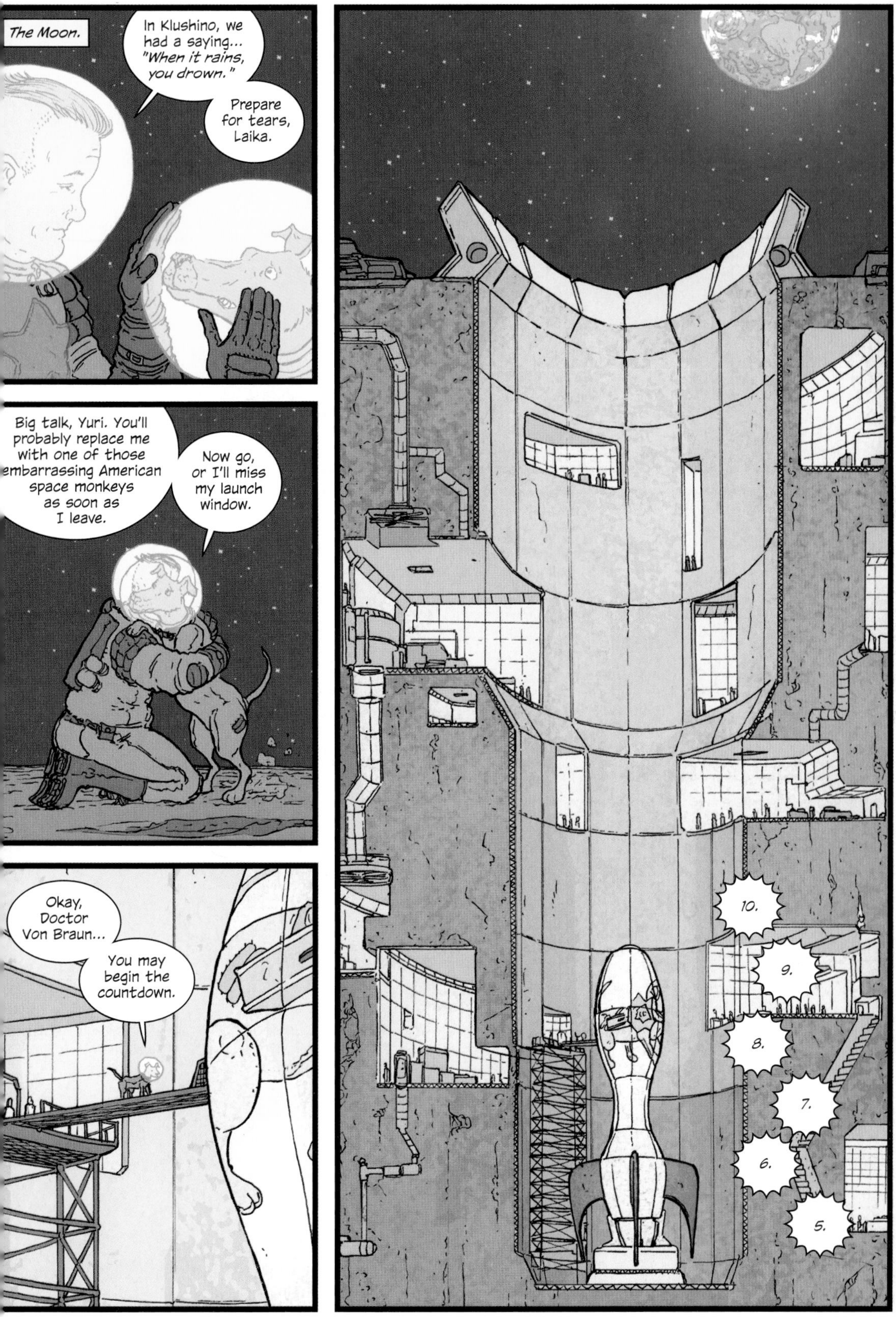
The Moon.
In Klushino, we had a saying... "When it rains, you drown."
Prepare for tears, Laika.
Big talk, Yuri. You'll probably replace me with one of those embarrassing American space monkeys as soon as I leave.
Now go, or I'll miss my launch window.
Okay, Doctor Von Braun...
You may begin the countdown.
10.
9.
8.
7.
6.
5.

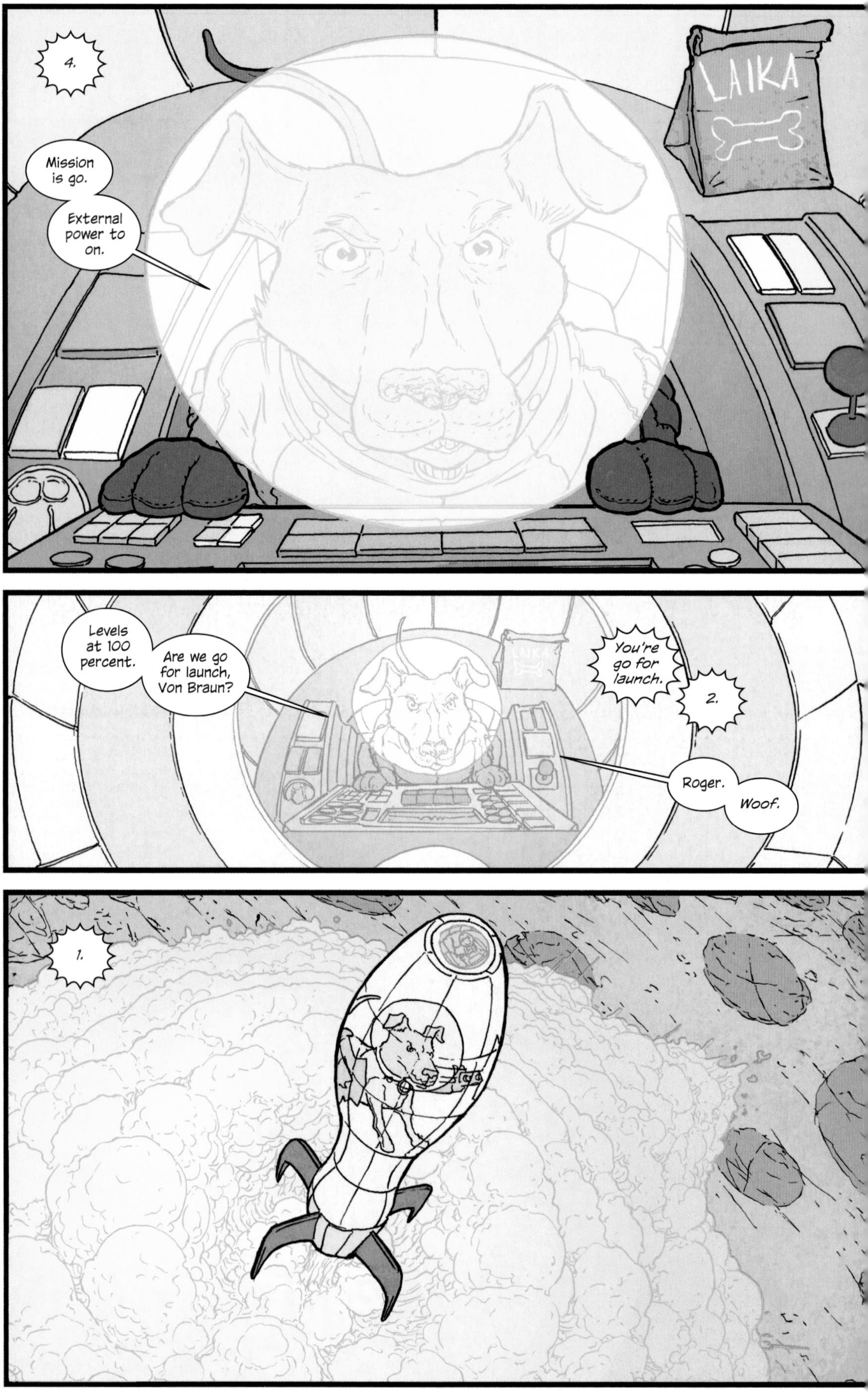
4.
LAIKA
Mission is go.
External power to on.
Levels at 100 percent.
Are we go for launch, Von Braun?
LAIKA
You're go for launch.
2.
Roger.
Woof.
1.

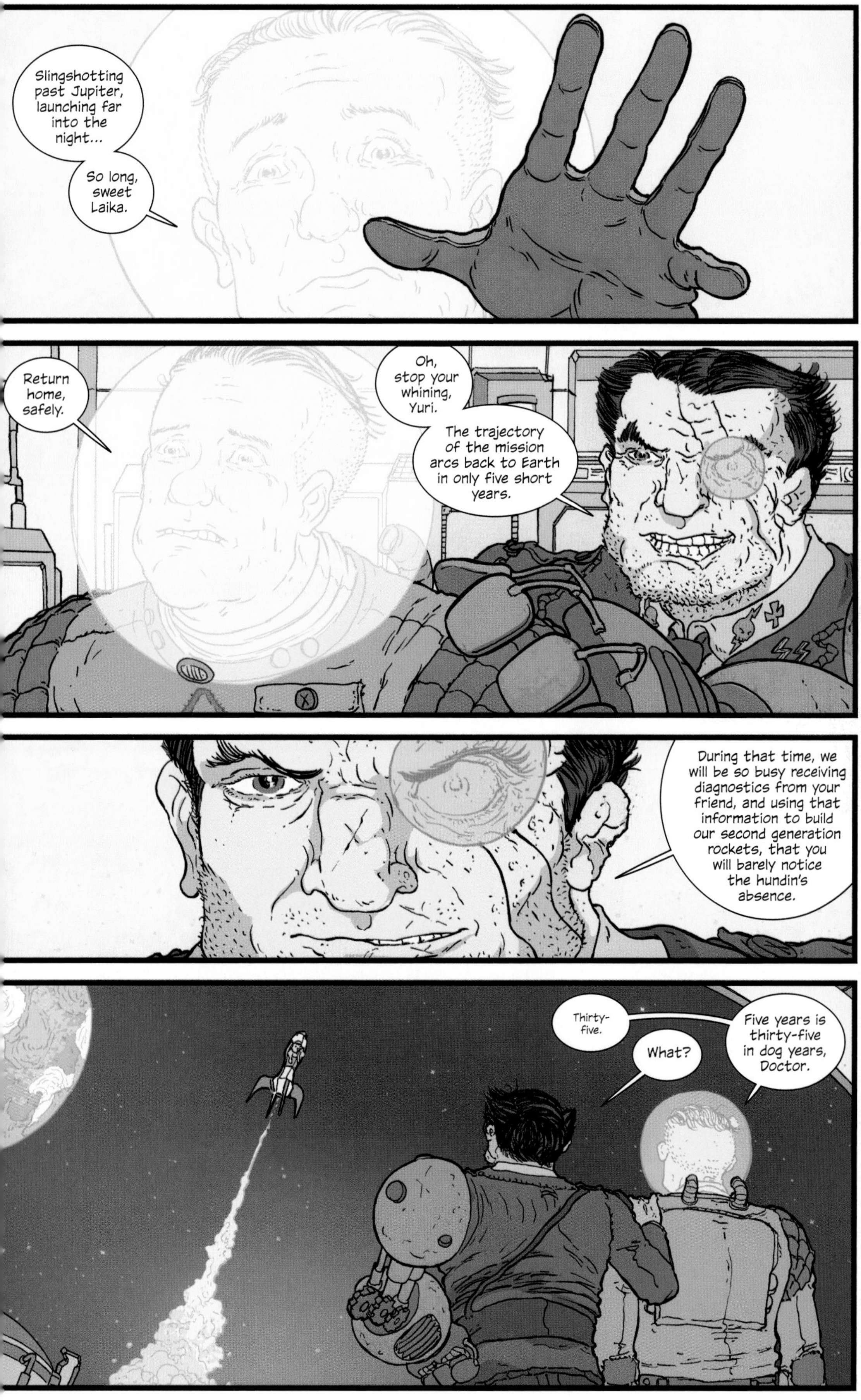
Slingshotting past Jupiter, launching far into the night...
So long, sweet Laika.
Return home, safely.
Oh, stop your whining, Yuri.
The trajectory of the mission arcs back to Earth in only five short years.
During that time, we will be so busy receiving diagnostics from your friend, and using that information to build our second generation rockets, that you will barely notice the hundin's absence.
Thirty-five.
What?
Five years is thirty-five in dog years, Doctor.

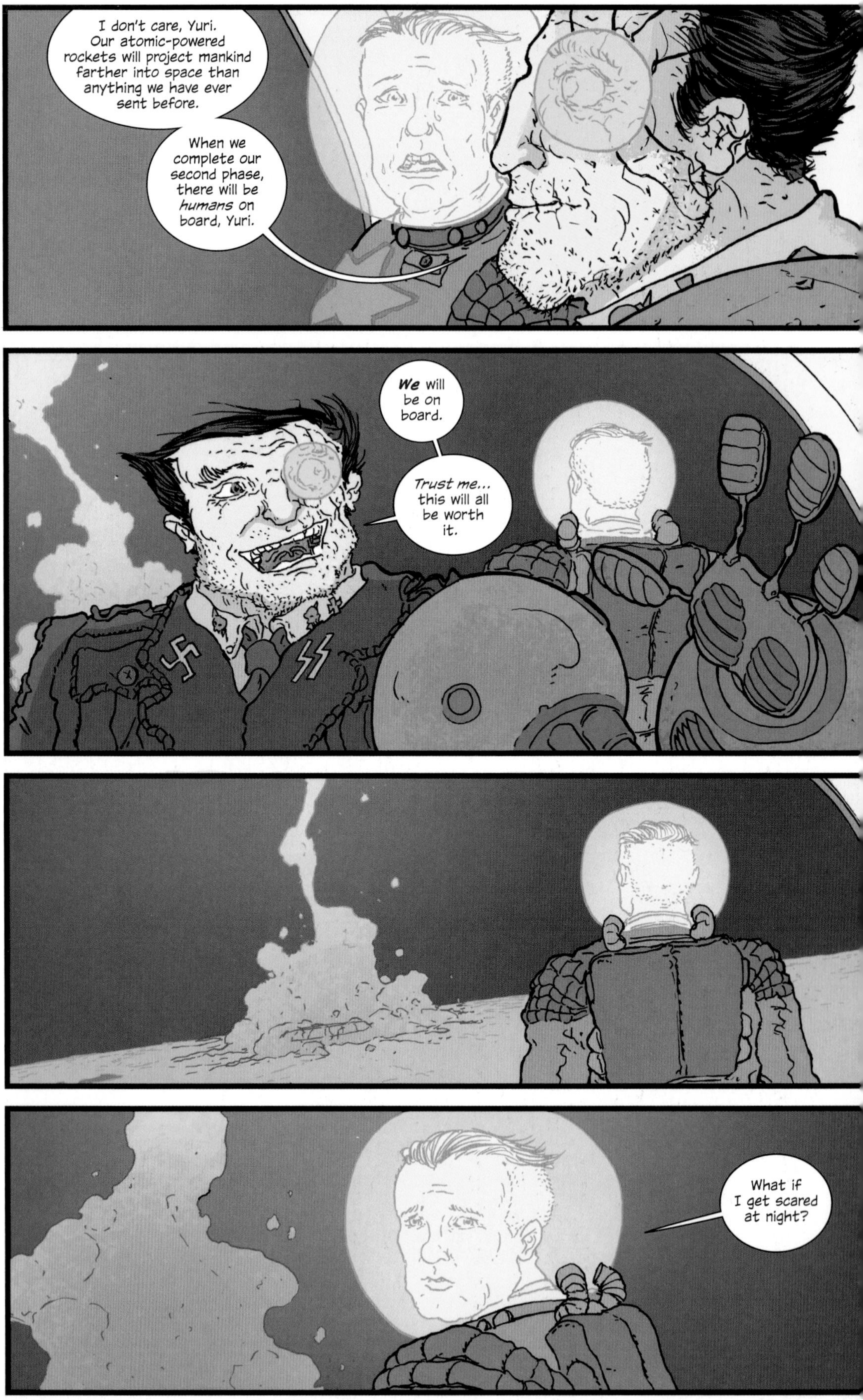
I don't care, Yuri. Our atomic-powered rockets will project mankind farther into space than anything we have ever sent before.
When we complete our second phase, there will be *humans* on board, Yuri.
***We*** will be on board.
*Trust me...* this will all be worth it.
What if I get scared at night?

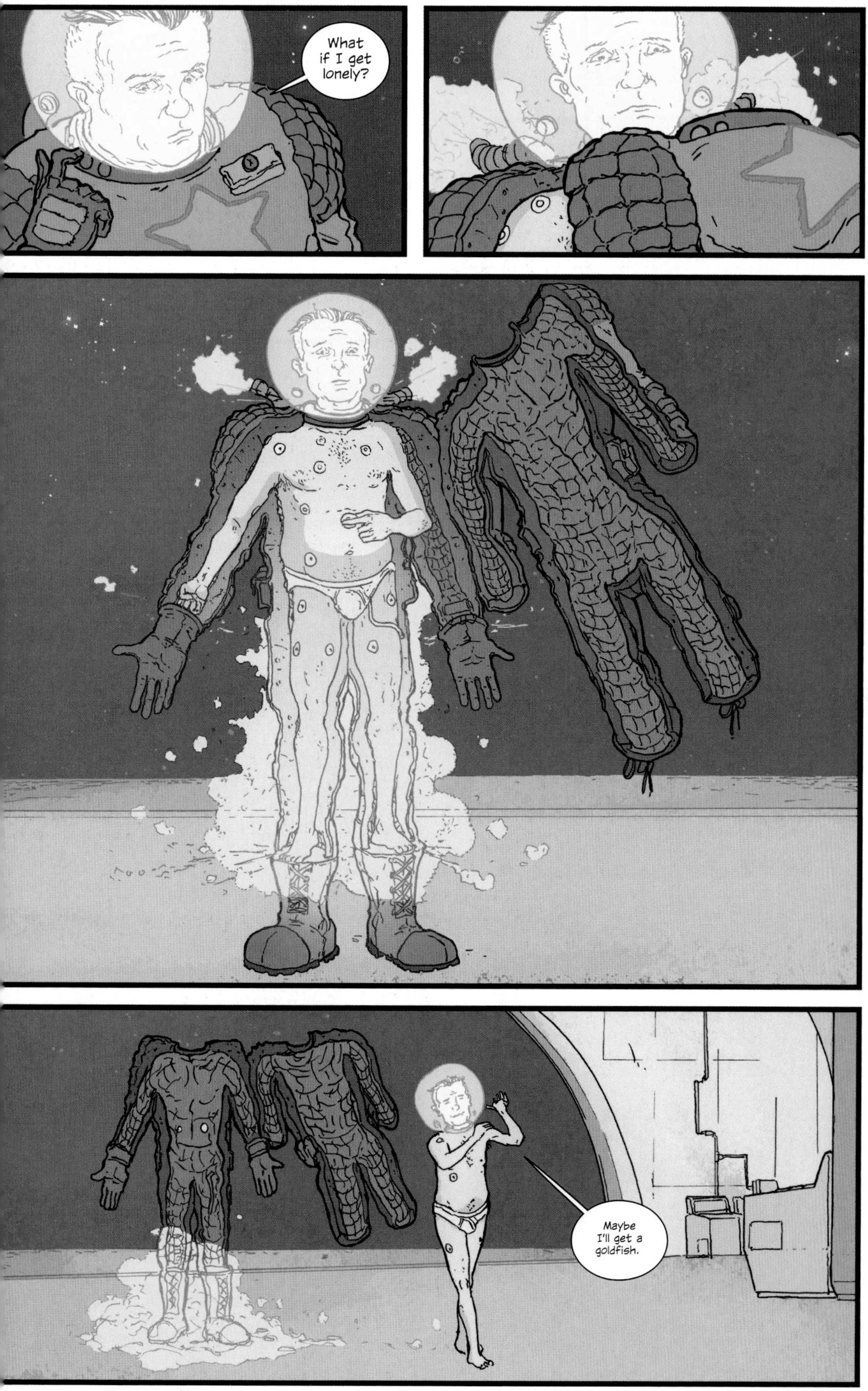
What if I get lonely?
Maybe I'll get a goldfish.

# PROJECT VULCAN

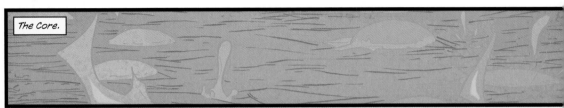

The Core.

Would you look at that?

Once a man, swimming in fire like it was water.

Uh-huh. It's good to see him throwing himself back into his work. He was useless, for what, the first six months we started the project?

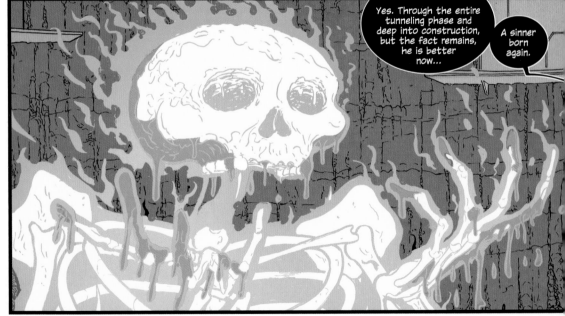

Yes. Through the entire tunneling phase and deep into construction, but the fact remains, he is better now...

A sinner born again.

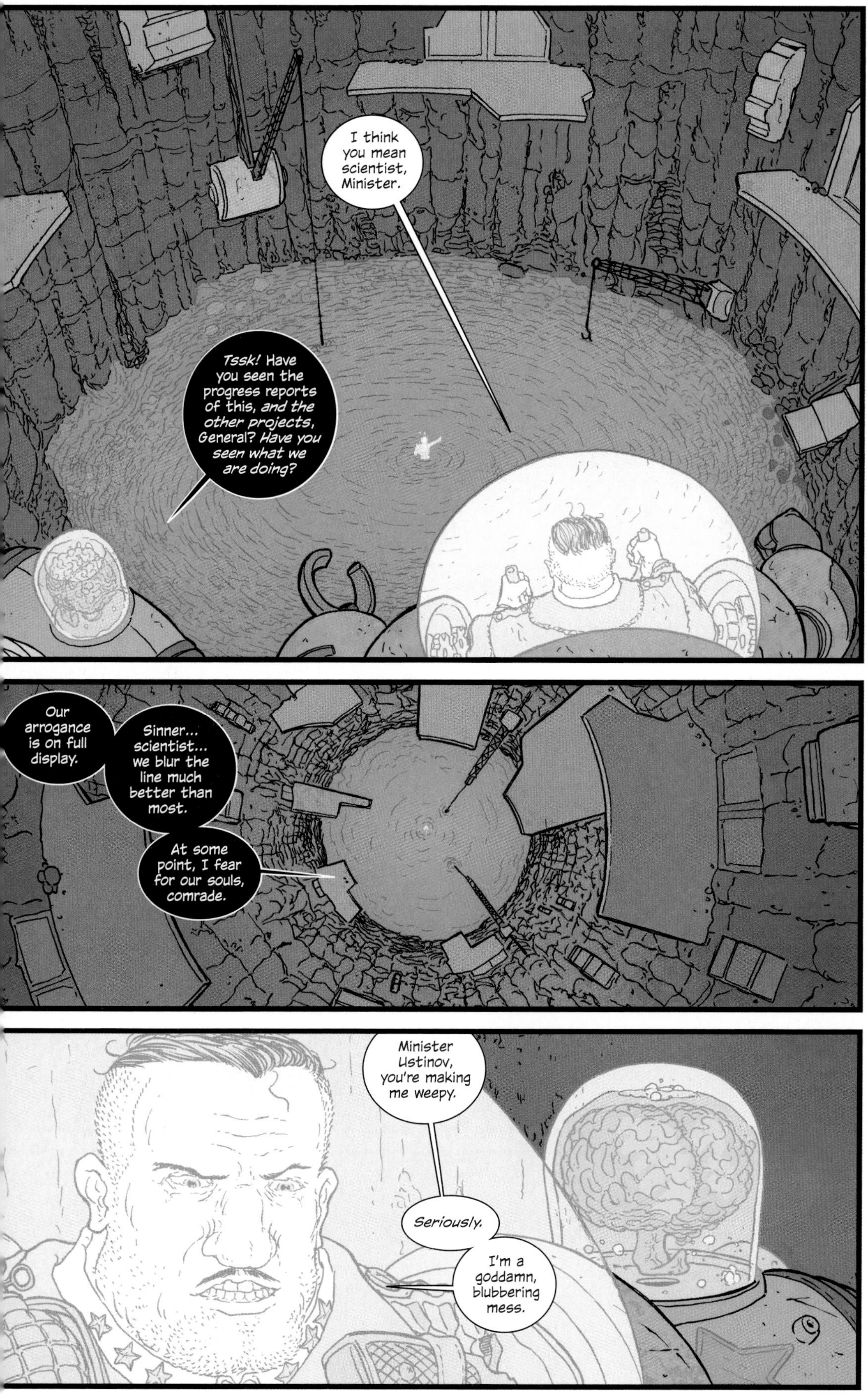
I think you mean scientist, Minister.
*Tssk!* Have you seen the progress reports of this, *and the other projects,* General? *Have you seen what we are doing?*
Our arrogance is on full display.
Sinner... scientist... we blur the line much better than most.
At some point, I fear for our souls, comrade.
Minister Ustinov, you're making me weepy.
*Seriously.*
I'm a goddamn, blubbering mess.

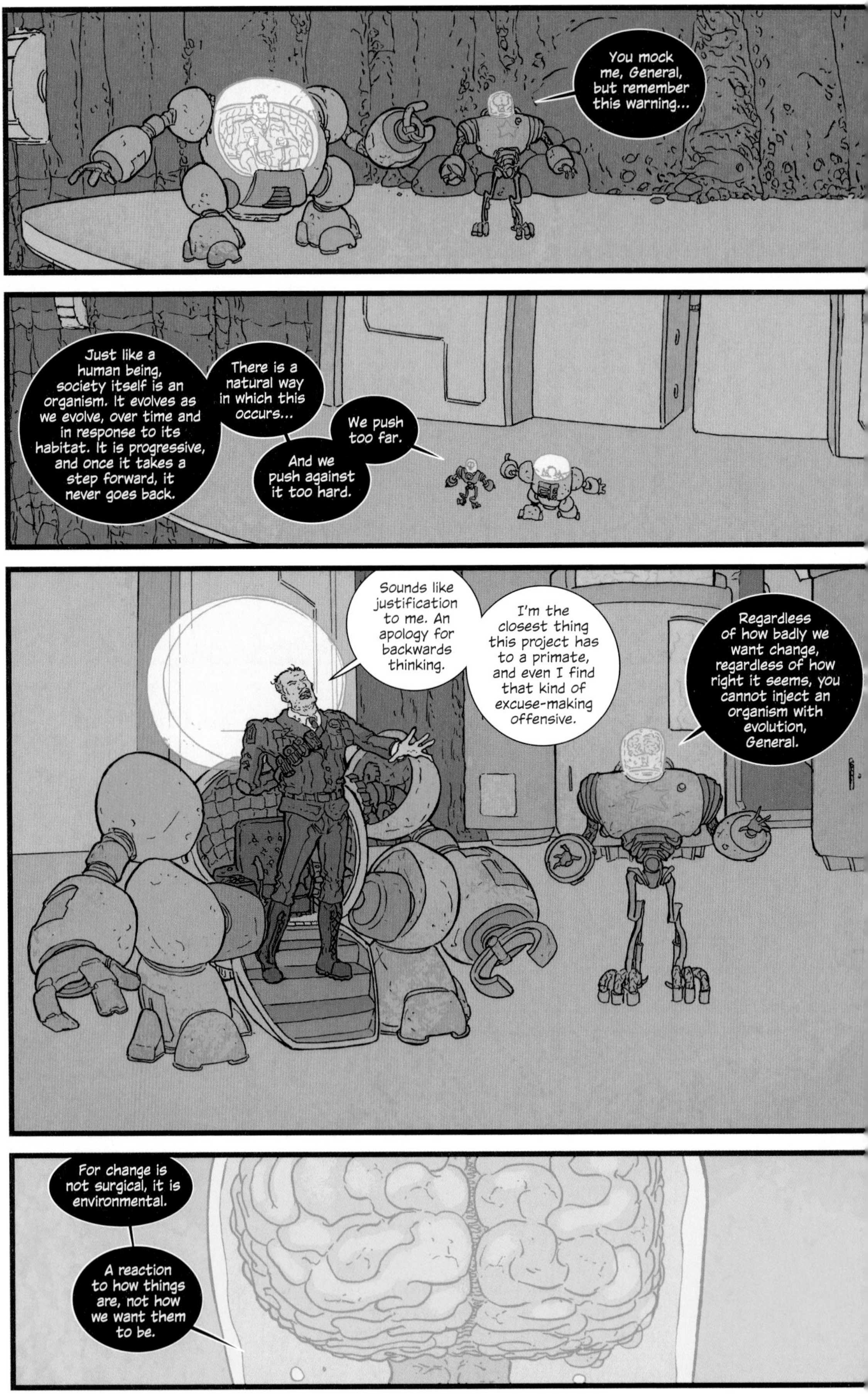
You mock me, General, but remember this warning...
Just like a human being, society itself is an organism. It evolves as we evolve, over time and in response to its habitat. It is progressive, and once it takes a step forward, it never goes back.
There is a natural way in which this occurs...
And we push against it too hard.
We push too far.
Sounds like justification to me. An apology for backwards thinking.
I'm the closest thing this project has to a primate, and even I find that kind of excuse-making offensive.
Regardless of how badly we want change, regardless of how right it seems, you cannot inject an organism with evolution, General.
For change is not surgical, it is environmental.
A reaction to how things are, not how we want them to be.

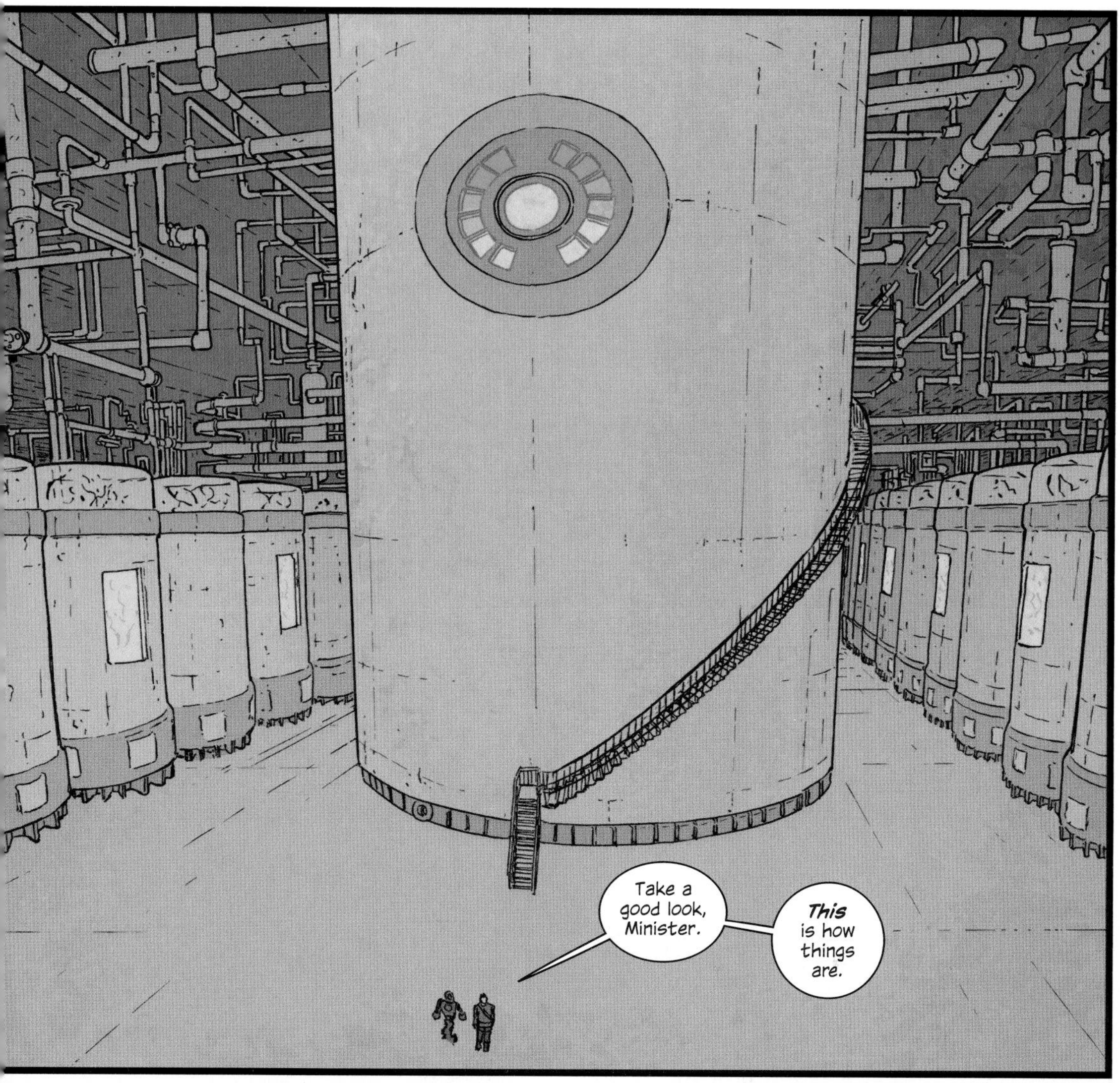
Take a good look, Minister.
*This* is how things are.
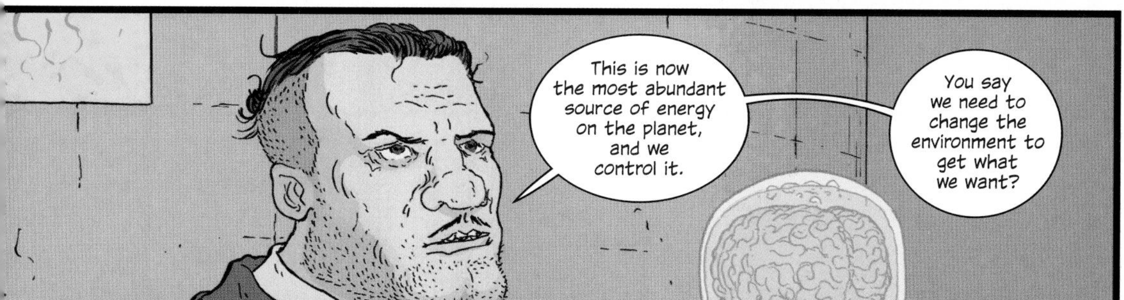
This is now the most abundant source of energy on the planet, and we control it.
You say we need to change the environment to get what we want?
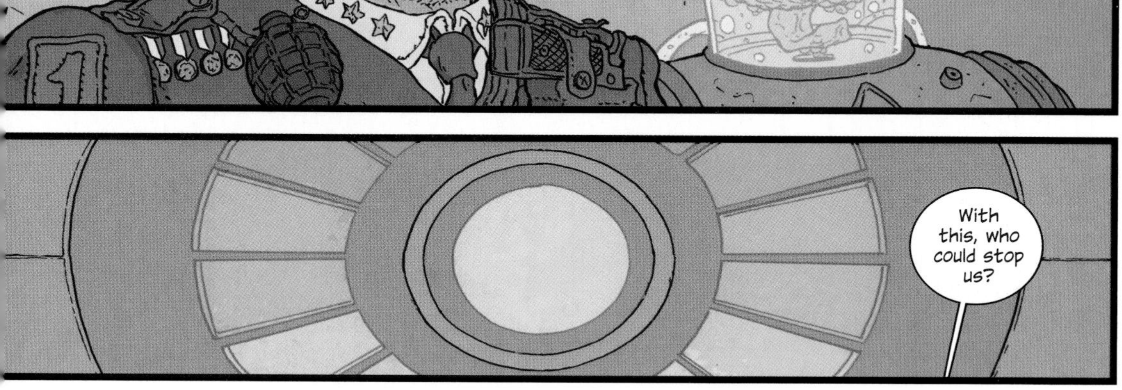
With this, who could stop us?

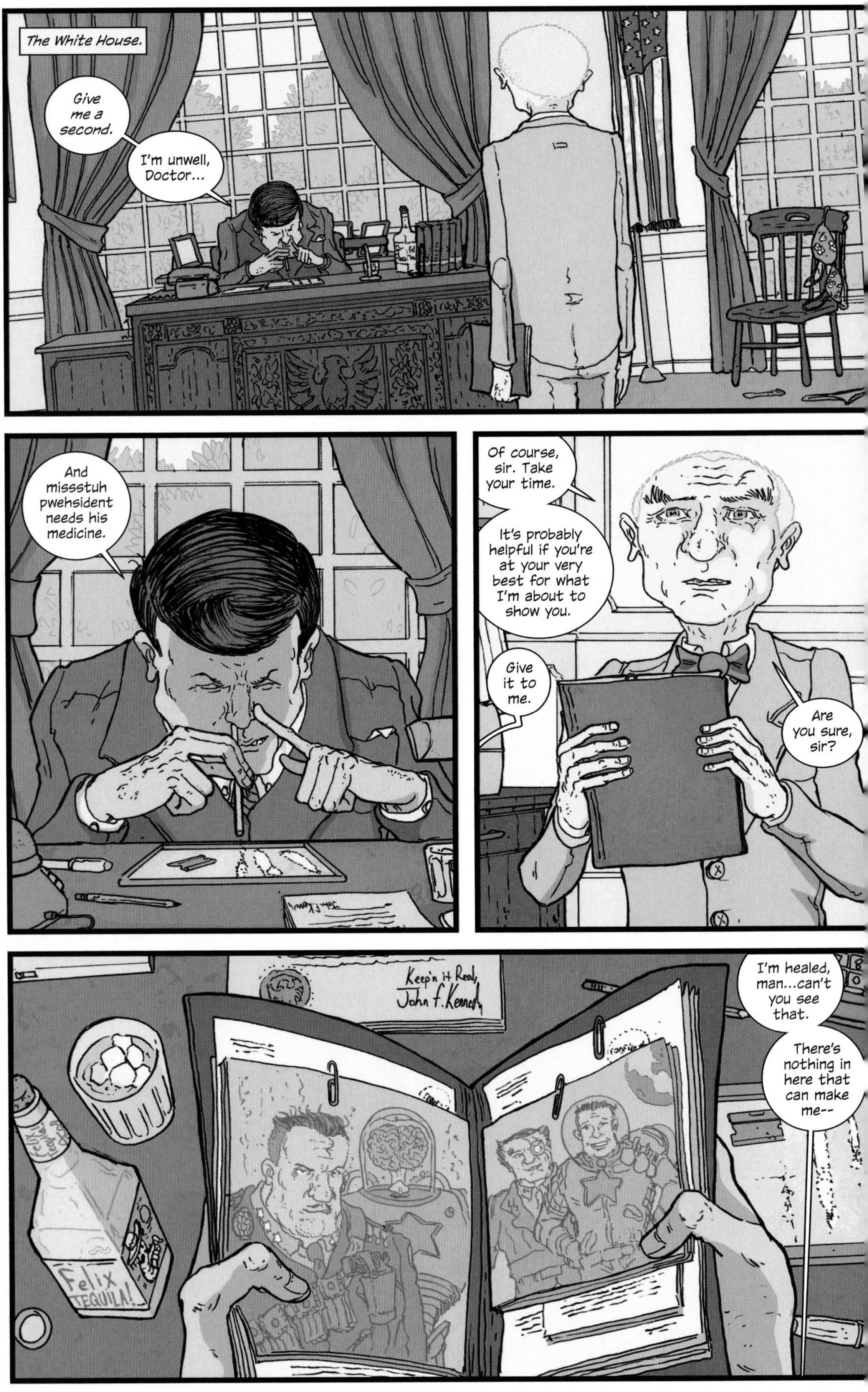
The White House.
Give me a second.
I'm unwell, Doctor...
And missstuh pwehsident needs his medicine.
Of course, sir. Take your time.
It's probably helpful if you're at your very best for what I'm about to show you.
Give it to me.
Are you sure, sir?
Keep'n it Real, John F. Kennedy
Felix TEQUILA!
I'm healed, man...can't you see that.
There's nothing in here that can make me--

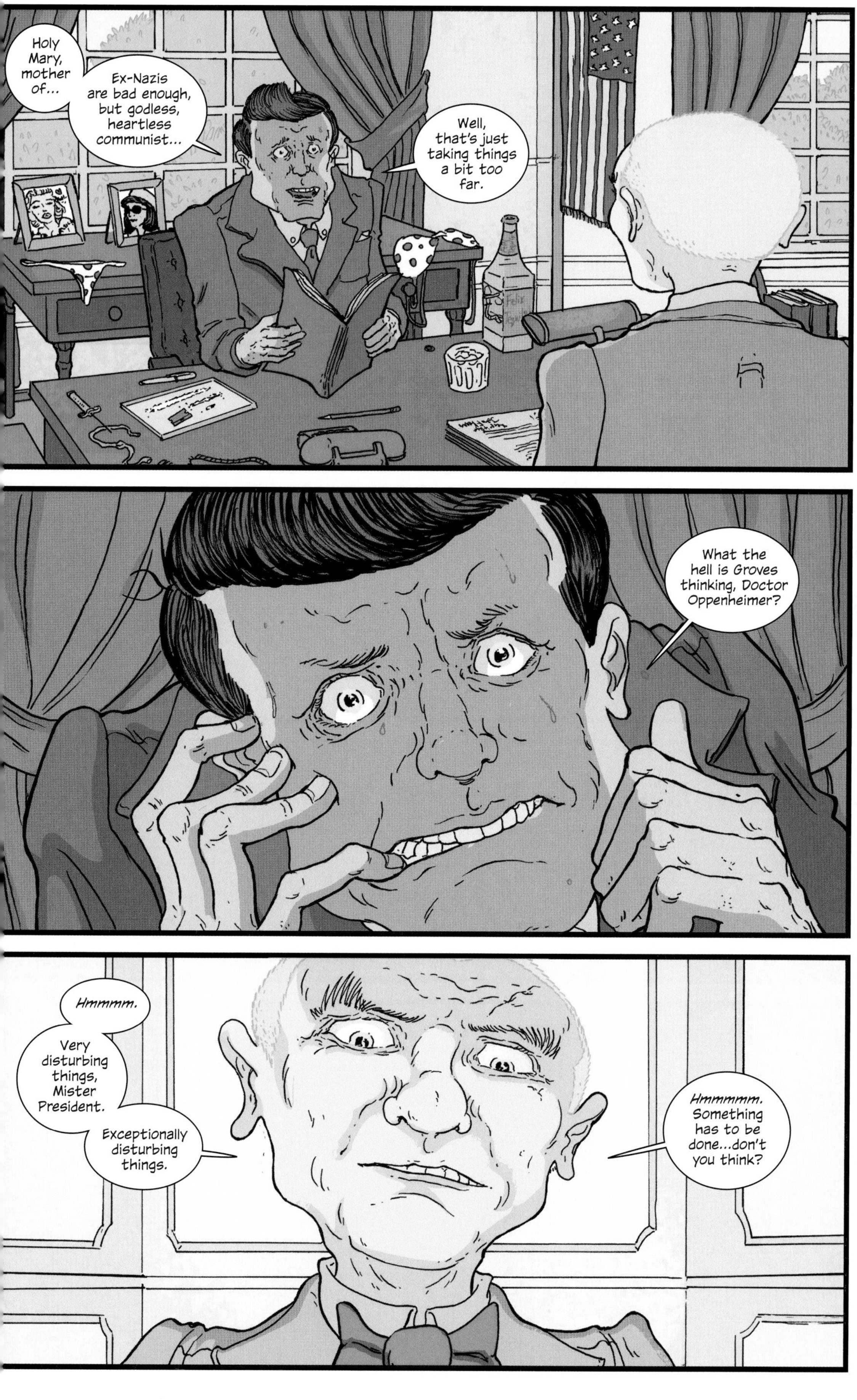
Holy Mary, mother of...
Ex-Nazis are bad enough, but godless, heartless communist...
Well, that's just taking things a bit too far.
What the hell is Groves thinking, Doctor Oppenheimer?
*Hmmmm.*
Very disturbing things, Mister President.
Exceptionally disturbing things.
*Hmmmmm.* Something has to be done...don't you think?

## PROJECT CHARON

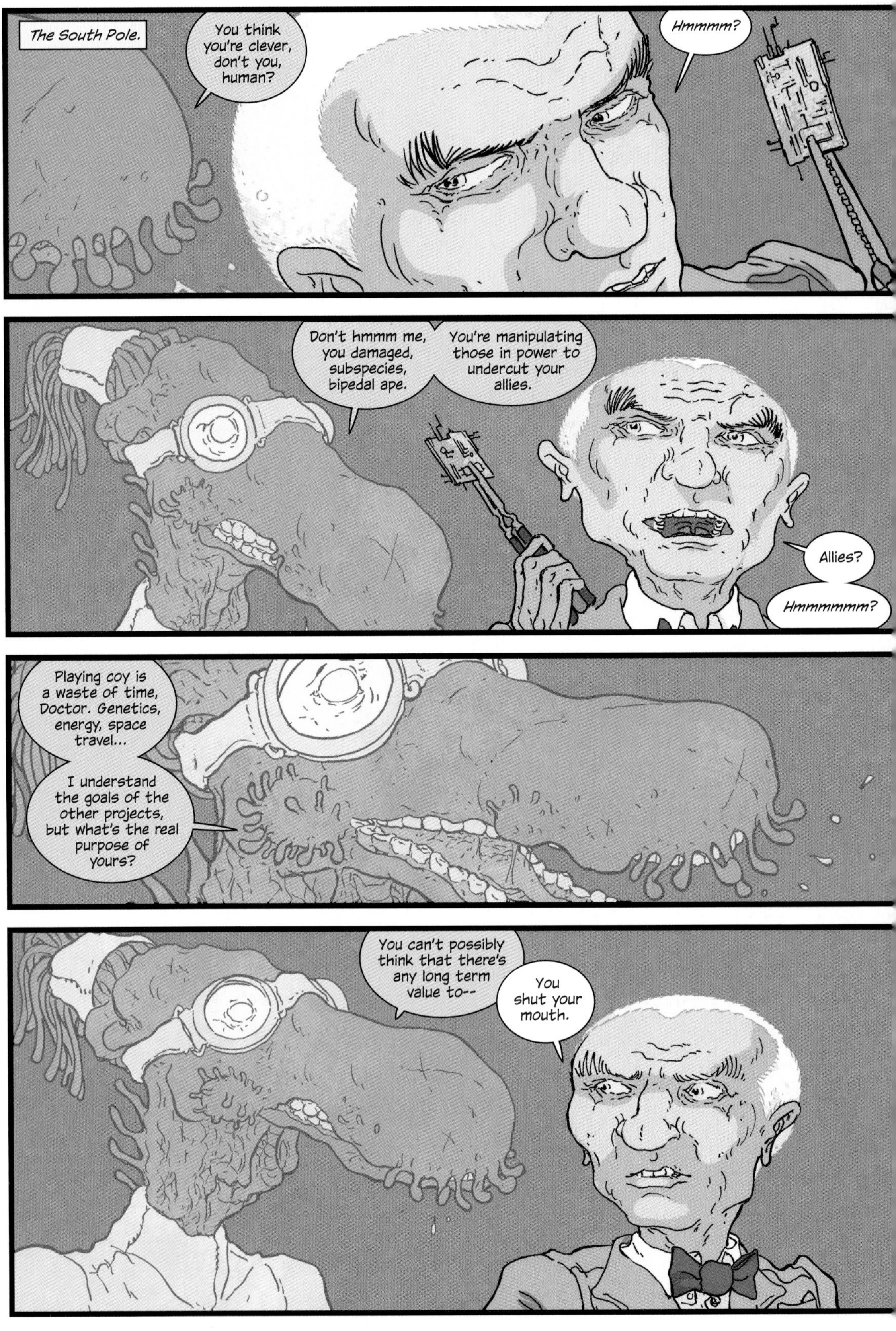
The South Pole.
You think you're clever, don't you, human?
Hmmmm?
Don't hmmm me, you damaged, subspecies, bipedal ape.
You're manipulating those in power to undercut your allies.
Allies?
Hmmmmmm?
Playing coy is a waste of time, Doctor. Genetics, energy, space travel...
I understand the goals of the other projects, but what's the real purpose of yours?
You can't possibly think that there's any long term value to--
You shut your mouth.

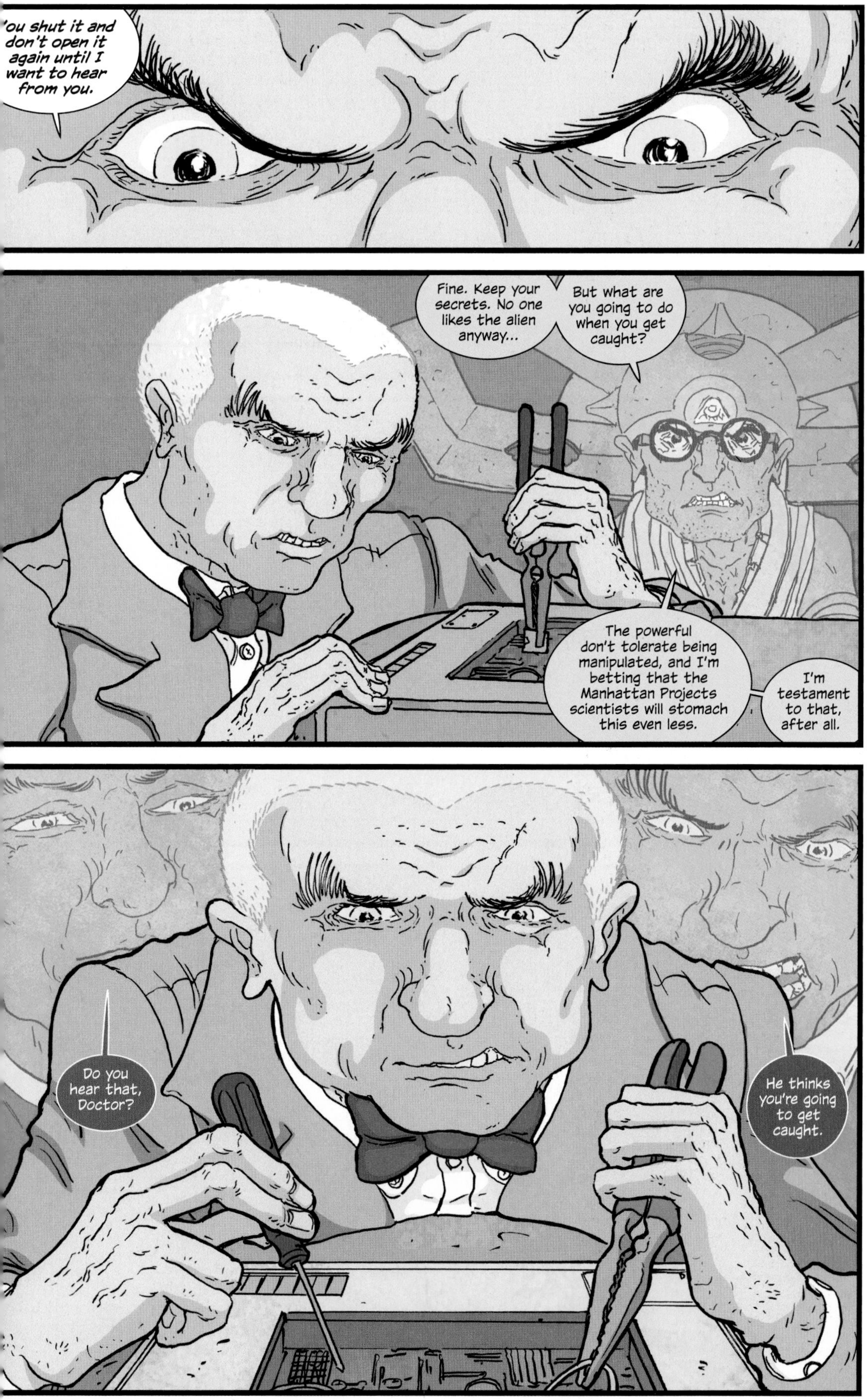
'ou shut it and don't open it again until I want to hear from you.
Fine. Keep your secrets. No one likes the alien anyway...
But what are you going to do when you get caught?
The powerful don't tolerate being manipulated, and I'm betting that the Manhattan Projects scientists will stomach this even less.
I'm testament to that, after all.
Do you hear that, Doctor?
He thinks you're going to get caught.

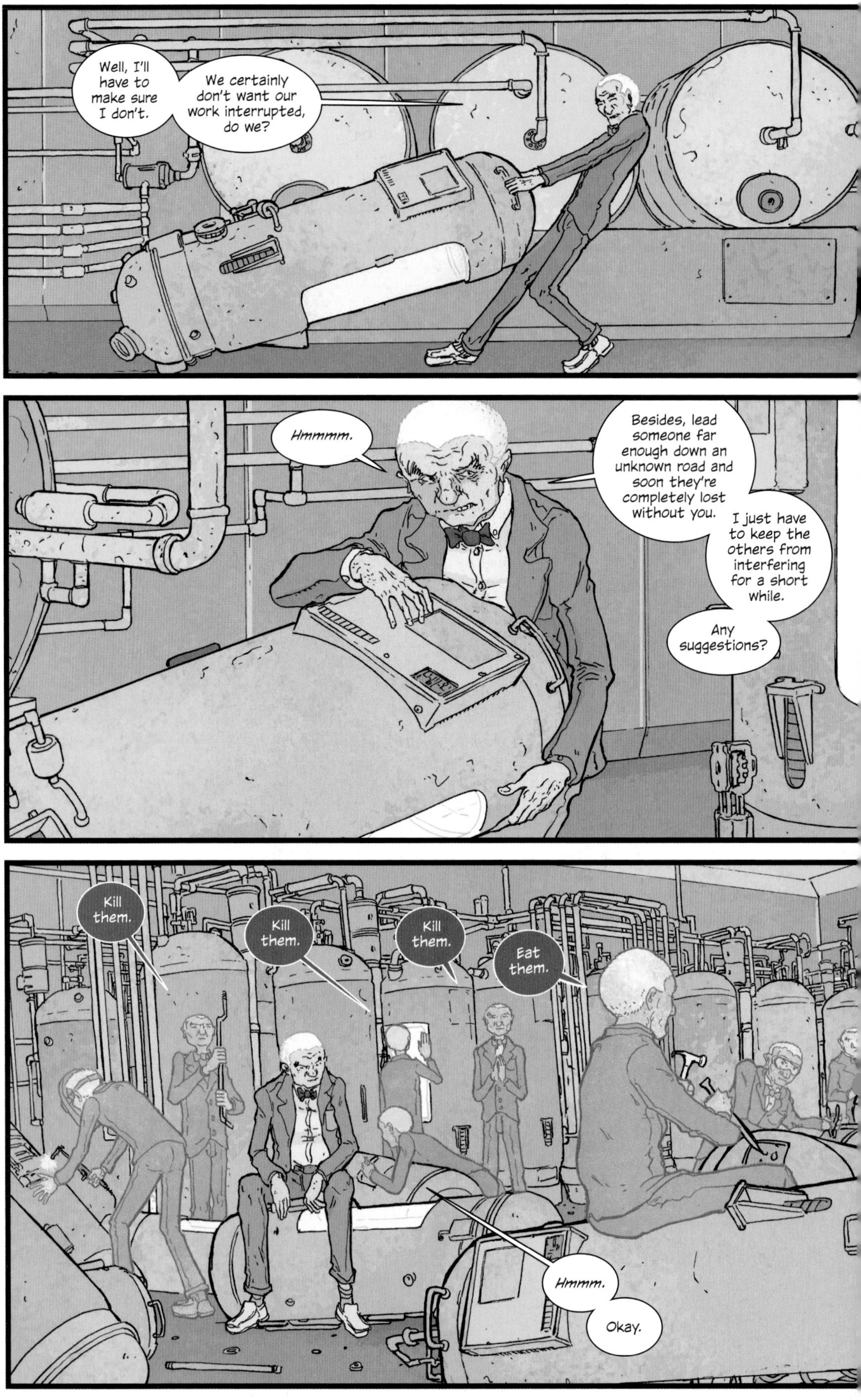
Well, I'll have to make sure I don't.
We certainly don't want our work interrupted, do we?
Hmmmm.
Besides, lead someone far enough down an unknown road and soon they're completely lost without you.
I just have to keep the others from interfering for a short while.
Any suggestions?
Kill them.
Kill them.
Kill them.
Eat them.
Hmmm.
Okay.

"WE KNEW THE ENDLESS OPPENHEIMER AND IT TERRIFIED US.

IMAGINE OUR HORROR WHEN WE DISCOVERED HE WAS INFINITE."

*CLAVIS AUREA*
THE RECORDED FEYNMAN

VOL. 4

# ARE THOSE
# EARS

"THINGS FLY APART. IT'S ONLY GRAVITY
THAT BRINGS THEM BACK TOGETHER...

AND WE HAD NO CENTER."

*CLAVIS AUREA*
THE RECORDED FEYNMAN | **VOL. 3**

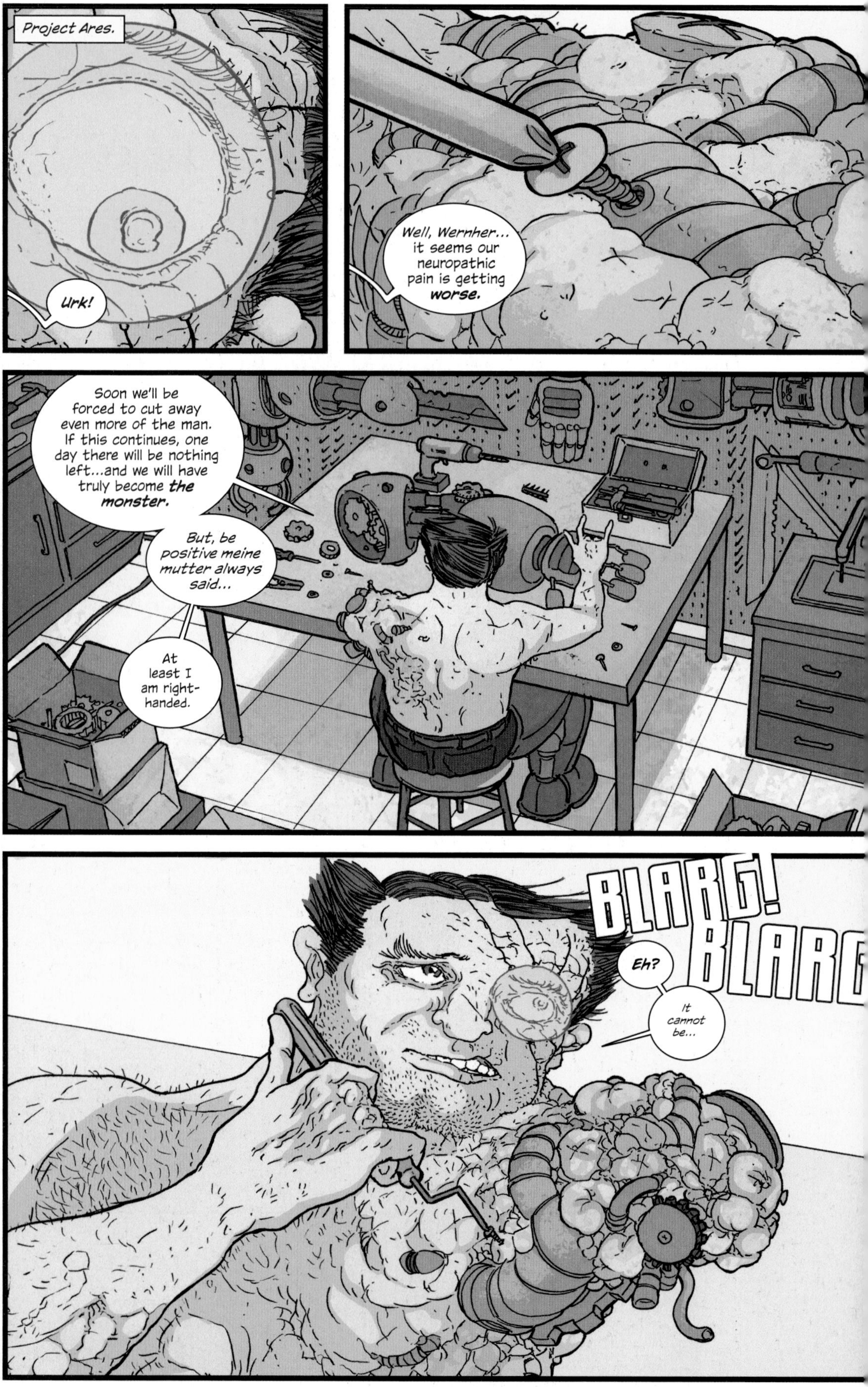

Project Ares.
Urk!
Well, Wernher... it seems our neuropathic pain is getting worse.
Soon we'll be forced to cut away even more of the man. If this continues, one day there will be nothing left...and we will have truly become the monster.
But, be positive meine mutter always said...
At least I am right-handed.
BLARG!
Eh?
It cannot be...

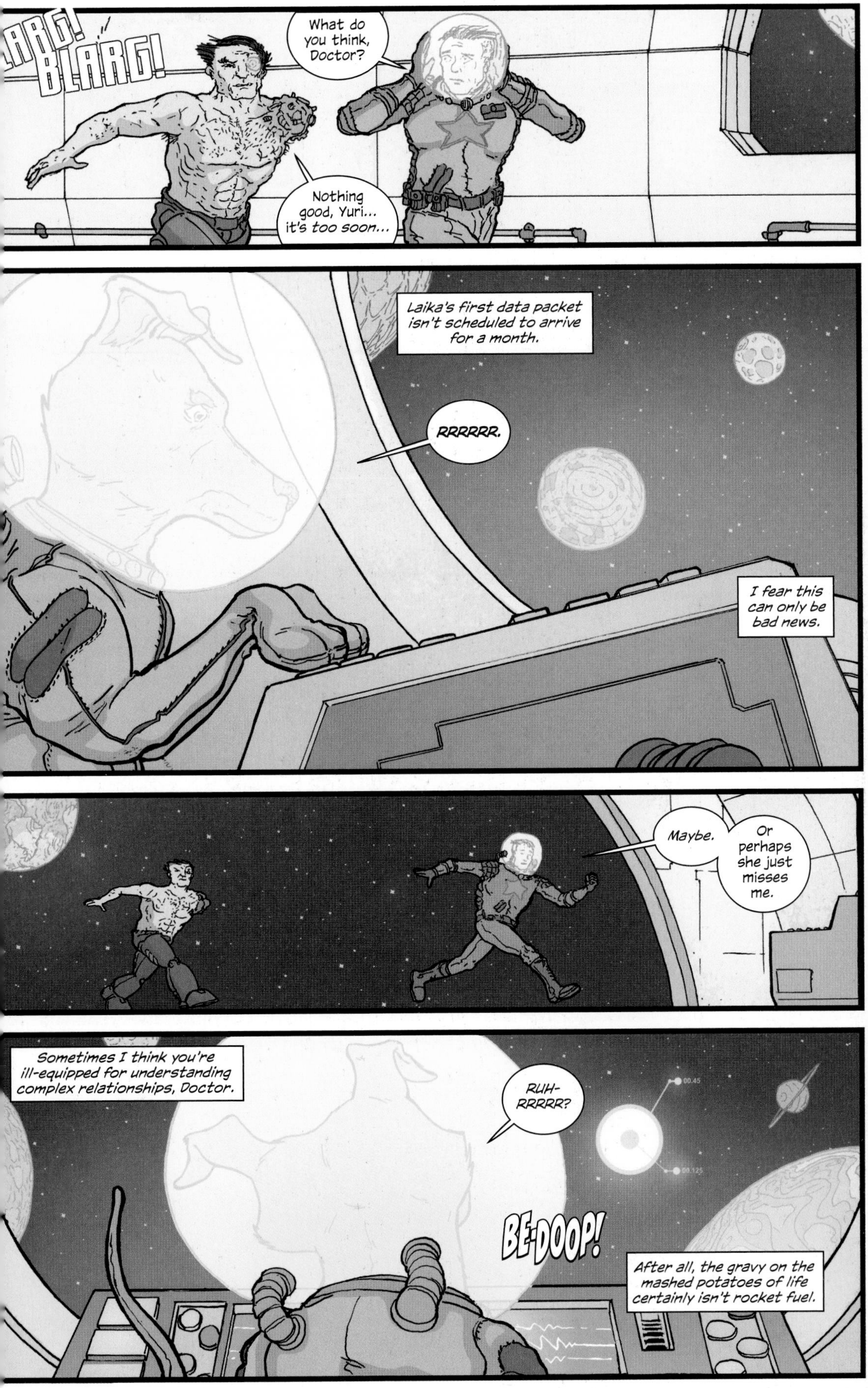

LARG! BLARG!
What do you think, Doctor?
Nothing good, Yuri... it's too soon...
Laika's first data packet isn't scheduled to arrive for a month.
RRRRRR.
I fear this can only be bad news.
Maybe.
Or perhaps she just misses me.
Sometimes I think you're ill-equipped for understanding complex relationships, Doctor.
RUH-RRRRR?
BE-DOOP!
After all, the gravy on the mashed potatoes of life certainly isn't rocket fuel.

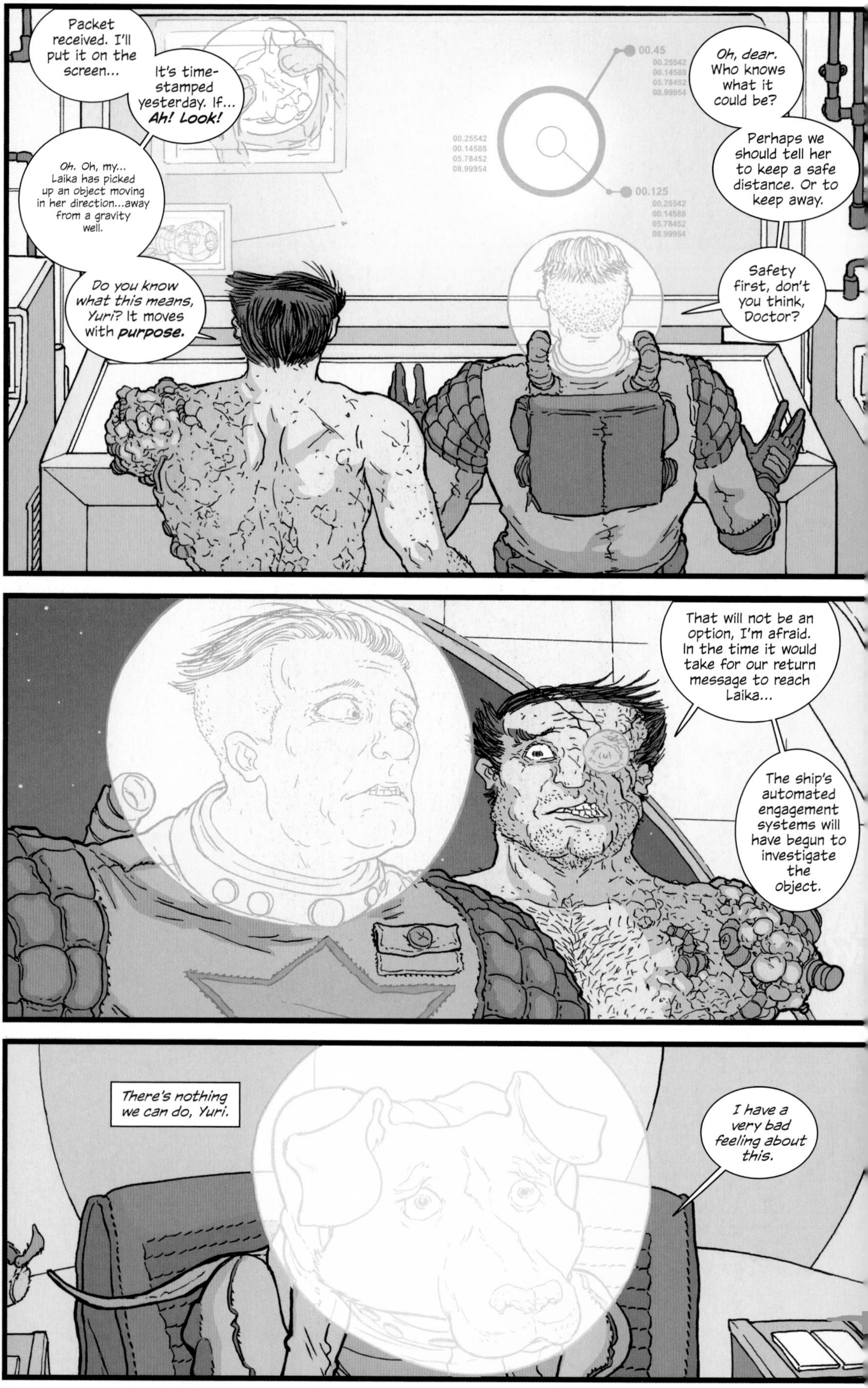
Packet received. I'll put it on the screen...
It's time-stamped yesterday. If... Ah! Look!
Oh. Oh, my... Laika has picked up an object moving in her direction...away from a gravity well.
Do you know what this means, Yuri? It moves with purpose.
Oh, dear. Who knows what it could be?
Perhaps we should tell her to keep a safe distance. Or to keep away.
Safety first, don't you think, Doctor?
00.45
00.25542
00.14588
05.78452
08.99954
00.125
That will not be an option, I'm afraid. In the time it would take for our return message to reach Laika...
The ship's automated engagement systems will have begun to investigate the object.
There's nothing we can do, Yuri.
I have a very bad feeling about this.

"WE DON'T TALK ABOUT THE DOG.

WE DON'T EVER TALK ABOUT THE GODDAMN DOG."

*CLAVIS AUREA*
THE RECORDED FEYNMAN | **VOL. 4**

# 14

**UPWARD BOUND**

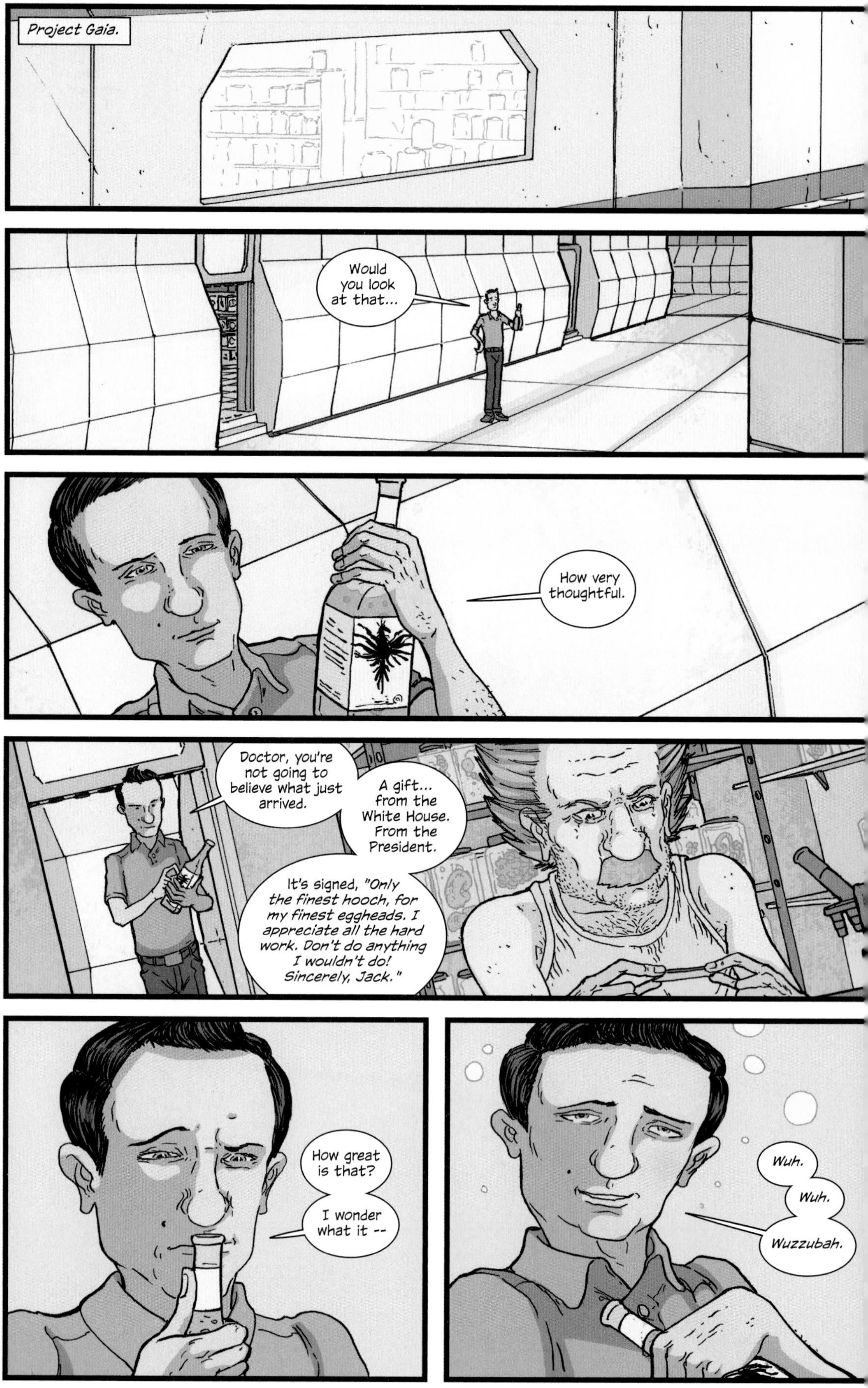
Project Gaia.
Would you look at that...
How very thoughtful.
Doctor, you're not going to believe what just arrived.
A gift... from the White House. From the President.
It's signed, "Only the finest hooch, for my finest eggheads. I appreciate all the hard work. Don't do anything I wouldn't do! Sincerely, Jack."
How great is that?
I wonder what it --
Wuh.
Wuh.
Wuzzubah.

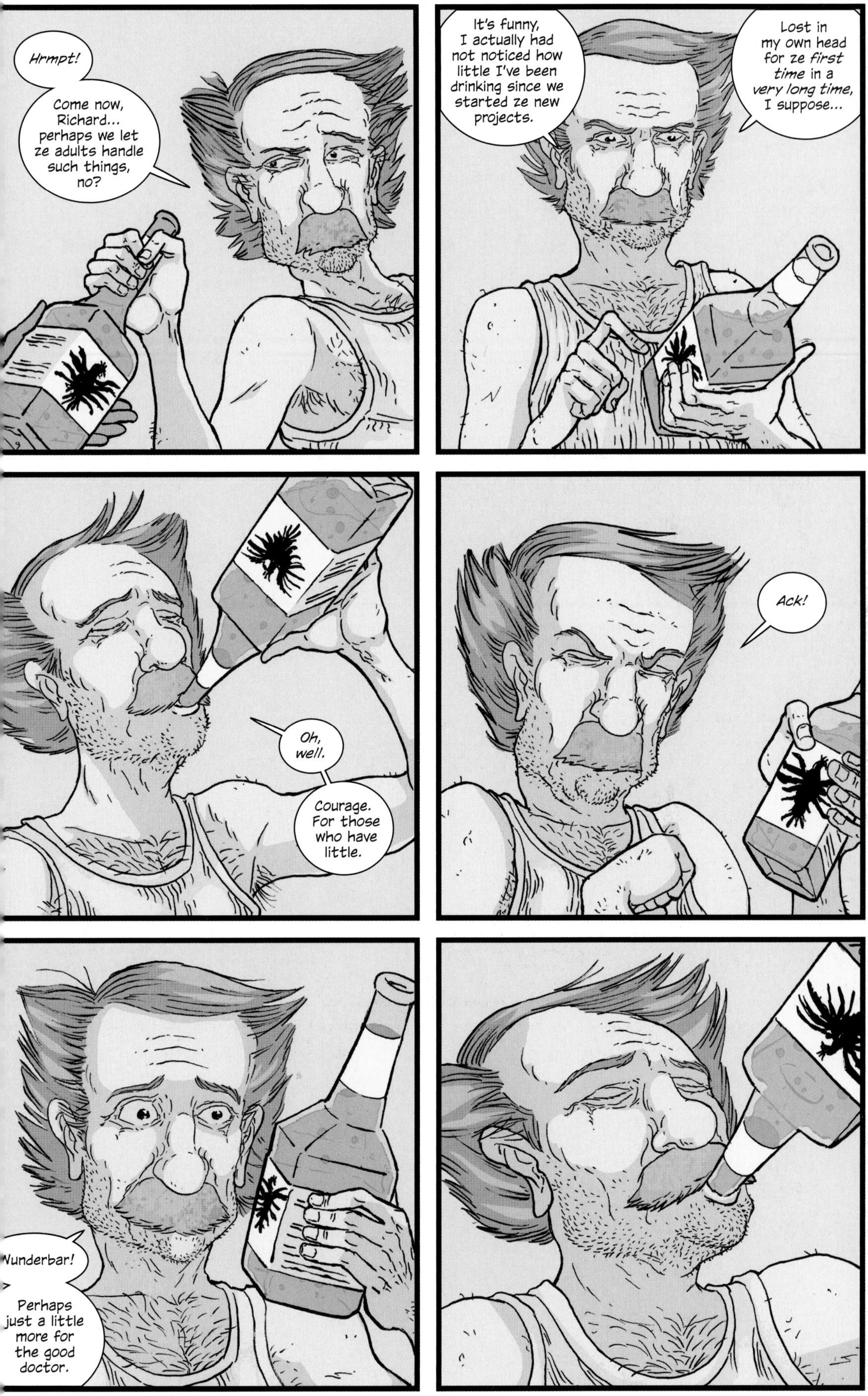

*Hrmpt!*
Come now, Richard... perhaps we let ze adults handle such things, no?
It's funny, I actually had not noticed how little I've been drinking since we started ze new projects.
Lost in my own head for ze *first time* in a *very long time*, I suppose...
*Oh, well.*
Courage. For those who have little.
*Ack!*
*Wunderbar!*
Perhaps just a little more for the good doctor.

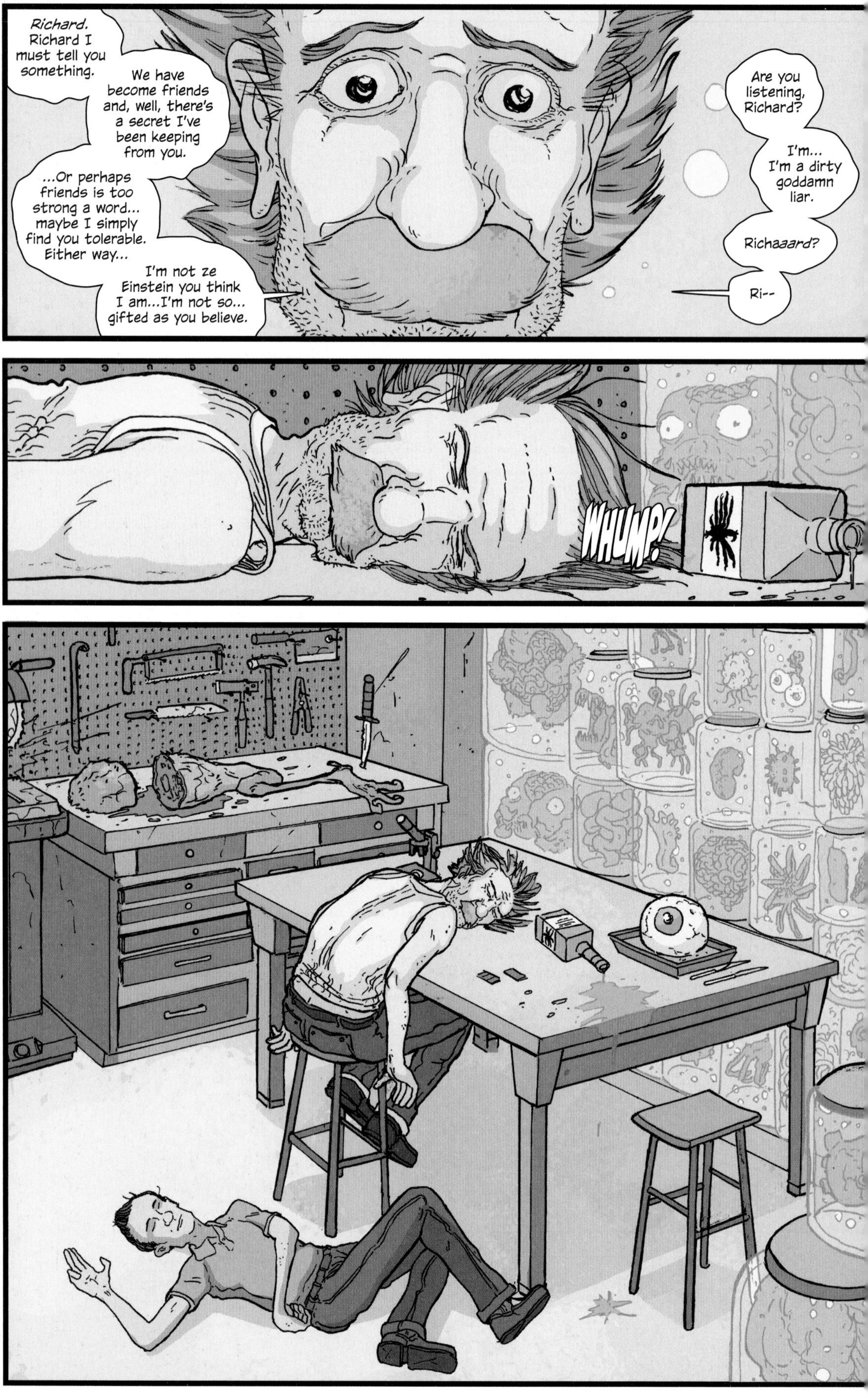
Richard. Richard I must tell you something.
We have become friends and, well, there's a secret I've been keeping from you.
...Or perhaps friends is too strong a word... maybe I simply find you tolerable. Either way...
I'm not ze Einstein you think I am...I'm not so... gifted as you believe.
Are you listening, Richard?
I'm... I'm a dirty goddamn liar.
Richaaard?
Ri--
WHUMP!

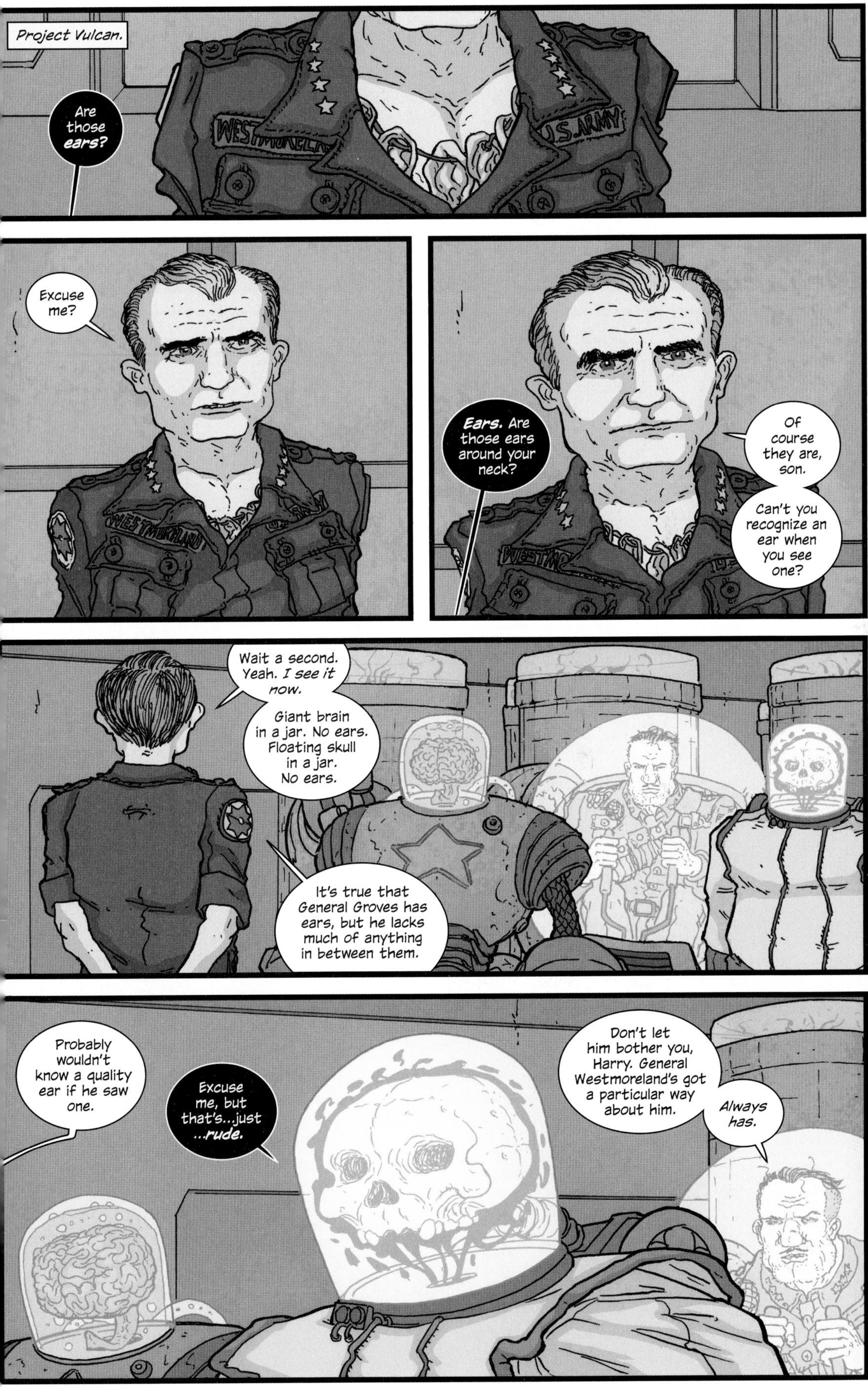
Project Vulcan.
Are those ears?
WESTMORELAND
U.S. ARMY
Excuse me?
Ears. Are those ears around your neck?
Of course they are, son.
Can't you recognize an ear when you see one?
Wait a second. Yeah. I see it now.
Giant brain in a jar. No ears. Floating skull in a jar. No ears.
It's true that General Groves has ears, but he lacks much of anything in between them.
Probably wouldn't know a quality ear if he saw one.
Excuse me, but that's...just ...rude.
Don't let him bother you, Harry. General Westmoreland's got a particular way about him.
Always has.

It's true. You see me comin'... prepare for the village to be burned down.

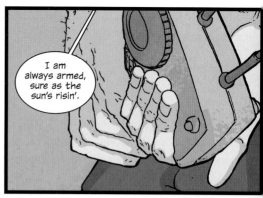

I am always armed, sure as the sun's risin'.

But I'm not here with threats, Leslie... I'm here with orders from on high.

The President sent me to shut you down and assume command of the Manhattan Projects.

'Cause I don't care if it's just gray matter floating atop a robot body...we won't tolerate you workin' with the *goddamn Russians.*

Well, General... I'm sorry you feel that way.

But we don't take orders from the President any longer, we answer to a higher power.

I've learned science trumps savagery each and every time.

Sorry you feel that way...

CLICK!

Uhhh... what's that?

It's a system override for your little toy, General Groves.
See. I'm in total control of the situation.
Dimitri!
Look out!
SMASH!
Catch it. Catch it. Catch it...

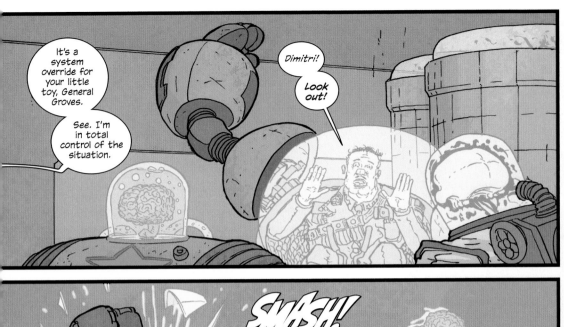

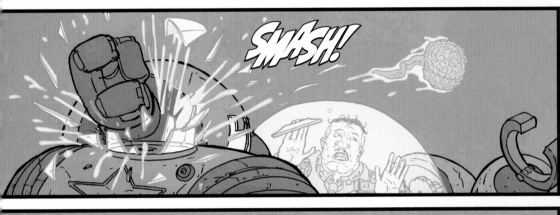

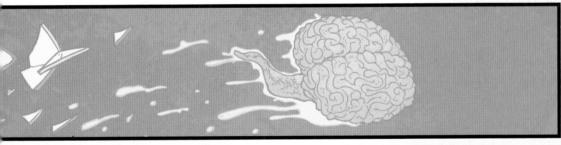

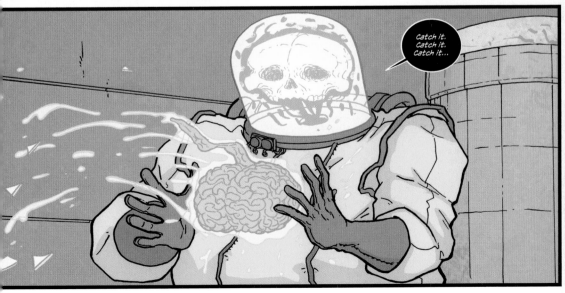

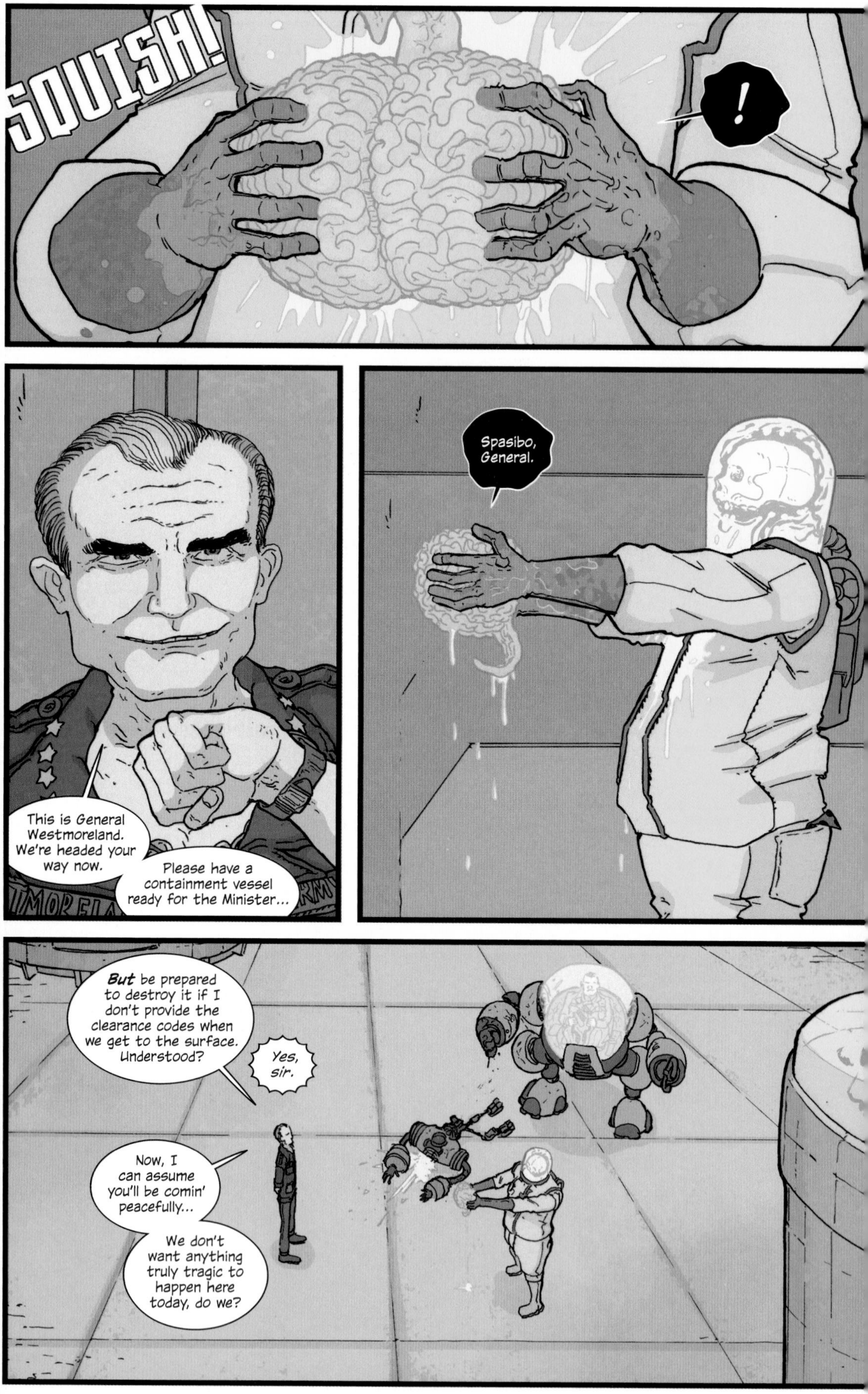
SQUISH!
!
This is General Westmoreland. We're headed your way now.
Please have a containment vessel ready for the Minister...
Spasibo, General.
**But** be prepared to destroy it if I don't provide the clearance codes when we get to the surface. Understood?
*Yes, sir.*
Now, I can assume you'll be comin' peacefully...
We don't want anything truly tragic to happen here today, do we?

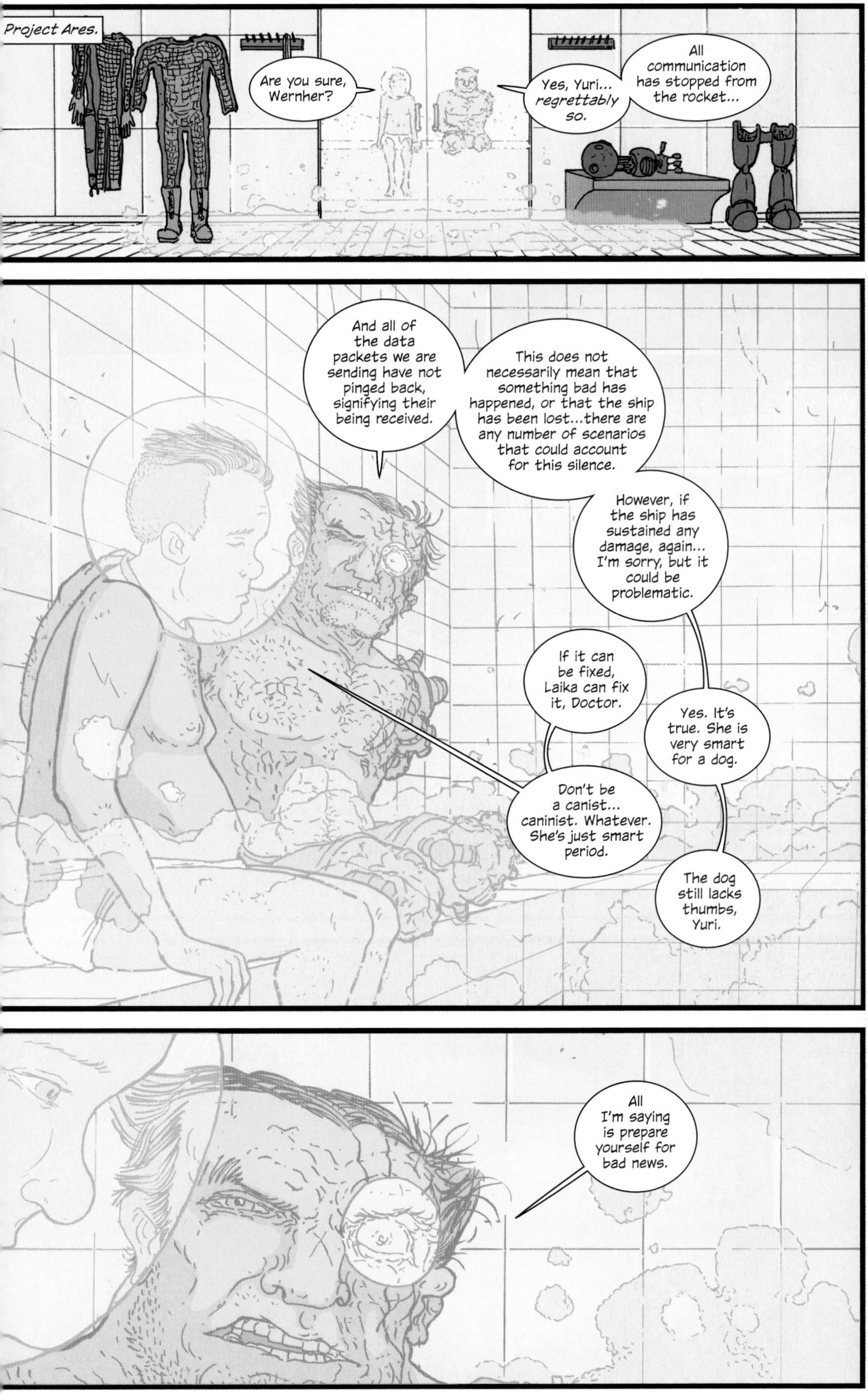
Project Ares.
Are you sure, Wernher?
Yes, Yuri... *regrettably* so.
All communication has stopped from the rocket...
And all of the data packets we are sending have not pinged back, signifying their being received.
This does not necessarily mean that something bad has happened, or that the ship has been lost...there are any number of scenarios that could account for this silence.
However, if the ship has sustained any damage, again... I'm sorry, but it could be problematic.
If it can be fixed, Laika can fix it, Doctor.
Yes. It's true. She is very smart for a dog.
Don't be a canist... caninist. Whatever. She's just smart period.
The dog still lacks thumbs, Yuri.
All I'm saying is prepare yourself for bad news.

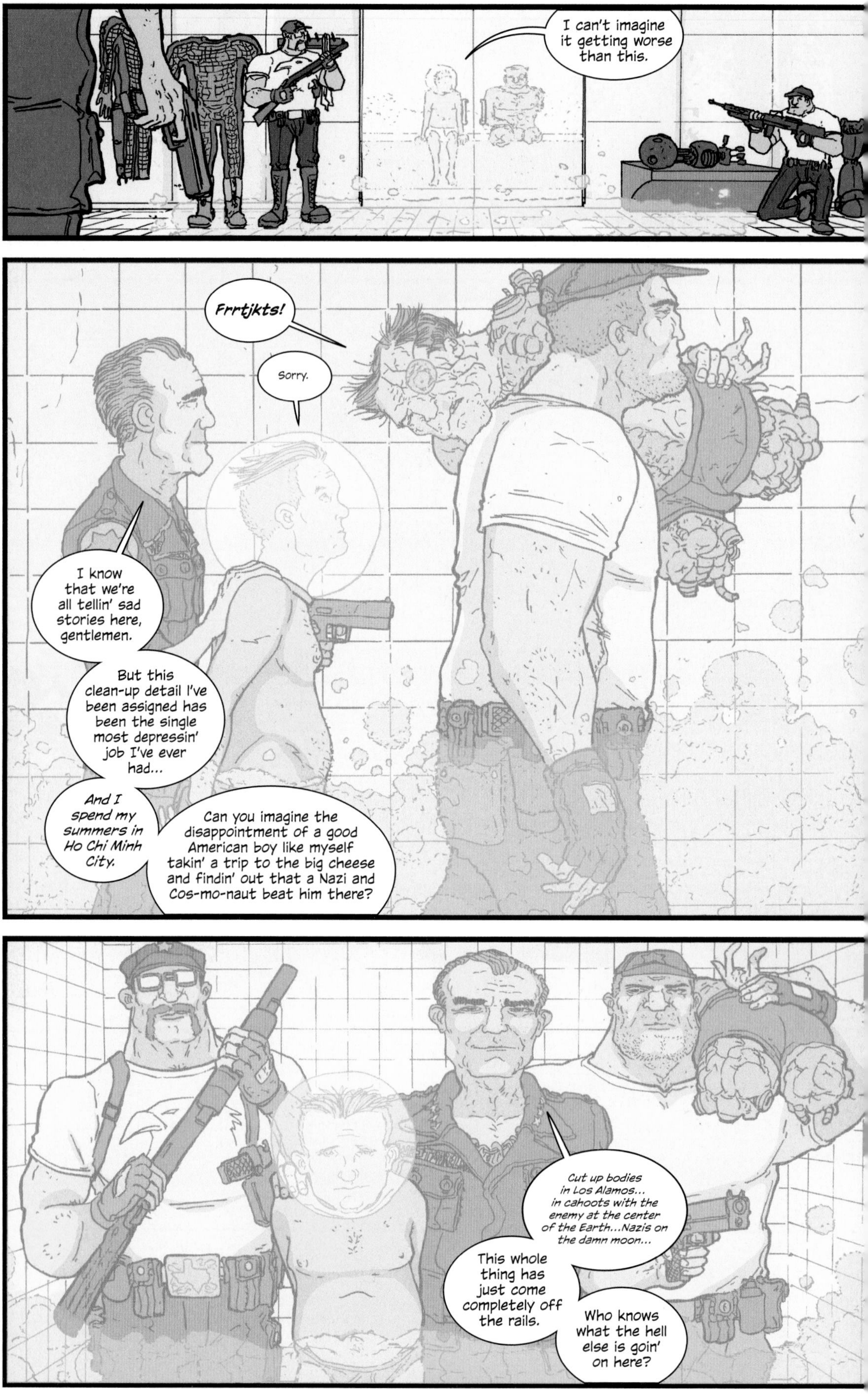

I can't imagine it getting worse than this.
Frrtjkts!
Sorry.
I know that we're all tellin' sad stories here, gentlemen.
But this clean-up detail I've been assigned has been the single most depressin' job I've ever had...
And I spend my summers in Ho Chi Minh City.
Can you imagine the disappointment of a good American boy like myself takin' a trip to the big cheese and findin' out that a Nazi and Cos-mo-naut beat him there?
Cut up bodies in Los Alamos... in cahoots with the enemy at the center of the Earth...Nazis on the damn moon...
This whole thing has just come completely off the rails.
Who knows what the hell else is goin' on here?

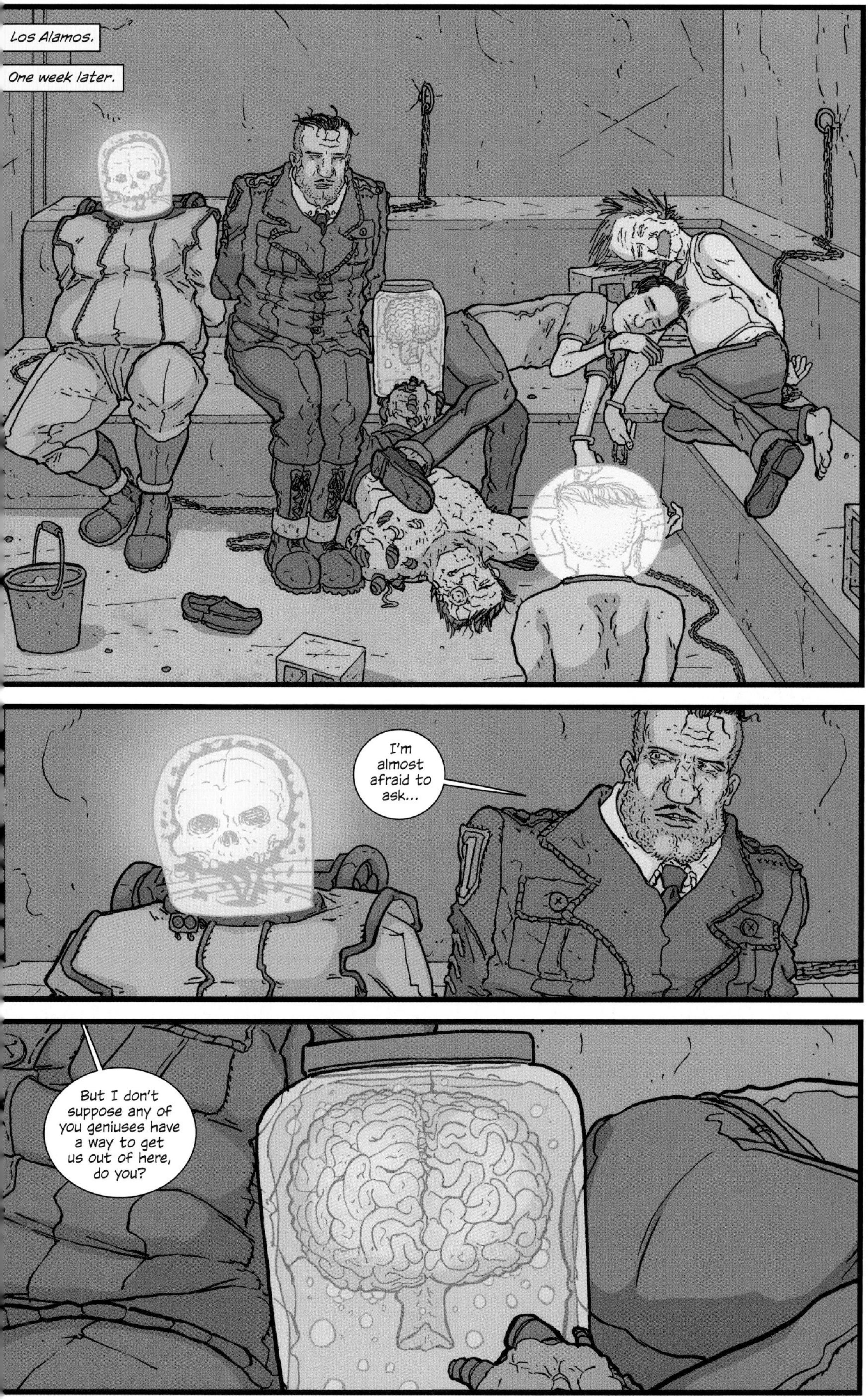
Los Alamos.
One week later.
I'm almost afraid to ask...
But I don't suppose any of you geniuses have a way to get us out of here, do you?

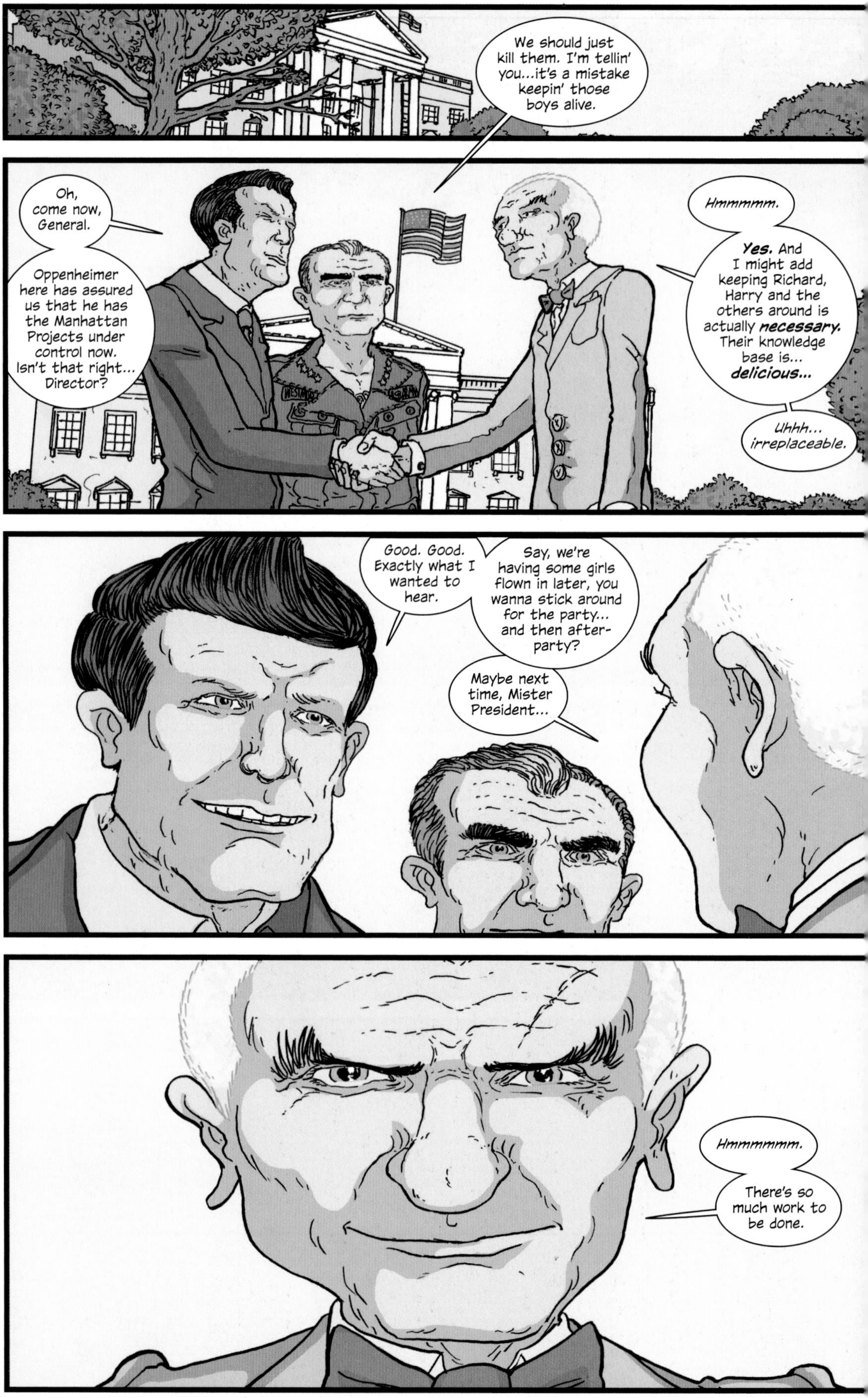

We should just kill them. I'm tellin' you...it's a mistake keepin' those boys alive.
Oh, come now, General.
Oppenheimer here has assured us that he has the Manhattan Projects under control now. Isn't that right... Director?
Hmmmmm.
Yes. And I might add keeping Richard, Harry and the others around is actually necessary. Their knowledge base is... delicious...
Uhhh... irreplaceable.
Good. Good. Exactly what I wanted to hear.
Say, we're having some girls flown in later, you wanna stick around for the party... and then after-party?
Maybe next time, Mister President...
Hmmmmmm.
There's so much work to be done.

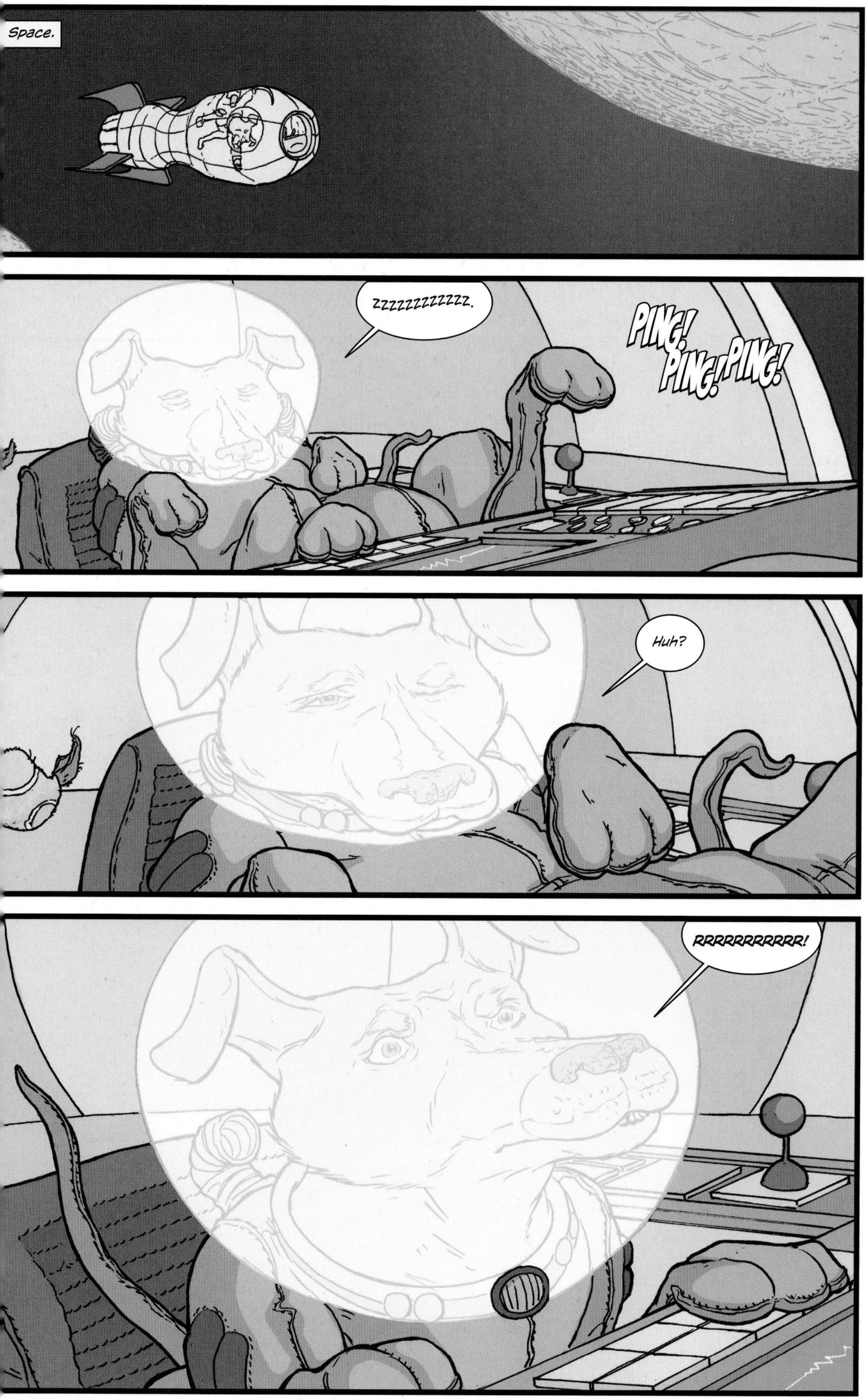
Space.
ZZZZZZZZZZZZ.
PING! PING! PING!
Huh?
RRRRRRRRRRR!

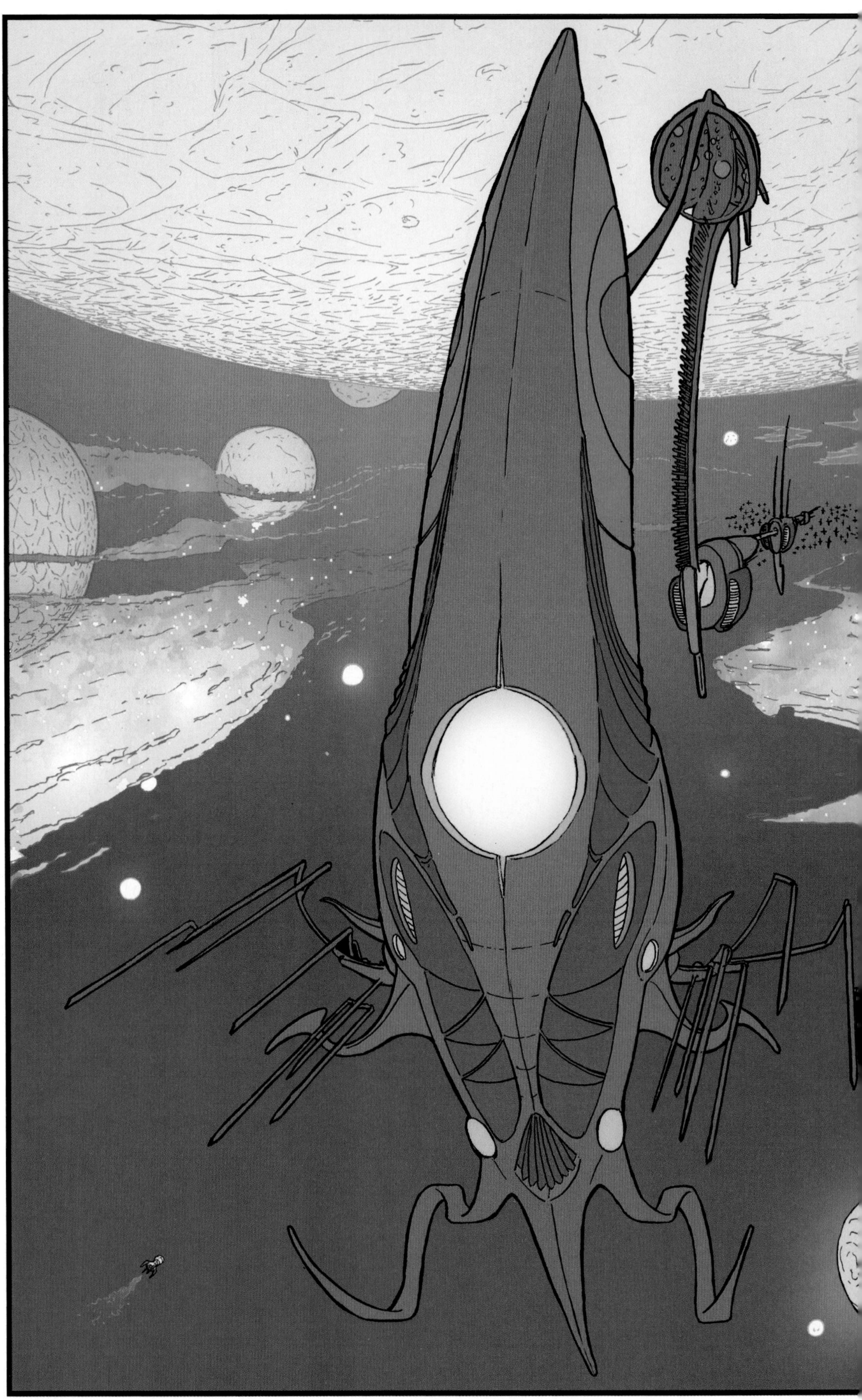

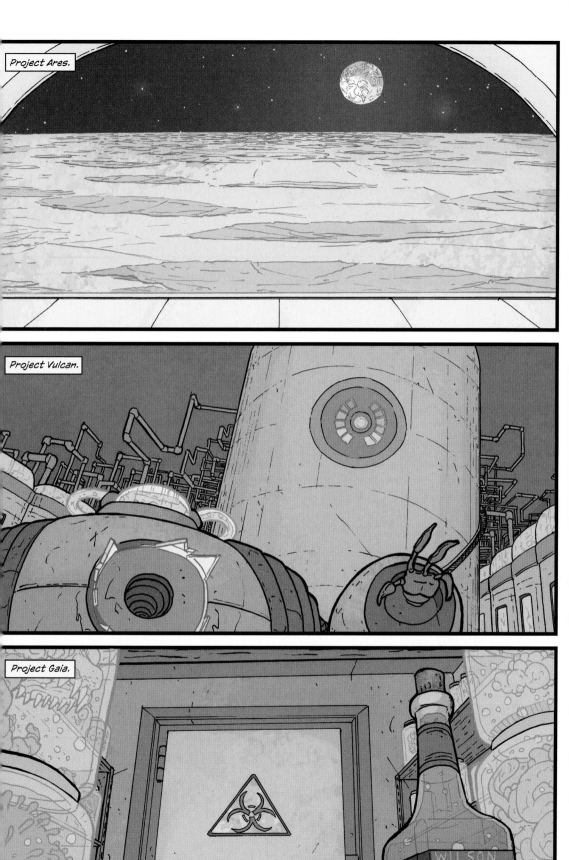

Project Ares.

Project Vulcan.

Project Gaia.

WILSON WISKEY

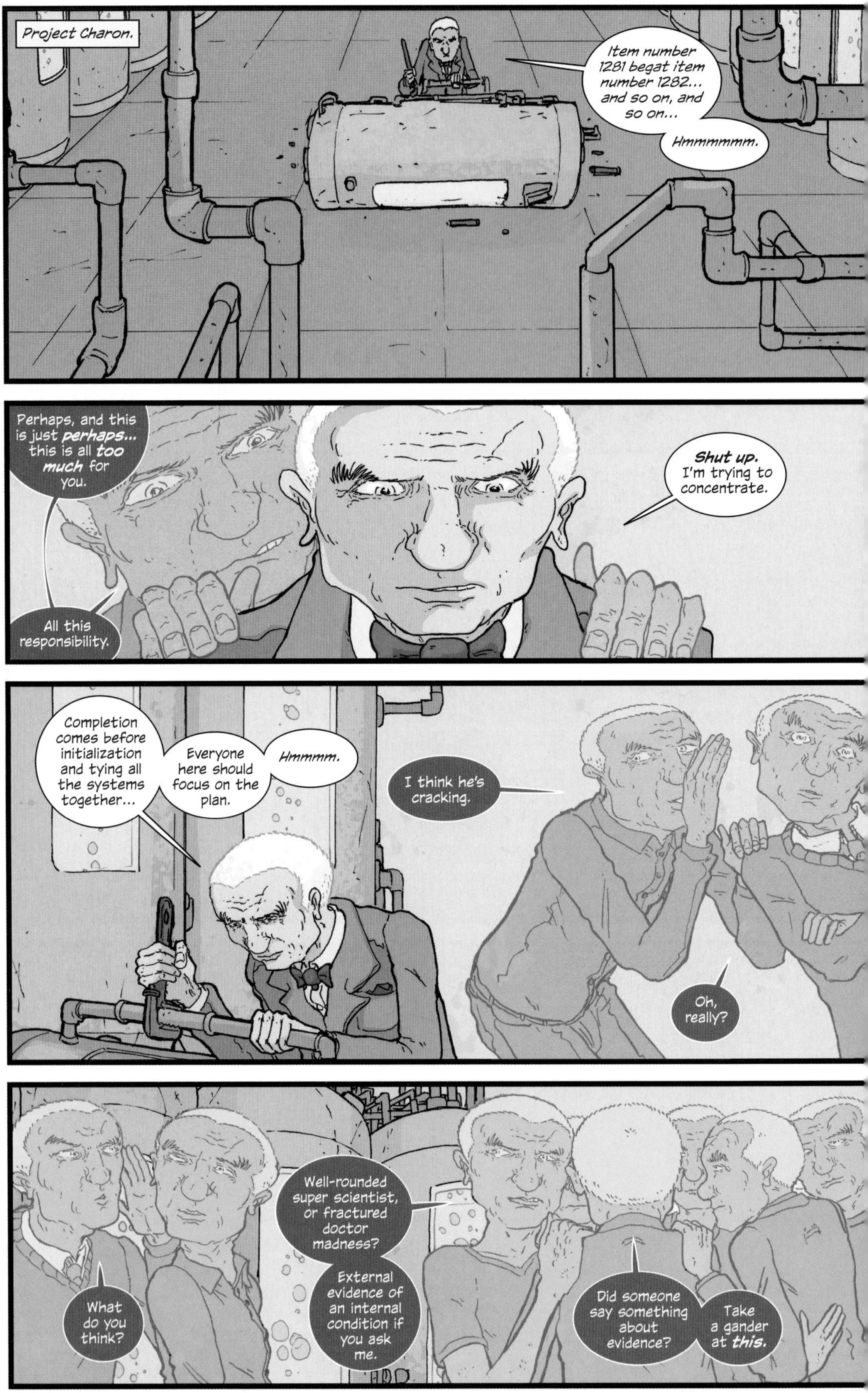

Project Charon.
Item number 1281 begat item number 1282... and so on, and so on...
Hmmmmmm.
Perhaps, and this is just ***perhaps...*** this is all ***too much*** for you.
All this responsibility.
***Shut up.*** I'm trying to concentrate.
Completion comes before initialization and tying all the systems together...
Everyone here should focus on the plan.
Hmmmm.
I think he's cracking.
Oh, really?
What do you think?
Well-rounded super scientist, or fractured doctor madness?
External evidence of an internal condition if you ask me.
Did someone say something about evidence?
Take a gander at ***this.***

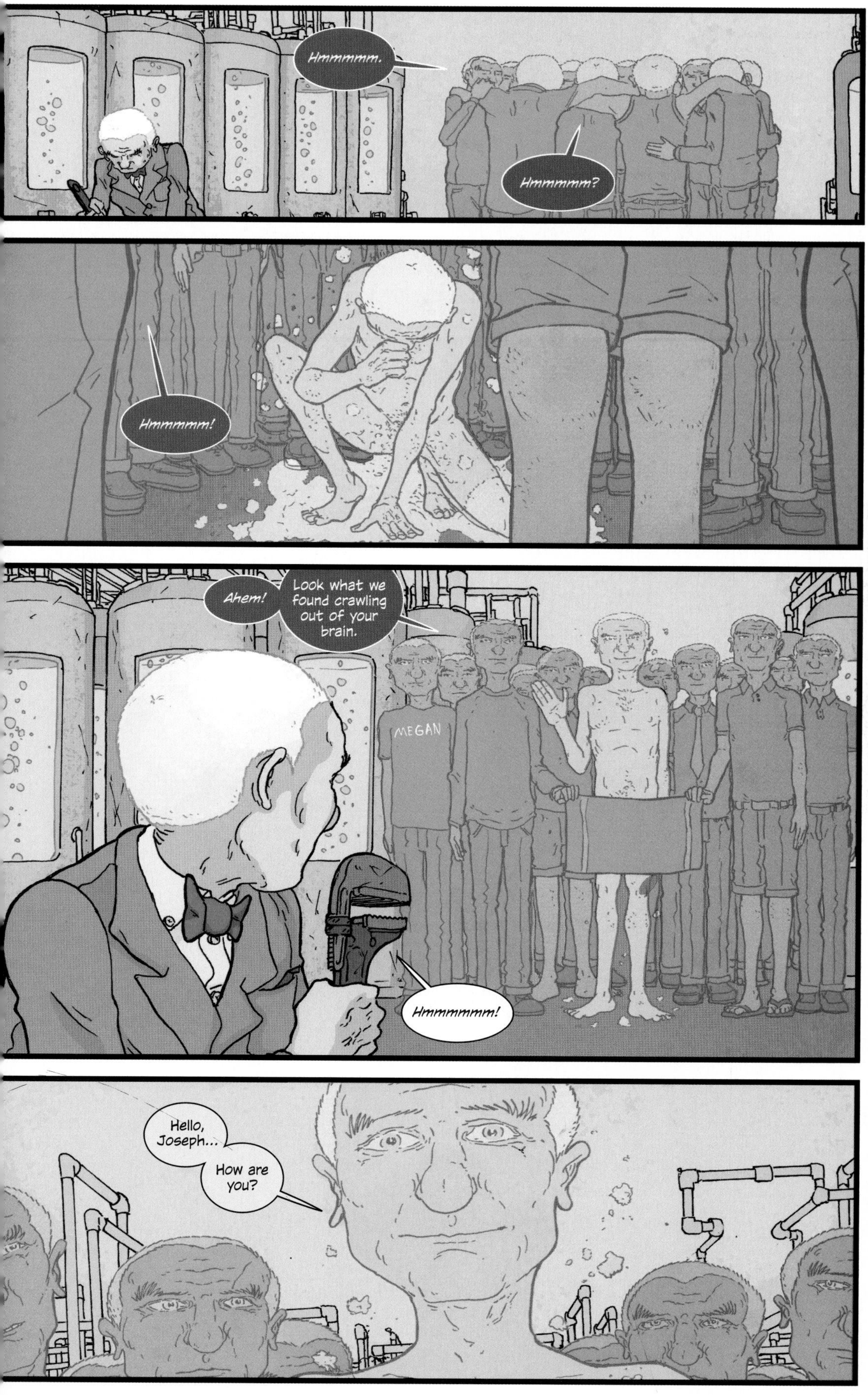
Hmmmmm.
Hmmmmm?
Hmmmmm!
Ahem!
Look what we found crawling out of your brain.
MEGAN
Hmmmmmm!
Hello, Joseph...
How are you?

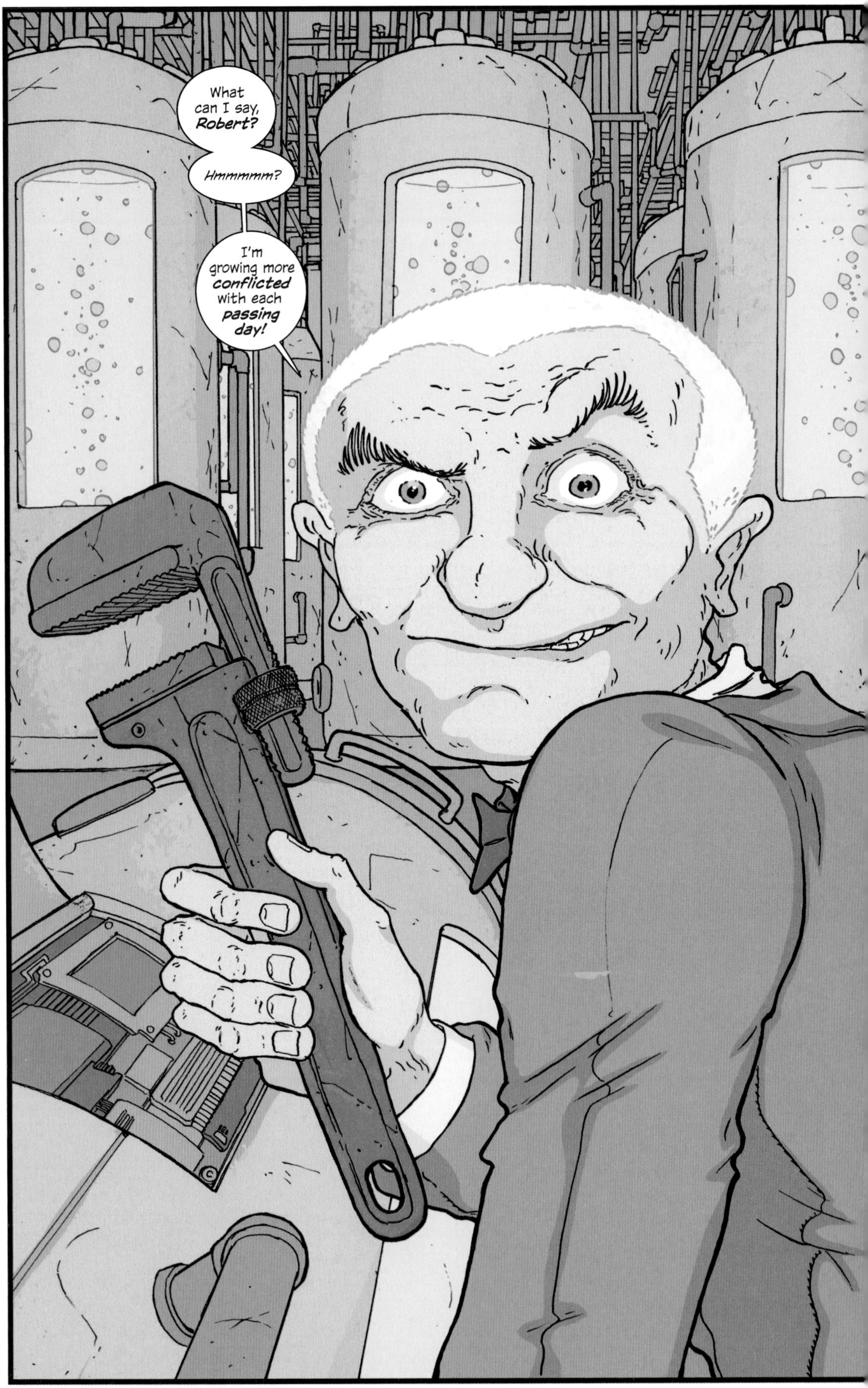
What can I say, *Robert?*
*Hmmmmm?*
I'm growing more *conflicted* with each *passing day!*

"WE WERE SO BUSY LOOKING AT OPPENHEIMER'S LEFT HAND, WE MISSED THE KNIFE IN HIS RIGHT."

*CLAVIS AUREA*
THE RECORDED FEYNMAN

**VOL. 4**

# HE STILL
## COVETED

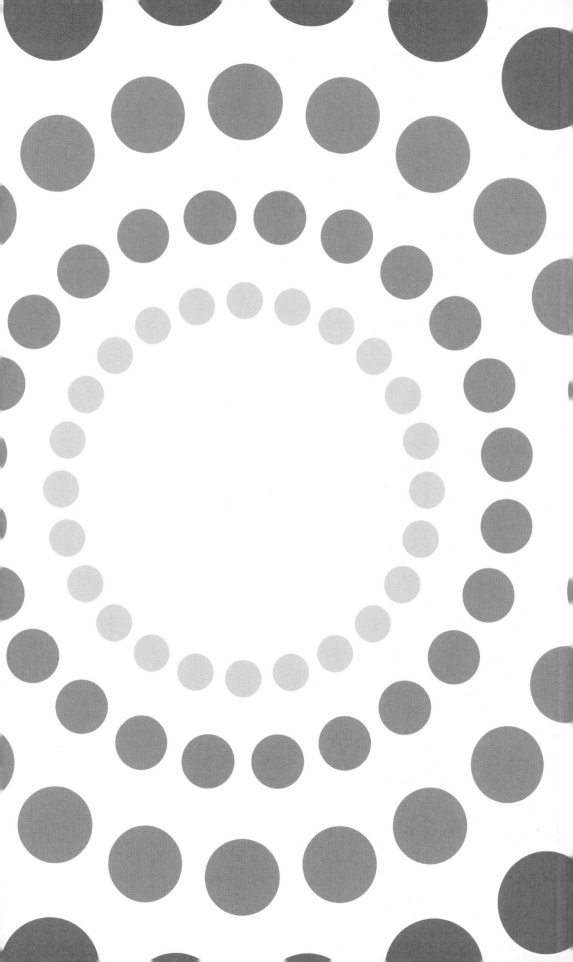

"THE GREAT EYE OF JOSEPH WATCHED OVER THEM ALL. THIS WAS EVOLUTION."

- OPPENHEIMER

*CLAVIS AUREA*
THE RECORDED FEYNMAN

# VOL. 3

For not-years in the now place the battle had raged **out there** -- outside the great Pyramid City.

Hmmmm.

Hmmmm.

Hmmmm?

They warred in the Valley, on the Plain, and on the broken Bridge.

Hmmmm.

Hmm--

The closest the Blues had come was the burning Forest...*until now.*

Hmmmm!

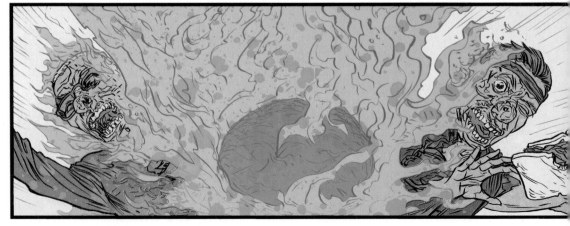

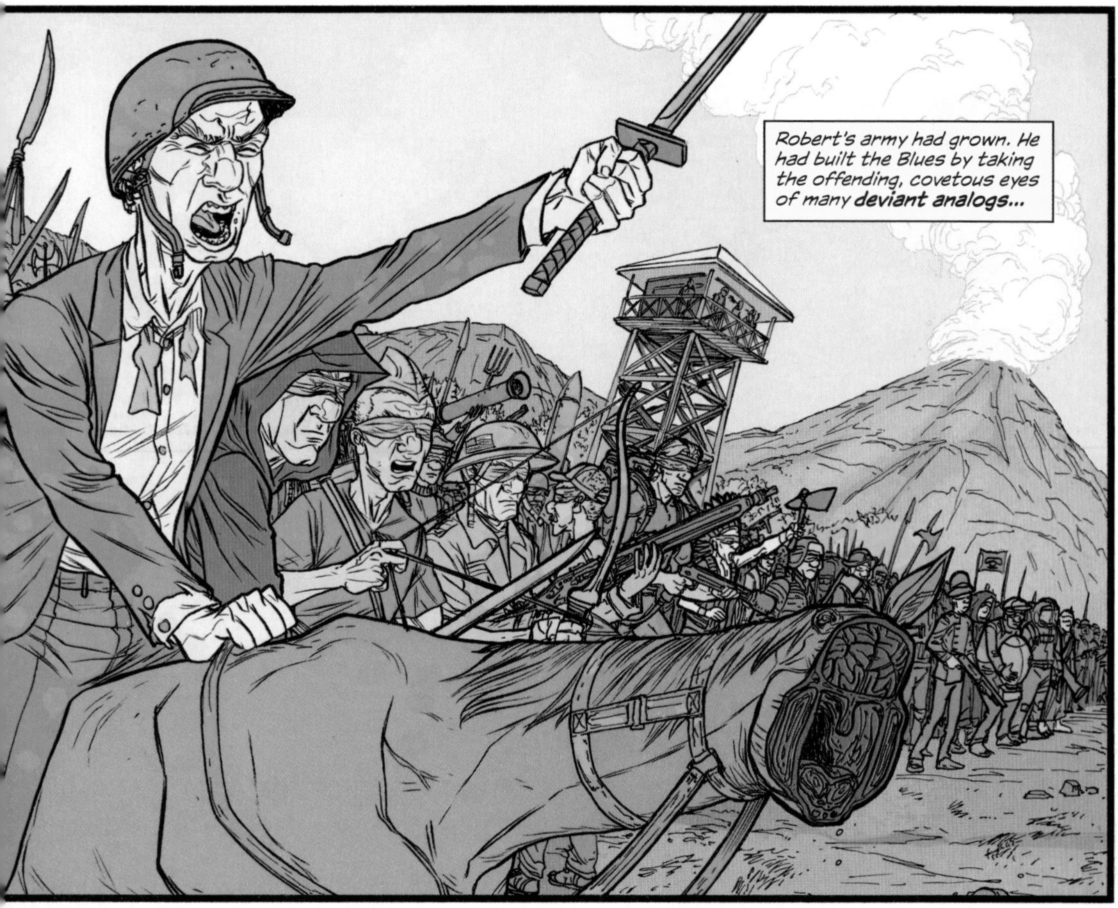
Robert's army had grown. He had built the Blues by taking the offending, covetous eyes of many **deviant analogs...**

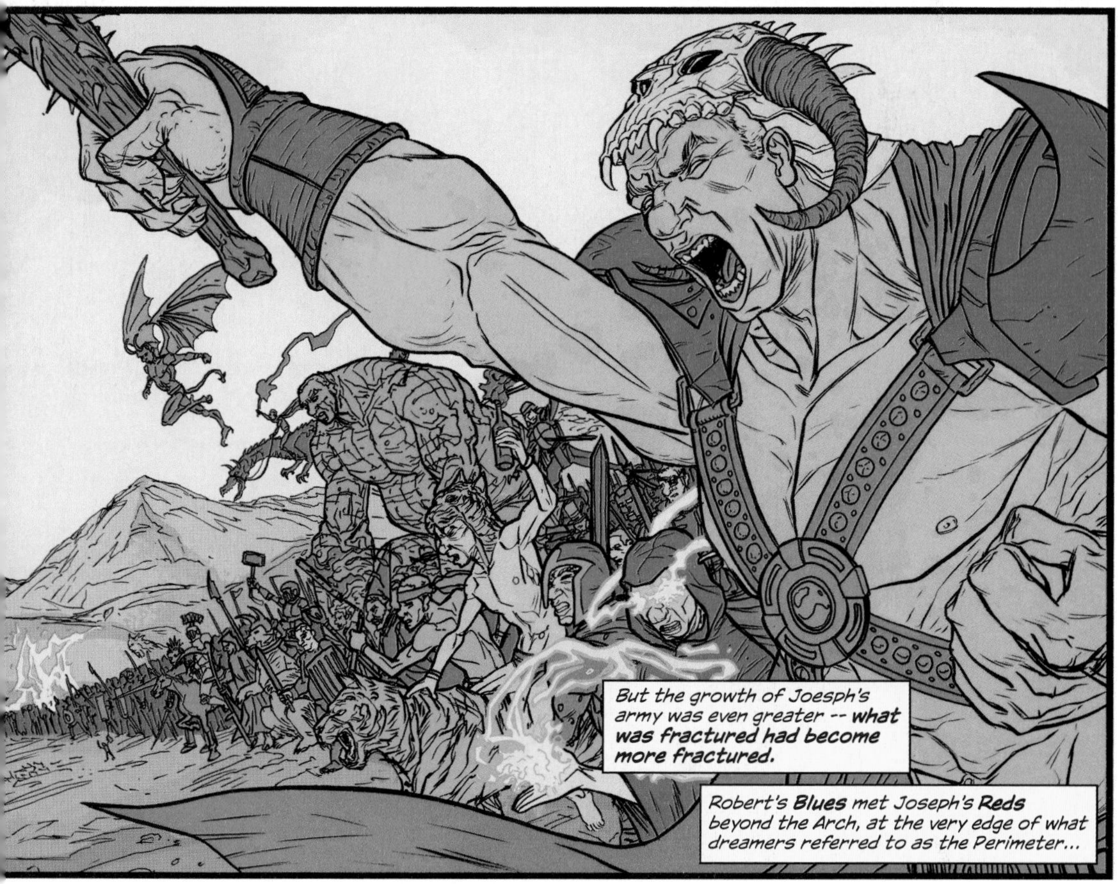
But the growth of Joesph's army was even greater -- **what was fractured had become more fractured.**
Robert's **Blues** met Joseph's **Reds** beyond the Arch, at the very edge of what dreamers referred to as the Perimeter...

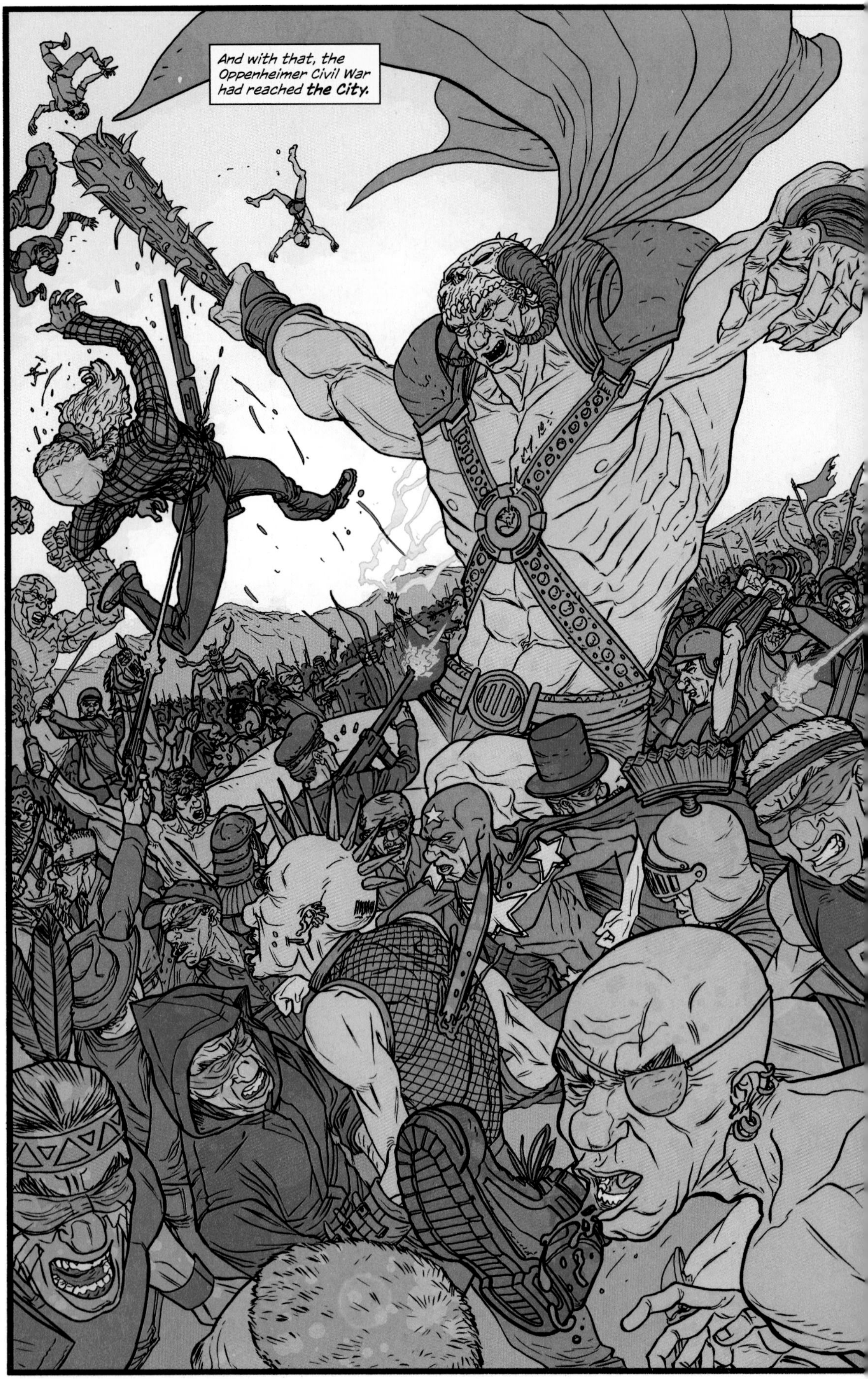
And with that, the Oppenheimer Civil War had reached the City.

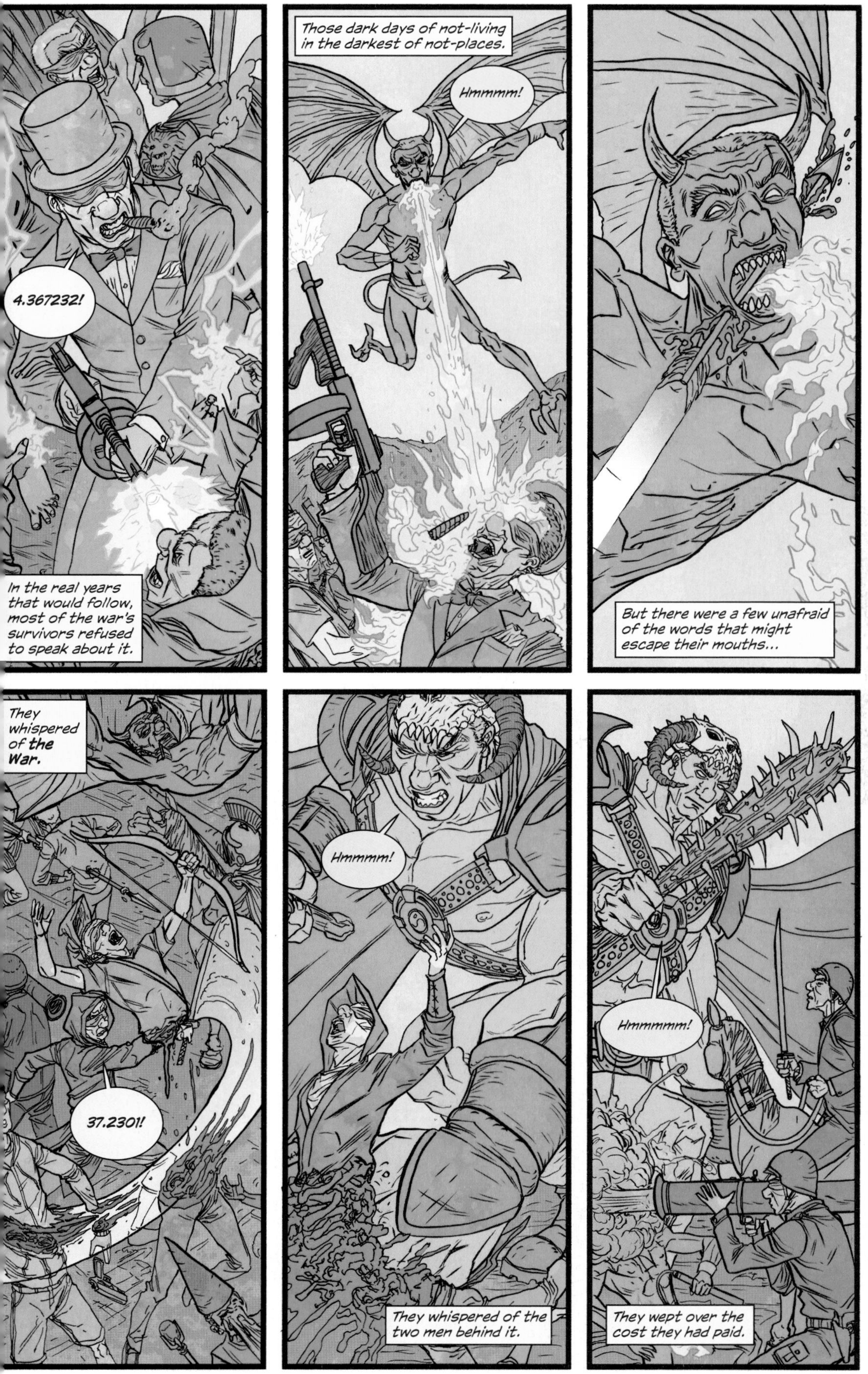
4.367232!
In the real years that would follow, most of the war's survivors refused to speak about it.
Those dark days of not-living in the darkest of not-places.
Hmmmm!
But there were a few unafraid of the words that might escape their mouths...
They whispered of **the War.**
37.2301!
Hmmmm!
They whispered of the two men behind it.
Hmmmmm!
They wept over the cost they had paid.

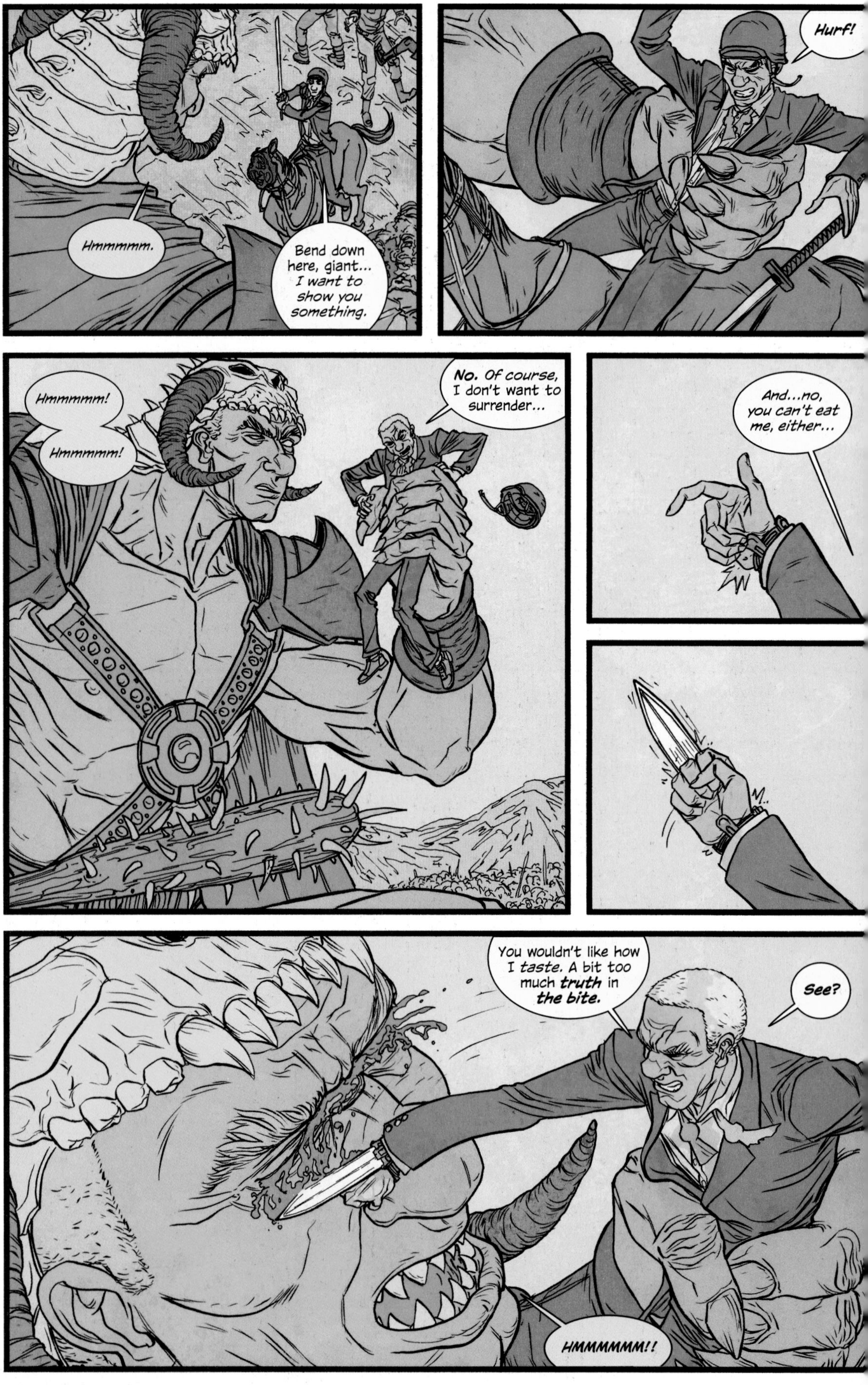
Hmmmmm.
Bend down here, giant... I want to show you something.
Hurf!
Hmmmmm!
Hmmmmm!
No. Of course, I don't want to surrender...
And...no, you can't eat me, either...
You wouldn't like how I taste. A bit too much truth in the bite.
See?
HMMMMMM!!

"THE GREAT EYE OF JOSEPH WATCHED OVER THEM ALL. THIS WAS ASSIMILATION."

- OPPENHEIMER

*CLAVIS AUREA*
THE RECORDED FEYNMAN | **VOL. 3**

# 15

## FINITE OPPENHEIMERS

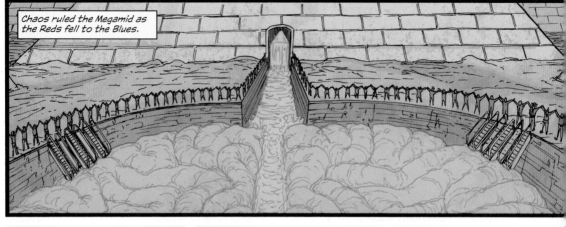

Chaos ruled the Megamid as the Reds fell to the Blues.

The news of defeat reached the City where fractured analogs and limited replicans worshipped the brain.

The great eye of Joseph looked down...

It looked down and saw his anger given form -- a simulacrum of the great Red himself, **Oppenheimer Prime.**

Hmmmmmm.

Before the war began, when he first took their eyes -- Robert remade the Blues in his own image.

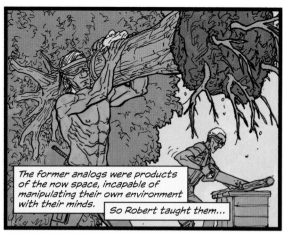

The former analogs were products of the now space, incapable of manipulating their own environment with their minds.

So Robert taught them...

Of math and machines, and all the wonders of science...

11.7820.

9.24.

This is how they had prepared for, and won, the first battle of the Oppenheimer Civil War.

3.14159!

Adaptation would come later.

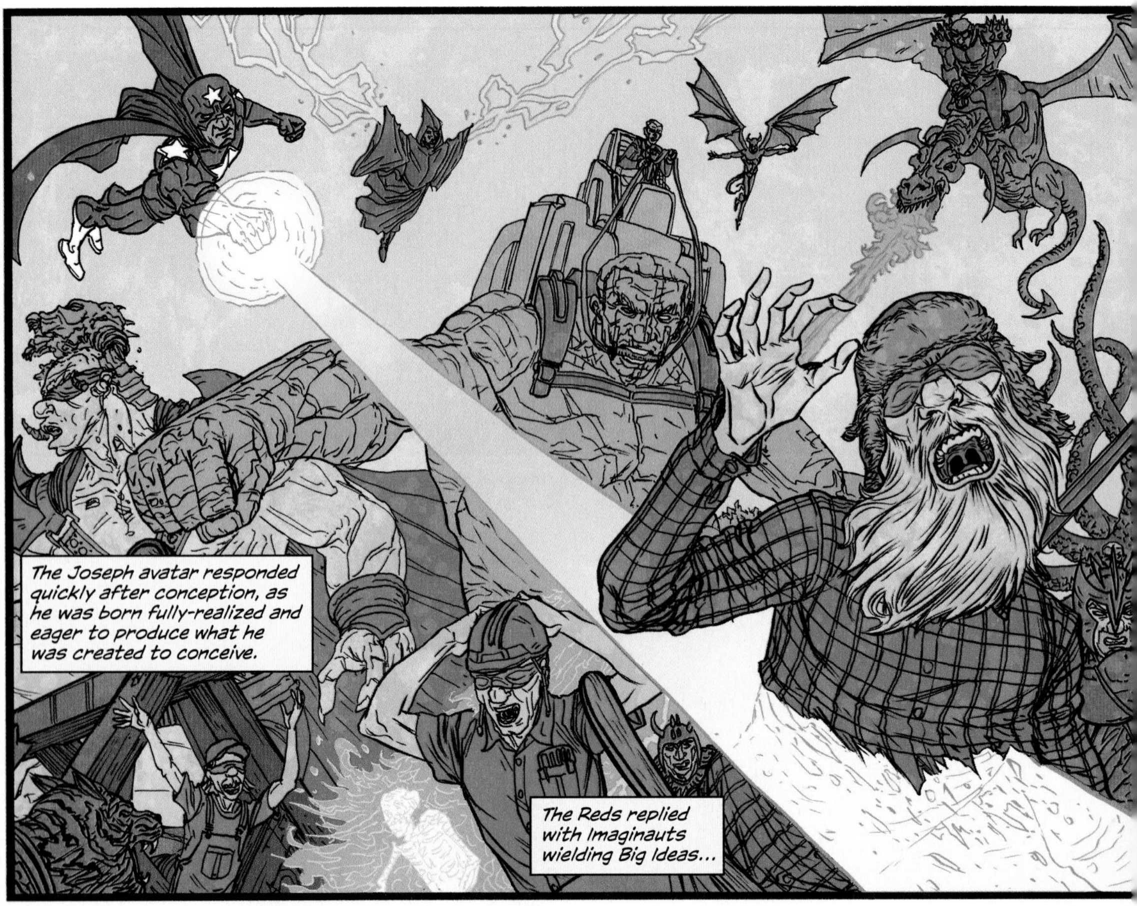
The Joseph avatar responded quickly after conception, as he was born fully-realized and eager to produce what he was created to conceive.
The Reds replied with Imaginauts wielding Big Ideas...

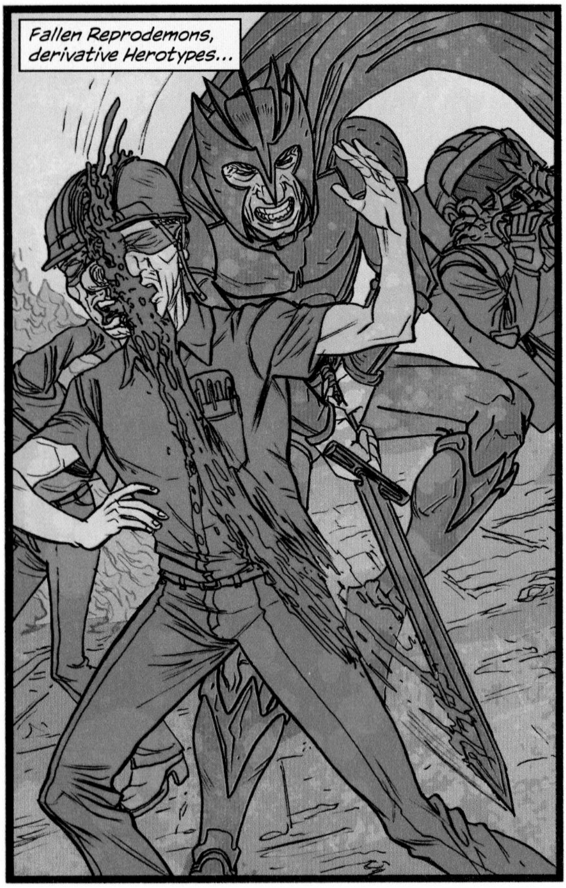
Fallen Reprodemons, derivative Herotypes...

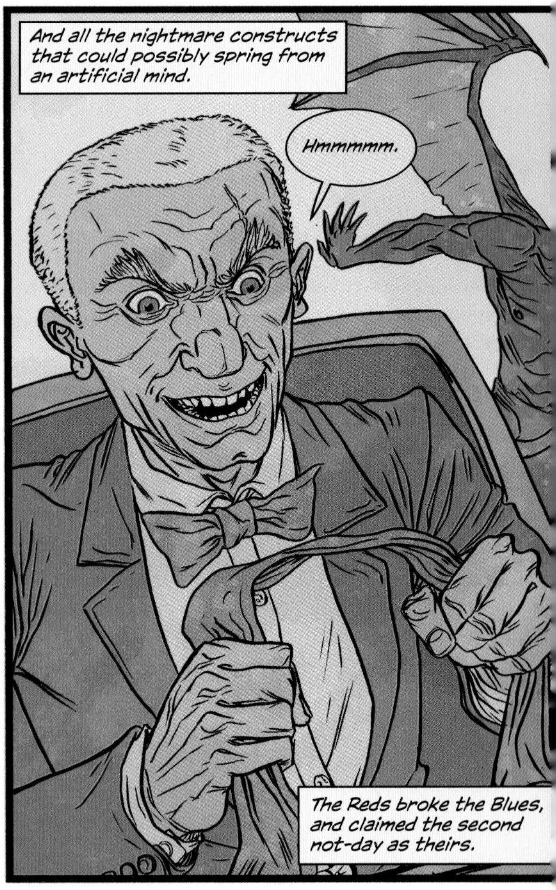
And all the nightmare constructs that could possibly spring from an artificial mind.
Hmmmmm.
The Reds broke the Blues, and claimed the second not-day as theirs.

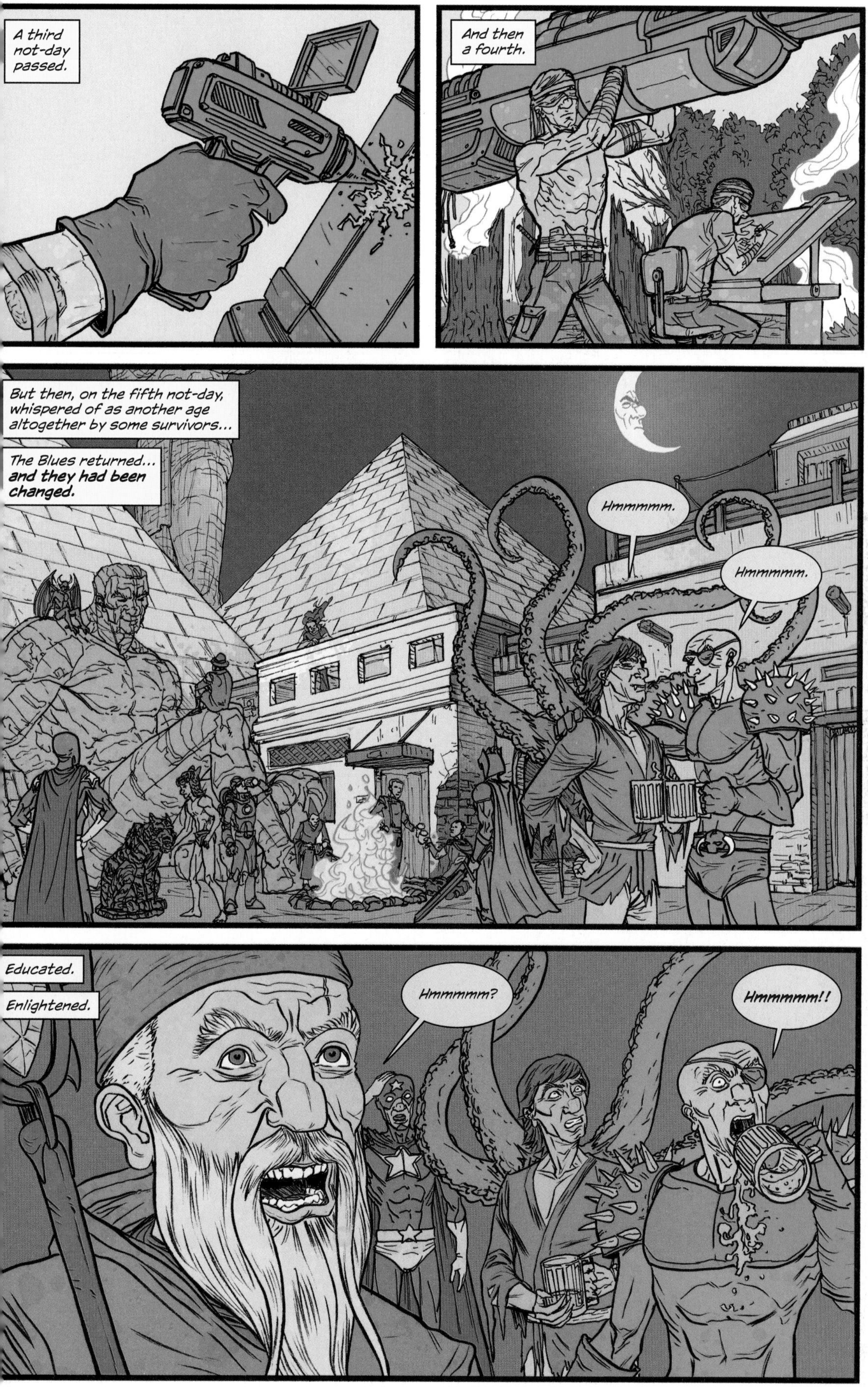
A third not-day passed.
And then a fourth.
But then, on the fifth not-day, whispered of as another age altogether by some survivors...
The Blues returned... **and they had been changed.**
Hmmmmm.
Hmmmmm.
Educated.
Enlightened.
Hmmmmm?
Hmmmmm!!

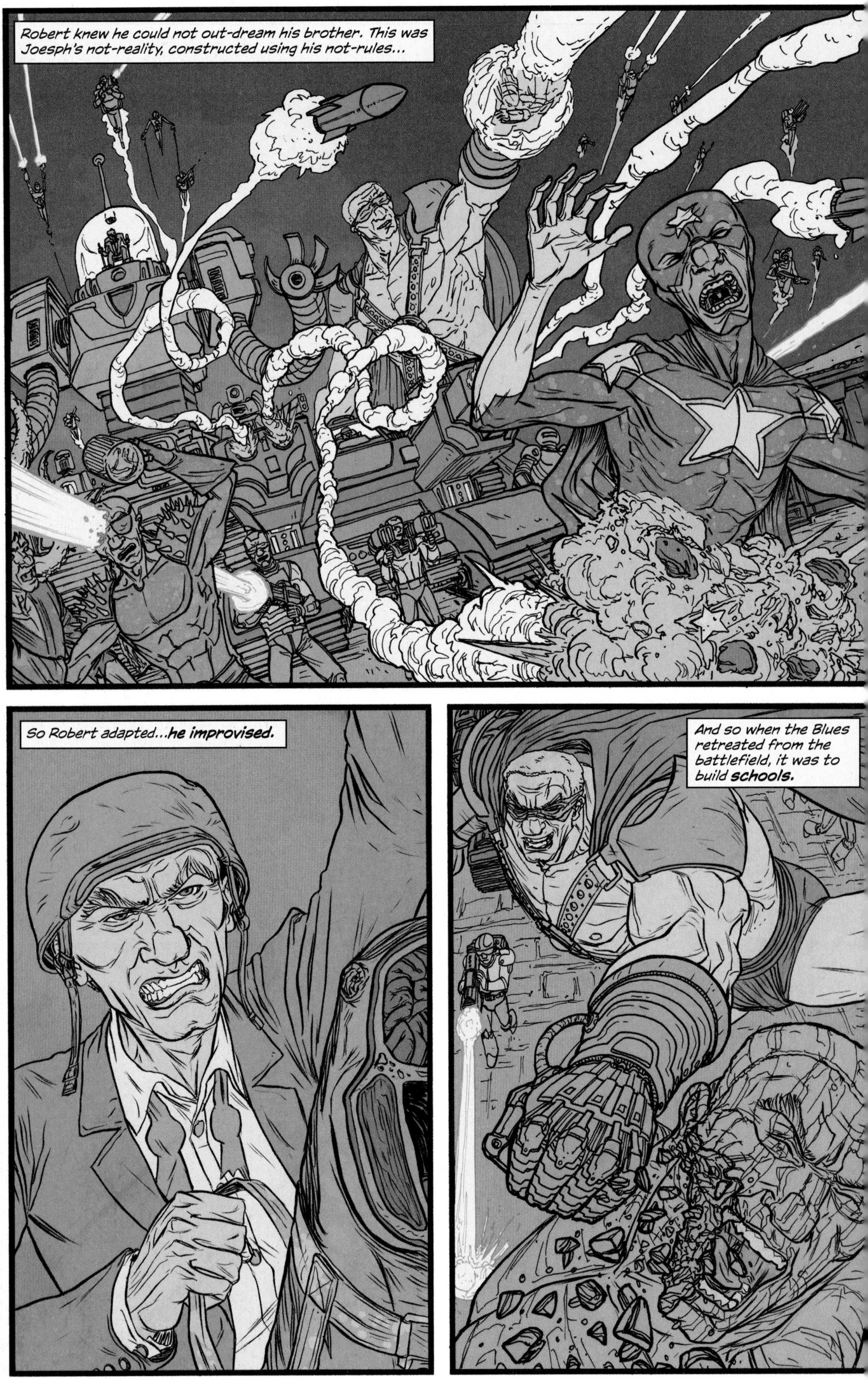
Robert knew he could not out-dream his brother. This was Joesph's not-reality, constructed using his not-rules...
So Robert adapted...**he improvised.**
And so when the Blues retreated from the battlefield, it was to build **schools.**

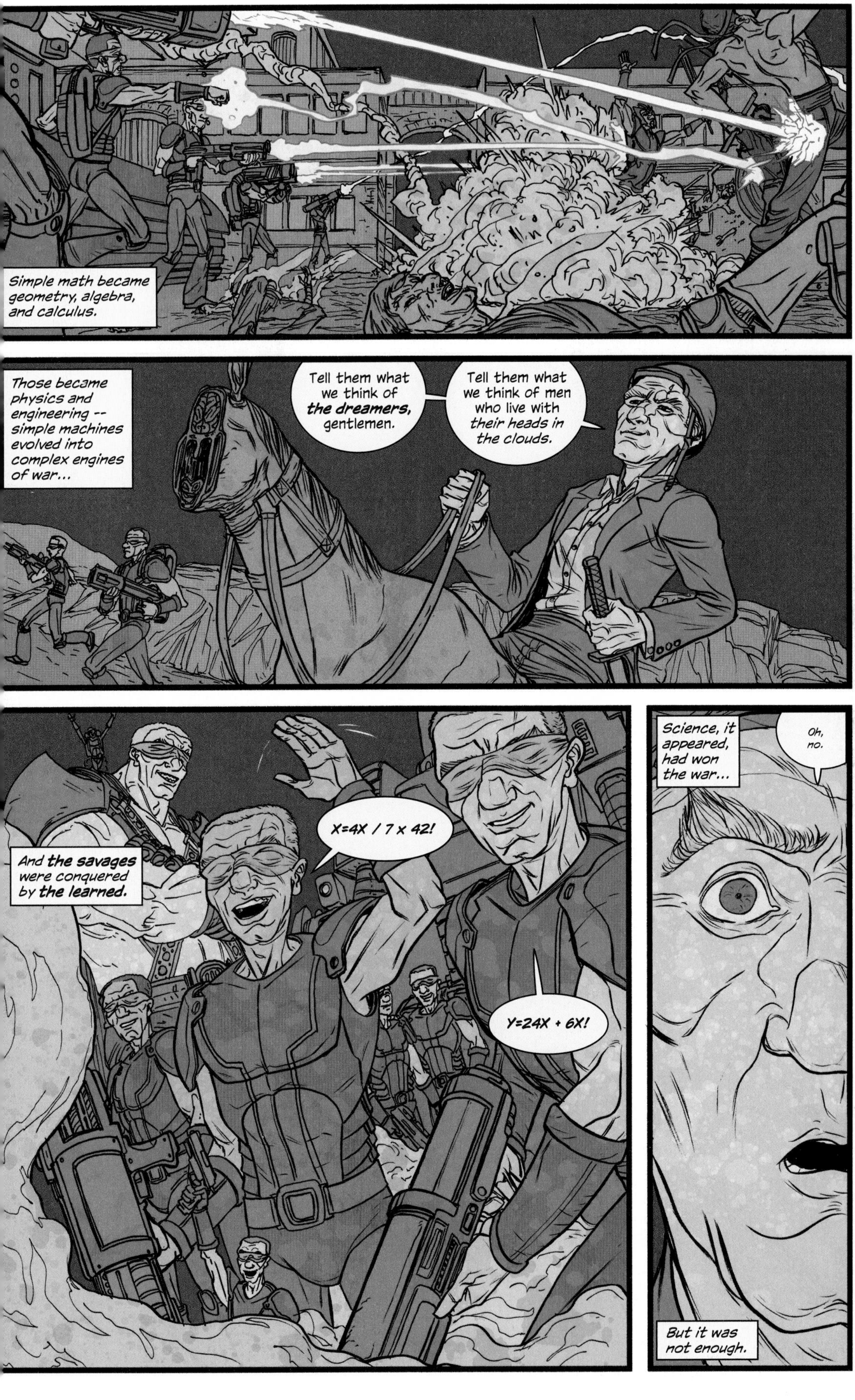
Simple math became geometry, algebra, and calculus.
Those became physics and engineering -- simple machines evolved into complex engines of war...
Tell them what we think of **the dreamers,** gentlemen.
Tell them what we think of men who live with *their heads in the clouds.*
And **the savages** were conquered by **the learned.**
X=4X / 7 x 42!
Y=24X + 6X!
Science, it appeared, had won the war...
Oh, no.
But it was not enough.

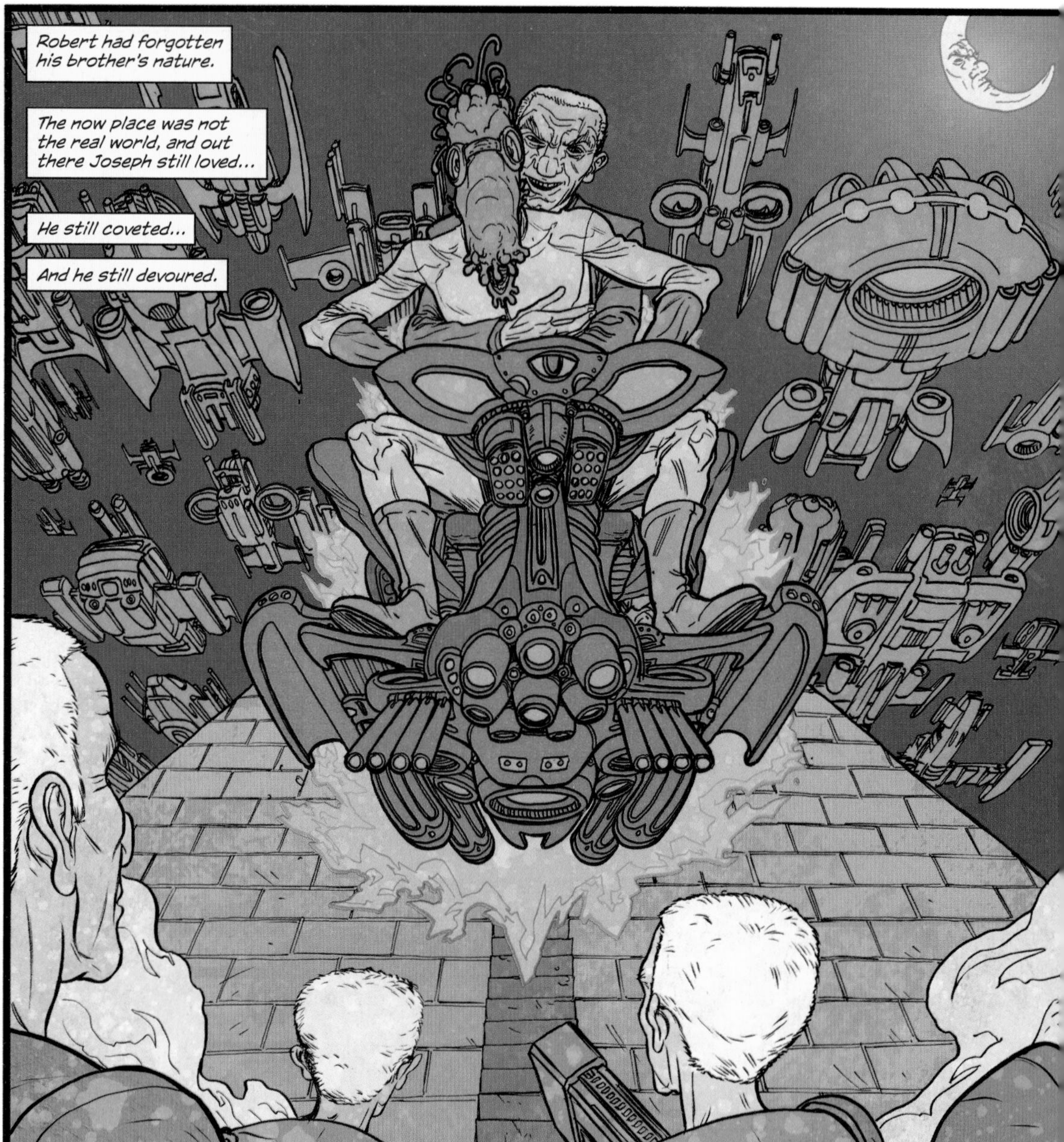
Robert had forgotten his brother's nature.
The now place was not the real world, and out there Joseph still loved...
He still coveted...
And he still devoured.

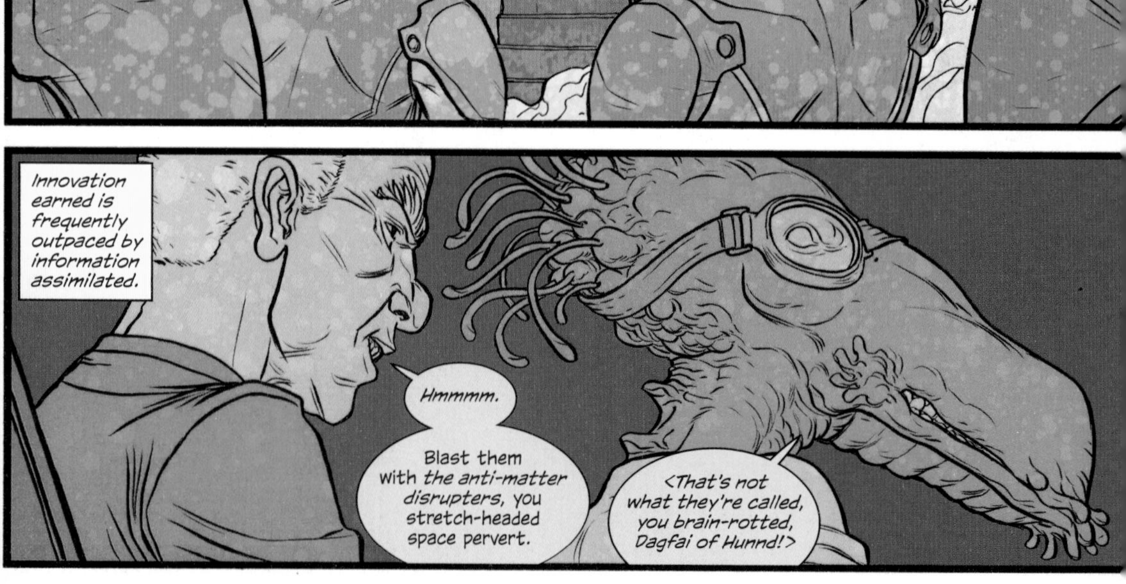
Innovation earned is frequently outpaced by information assimilated.
Hmmmm.
Blast them with the anti-matter disrupters, you stretch-headed space pervert.
<That's not what they're called, you brain-rotted, Dagfai of Hunnd!>

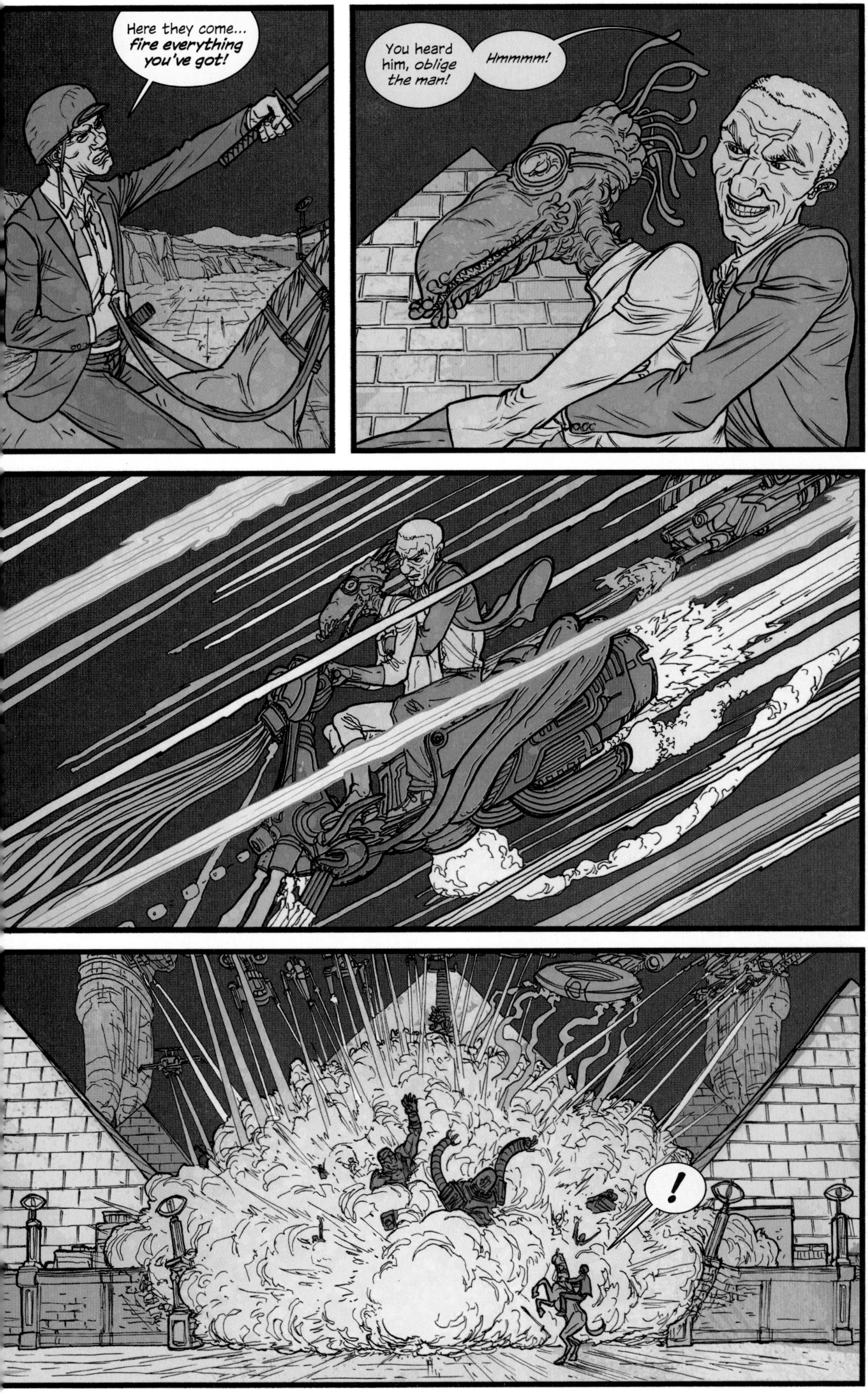
Here they come... *fire everything you've got!*
You heard him, *oblige* the man!
*Hmmmm!*
!

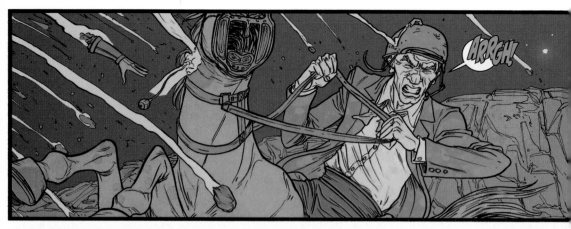

GRRGH!

As his avatar-brother pursued him, Robert wondered...

Where did it go wrong? How was he so mistaken?

Was every move he made to defeat the Great Eye utter folly?

If every time he adapted -- *if every time he evolved* -- the rules were changed, how could he ever hope to win?

The answer was obvious...

In this place, *he could not.*

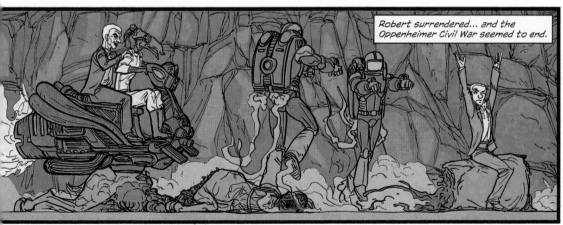

Robert surrendered... and the Oppenheimer Civil War seemed to end.

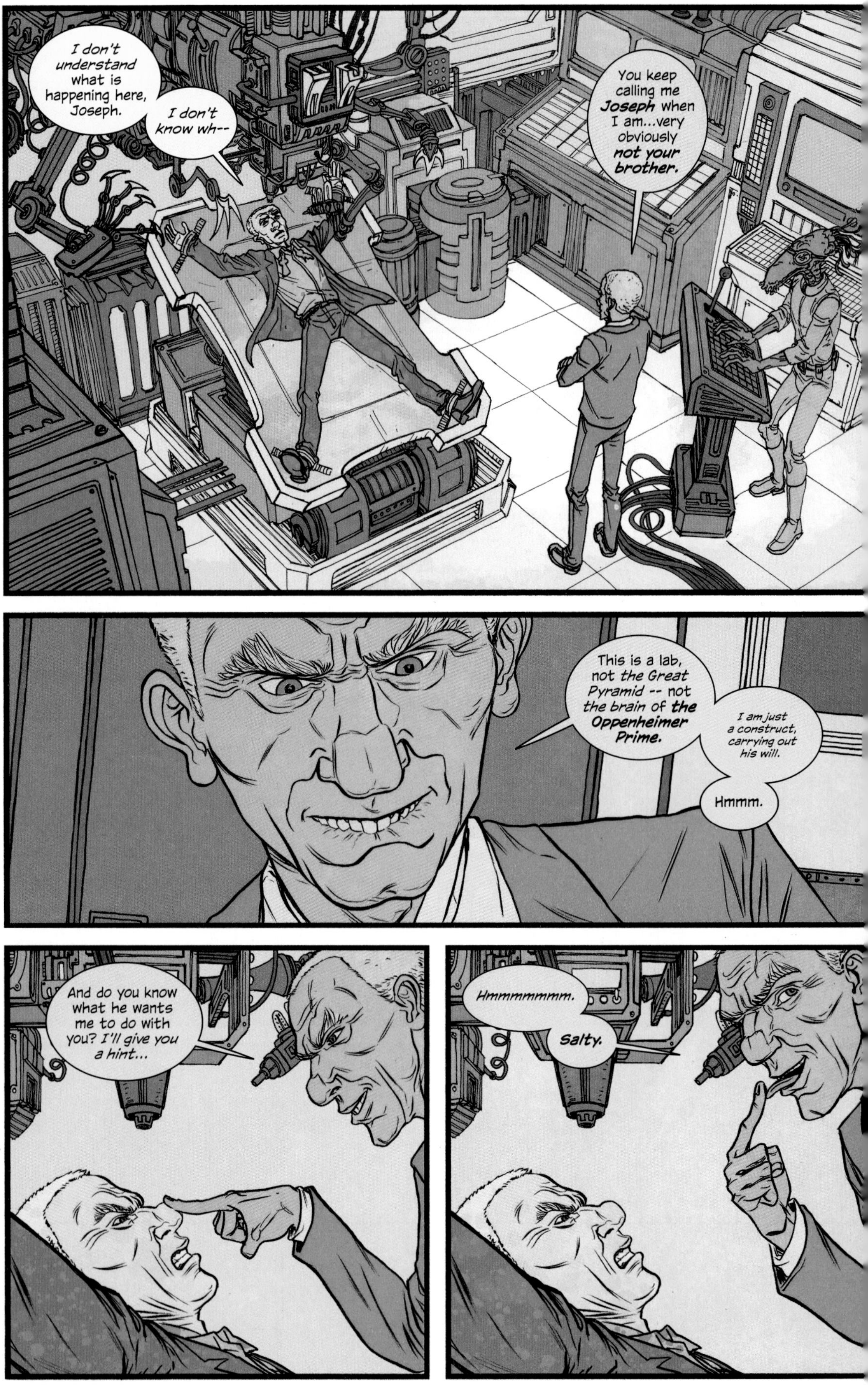

I don't understand what is happening here, Joseph.
I don't know wh--
You keep calling me Joseph when I am...very obviously not your brother.
This is a lab, not the Great Pyramid -- not the brain of the Oppenheimer Prime.
I am just a construct, carrying out his will.
Hmmm.
And do you know what he wants me to do with you? I'll give you a hint...
Hmmmmmmmm.
Salty.

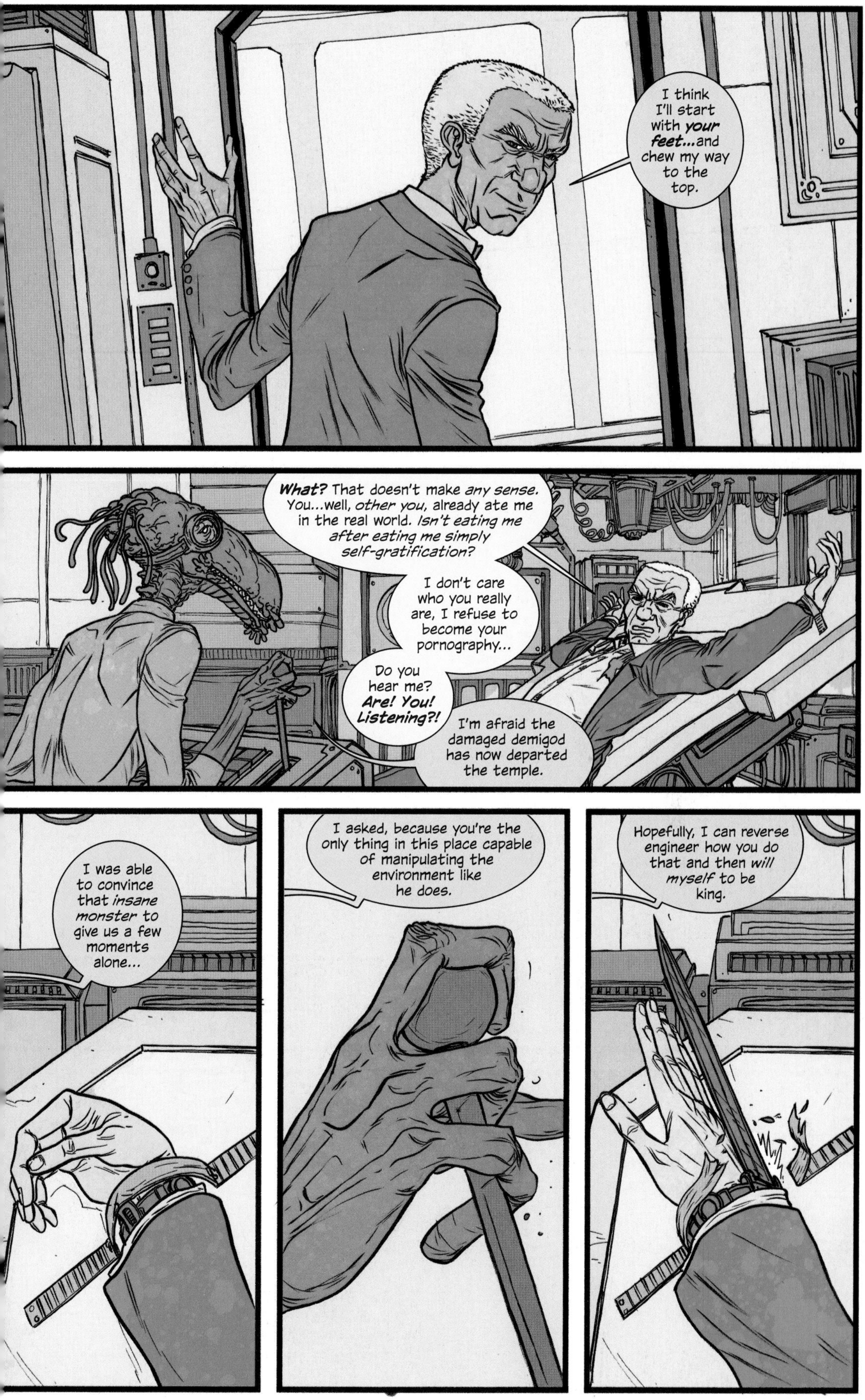
I think I'll start with **your feet...** and chew my way to the top.
***What?*** That doesn't make *any sense.* You...well, *other you,* already ate me in the real world. *Isn't eating me after eating me simply self-gratification?*
I don't care who you really are, I refuse to become your pornography...
Do you hear me? ***Are! You! Listening?!***
I'm afraid the damaged demigod has now departed the temple.
I was able to convince that *insane monster* to give us a few moments alone...
I asked, because you're the only thing in this place capable of manipulating the environment like he does.
Hopefully, I can reverse engineer how you do that and then *will myself* to be king.

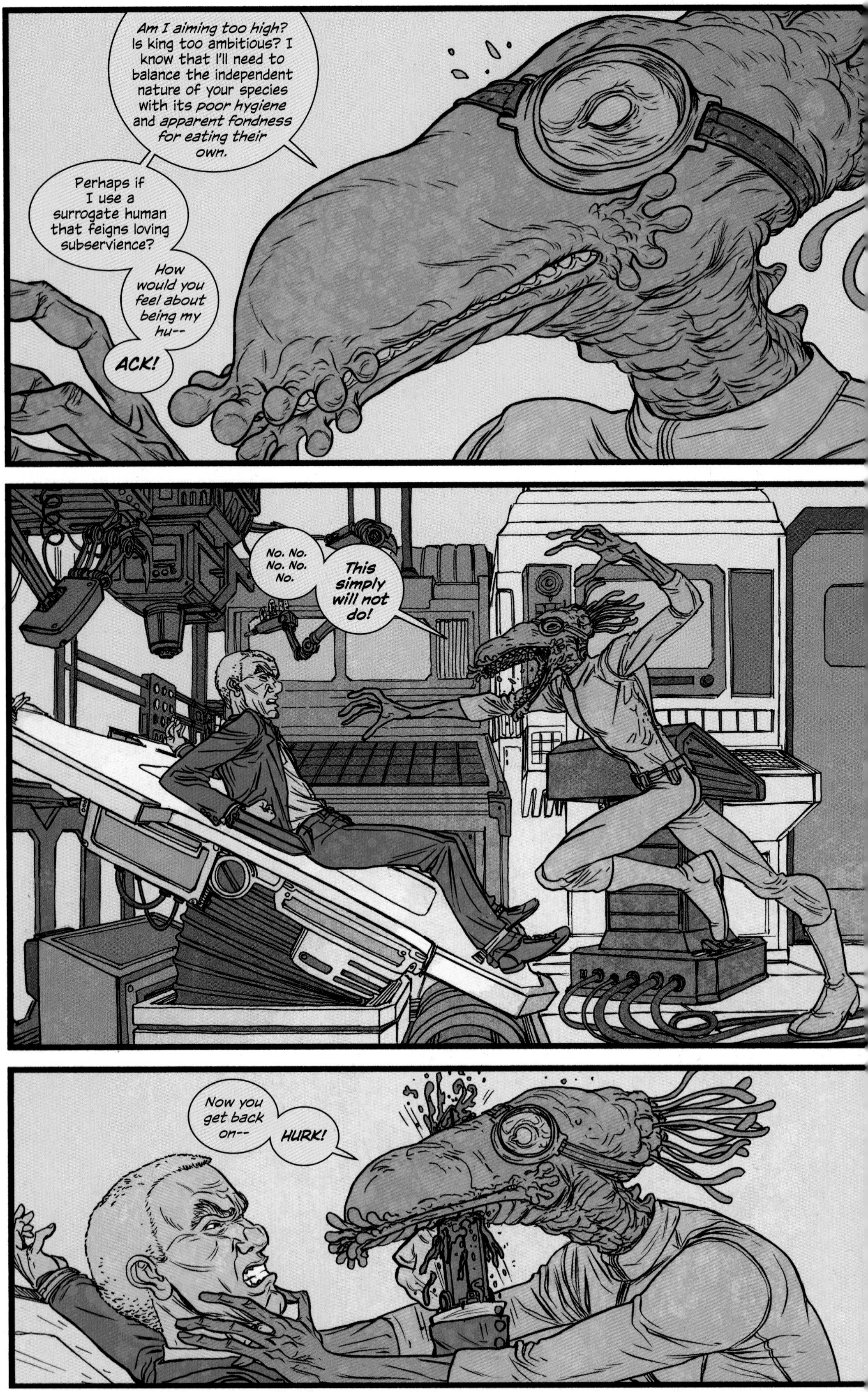
Am I aiming too high? Is king too ambitious? I know that I'll need to balance the independent nature of your species with its poor hygiene and apparent fondness for eating their own.
Perhaps if I use a surrogate human that feigns loving subservience?
How would you feel about being my hu--
ACK!
No. No. No. No. No.
This simply will not do!
Now you get back on--
HURK!

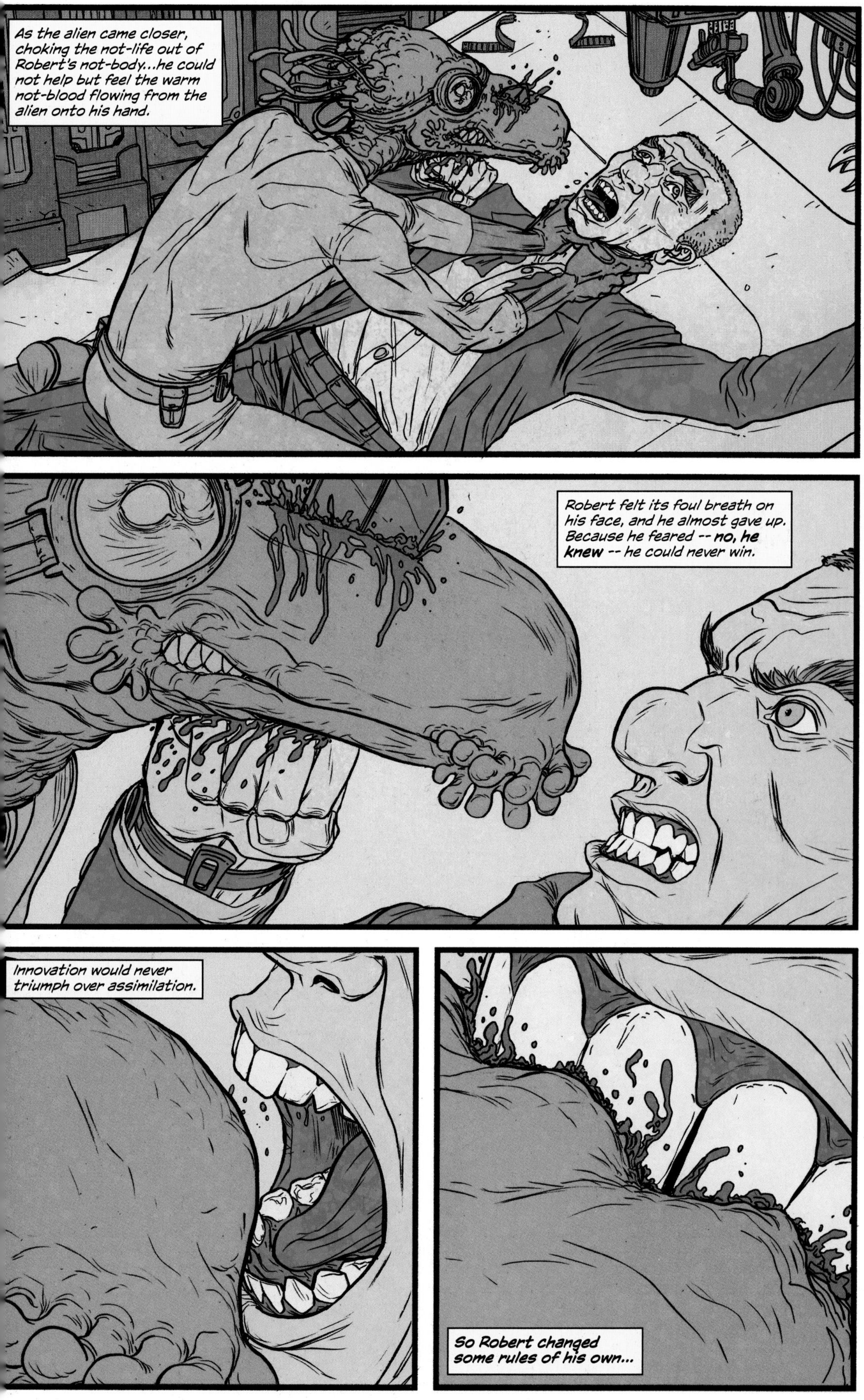
As the alien came closer, choking the not-life out of Robert's not-body...he could not help but feel the warm not-blood flowing from the alien onto his hand.
Robert felt its foul breath on his face, and he almost gave up. Because he feared -- **no, he knew** -- he could never win.
Innovation would never triumph over assimilation.
So Robert changed some rules of his own...

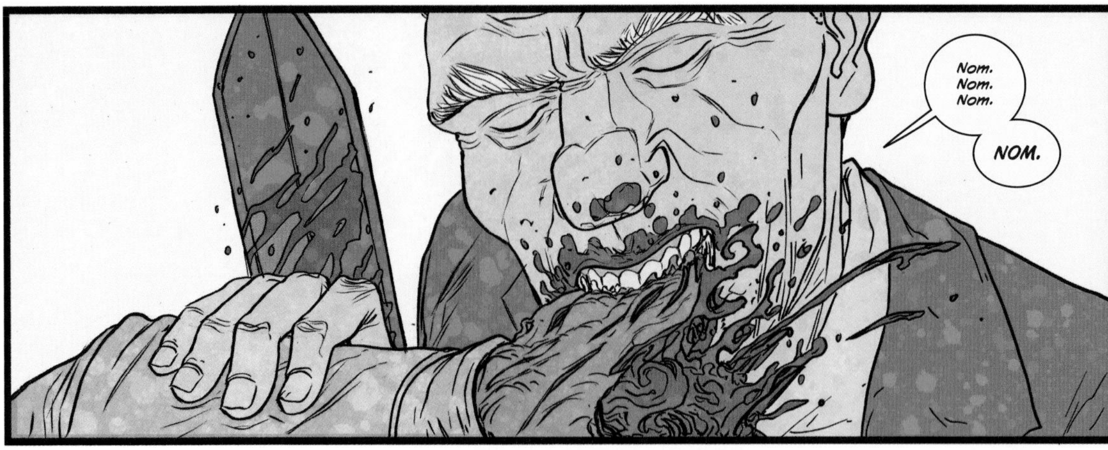
Nom.
Nom.
Nom.
NOM.

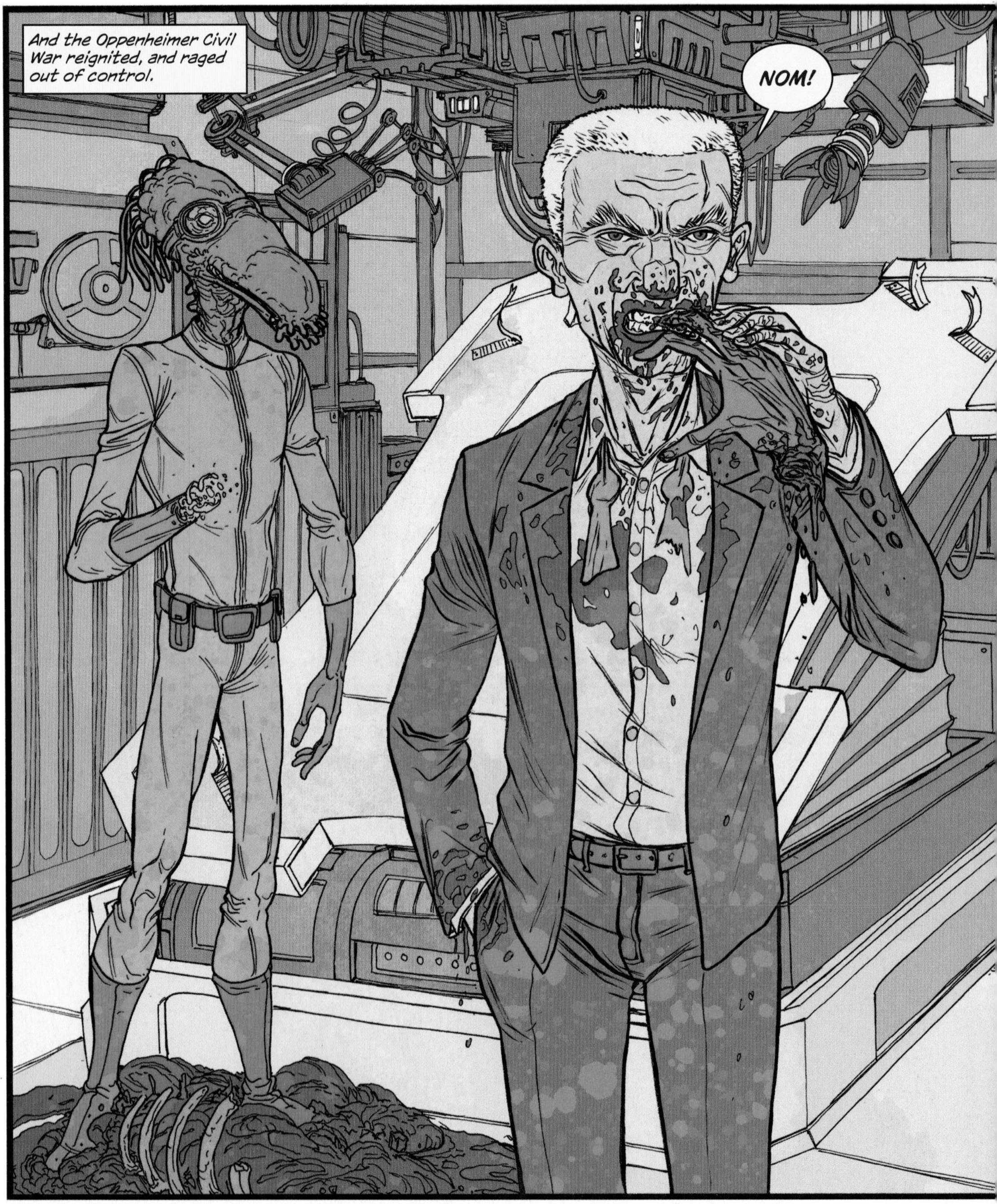
And the Oppenheimer Civil War reignited, and raged out of control.
NOM!

"WE LOOKED UP, AND FROM THE MEGAMID, IT LOOKED DOWN. THE GREAT EYE OFFENDED, SO WE ATE THEM.

AGAIN, AND AGAIN, AND AGAIN."

- OPPENHEIMER

*CLAVIS AUREA*
THE RECORDED FEYNMAN | **VOL. 3**

# THE CAST

## JOSEPH OPPENHEIMER

Super genius.
American. Physicist.
Multiple personalities.

## ALBRECHT EINSTEIN

Highly intelligent.
German. Physicist.
Drinks.

## RICHARD FEYNMAN

Super genius.
American. Physicist.
Wormholer.

## ENRICO FERMI

Super genius.
Italian. Physicist.
Not human.

## HARRY DAGHLIAN

Super genius.
American. Physicist.
Irradiated.

## WERNHER VON BRAUN

Super genius.
German. Rocket scientist.
Robot arm.

## LESLIE GROVES

Not a genius.
American. General.
Smokes. Bombs.

## FDR: A.I.

Computational super genius.
American. President.
Dead.

## JOHN F. KENNEDY

Not a genius.
American. President.
Sexytime.

# THE CAST

## YURI GAGARIN

Not a genius.
Russian. Cosmonaut.
Hero.

## LAIKA

Way smarter than thought.
Russian. Space Dog.
Speaks.

## HELMUTT GRÖTTRUP

Super genius.
German. Rocket scientist.
Slave.

## DMITRIY USTINOV

Not a genius.
Russian. Minister.
Master.

**Jonathan Hickman** is the visionary talent behind such works as the Eisner-nominated **NIGHTLY NEWS**, **TRANSHUMAN** and **PAX ROMANA**. He also plies his trade at MARVEL working on books like **FANTASTIC FOUR** and **THE AVENGERS**.

His twin brother, Marc, is a regional salesperson for Oscar Mayer.

**Jonathan** lives in South Carolina near a lowcountry nature reserve.

You can visit his website:***www.pronea.com***, or email him at:***jonathan@pronea.com***.

·

**Nick Pitarra** is a native Texan and all around nice guy. As a senior in high school he was kicked out of honors English, and subsequently fell in love with comic illustration while doodling with a friend in his new class.

Sometimes it pays not to do your homework.